THE HEAVENLY LAND AND THE LAND OF THE RISING SUN

Historical Linkages, Security Cooperation and Strategic Partnership

THE HEAVENLY LAND AND THE LAND OF THE RISING SUN

Historical Linkages, Security Cooperation and Strategic Partnership

Adarsha Verma

KNOWLEDGE WORLD
KW Publishers Pvt Ltd
New Delhi

MANOHAR PARRIKAR idsa
MANOHAR PARRIKAR INSTITUTE FOR DEFENCE STUDIES AND ANALYSES
मनोहर पर्रिकर रक्षा अध्ययन एवं विश्लेषण संस्थान

Manohar Parrikar Institute for Defence Studies and Analyses
No. 1, Development Enclave, Delhi Cantt.
New Delhi-110 010
Phone: +91-11-26717983
Website: www.idsa.in

ISBN 978-93-89137-45-3 Hardback

Published in India by Kalpana Shukla

KW Publishers Pvt Ltd
4676/21, First Floor, Ansari Road
Daryaganj, New Delhi 110 002
Phone: +91 11 23263498/43528107
Marketing: kw@kwpub.com
Editorial: production@kwpub.com
Website: www.kwpub.com

Printed and bound in India

Contents

List of Tables, Figures and Maps

Tables

Figures

Maps

Preface

India-Japan cultural and security relations is a subject that has always been intriguing considering the potential it holds for the future security architecture in the Indo-Pacific region. The opportunity to do a research fellowship at the Manohar Parrikar Institute for Defence Studies and Analyses (Manohar Parrikar IDSA) came as a blessing and gave direction to my interest of writing on the subject.

This research provided a suitable platform to understand the deep cultural relations between the people of both nations. The past decade has witnessed rapid strides in economic engagement between India and Japan. The relations between the two countries are now one of the fastest developing relations. However, the present times being hailed as the 'new era in Japan-India relationship', there has not been substantial progress in the security domain.[1] The book is intended to educate the reader on the security aspects of the relationship between the two countries and how this relationship can be enhanced further especially in the context of the present security environment of East Asia, which is fluid and unpredictable with a number of flashpoints. Set in both, a bilateral as well as a regional context, the security relationship has been analysed to arrive at pragmatic recommendations that must be implemented for an enhanced relationship in the security realm.

The journey of writing this book started two years back as part of my research work in the Manohar Parrikar IDSA. Over these two years one has matured as an analytic writer and followed events in Japan closely, from varied angles. Though two years may be considered a very miniscule time in the history of a nation, the relationship that has evolved between India and Japan within this time frame has been noteworthy and exhibits that results can be achieved through resolve, by political leaders.

In order to write this book, many primary sources were tapped, which included personnel in the Indian defence establishment and the Japanese Embassy in India. Japanese and other foreign scholars visiting India were also interacted with and interviewed for their insights. Interactions with various Japanese experts and military experts gave an understanding into the way Japan looks at security and the Japanese understanding of strategic aspects. To my knowledge, there has been no previous work carried out that focussed solely on security issues right from the tactical level to the strategic level. A lot of research has however been carried out in the overall theme of international relations, with security cooperation and strategic partnerships being part of the literature.

The book comprises of four parts, each part dealing with a different aspect of the security relationship. An attempt has also been made to quantitatively define the qualitative aspect of the level of security cooperation between the two countries. In order to arrive at strategies for enhancement of security cooperation between India and Japan a SWOT analysis has been carried out in Part II of this book. The SWOT analysis compares the strengths and weakness of India in security aspects with the opportunities and threats in the security realm of Japan. The issues that can complement each other have been brought together to form strategies that will enhance and complement this relationship.

Though it has been widely mentioned in a number of literary works that the India-Japan cooperation is a work in progress, there has been no research work to figuratively assess the levels of security relationship. This inspired me to work out a security model which can arrive at a quantitative assessment of the same.

The book has been the result of a thorough research on the subject over the past two years. The views expressed here and any factual errors are entirely my own. They bear no relation to any government policy or the Institute for Defence Studies and Analyses.

Note

1. Ministry of Foreign Affairs of Japan, Japan-India Relations, available at https://www.mofa.go.jp/region/asia-paci/india/data.html, accessed on February 6, 2019. Prime Ministers Modi and Shinzo Abe announced, 'Japan and India Vision 2025 Special Strategic and Global Partnership Working Together for Peace and Prosperity of the Indo-Pacific Region and the World'—a joint statement that would serve as a guide post for the "new era in Japan-India relations".

Acknowledgements

At the outset, I wish to thank KW Publishers for assisting me in writing this book on India-Japan Security Cooperation. I also wish to acknowledge with gratitude the assistance provided to me by the Manohar Parrikar Institute for Defence Studies and Analyses (Manohar Parrikar IDSA) in writing this book, which took two years of intensive research to complete. My sincere thanks to then Director General of Manohar Parrikar IDSA Mr Jayant Prasad and the Deputy Director General Maj Gen Alok Deb (Retired) whose guidance and encouragement made this book possible. Dr Jagannath P. Panda, the Centre Coordinator, Dr Titli Basu and the entire team of the East Asia Centre deserve a special mention for the continuous guidance provided during our periodic meetings.

I also wish to highlight the assistance provided by the entire library staff, especially Mr Suresh Sevangi and the Library-in-charge, Ms Hitakshi.

In the end, I wish to thank my wife, Pooja for her patience in bearing with my long absence at times and without whose encouragement this book would not have been a reality.

Map of Japan in East Asia

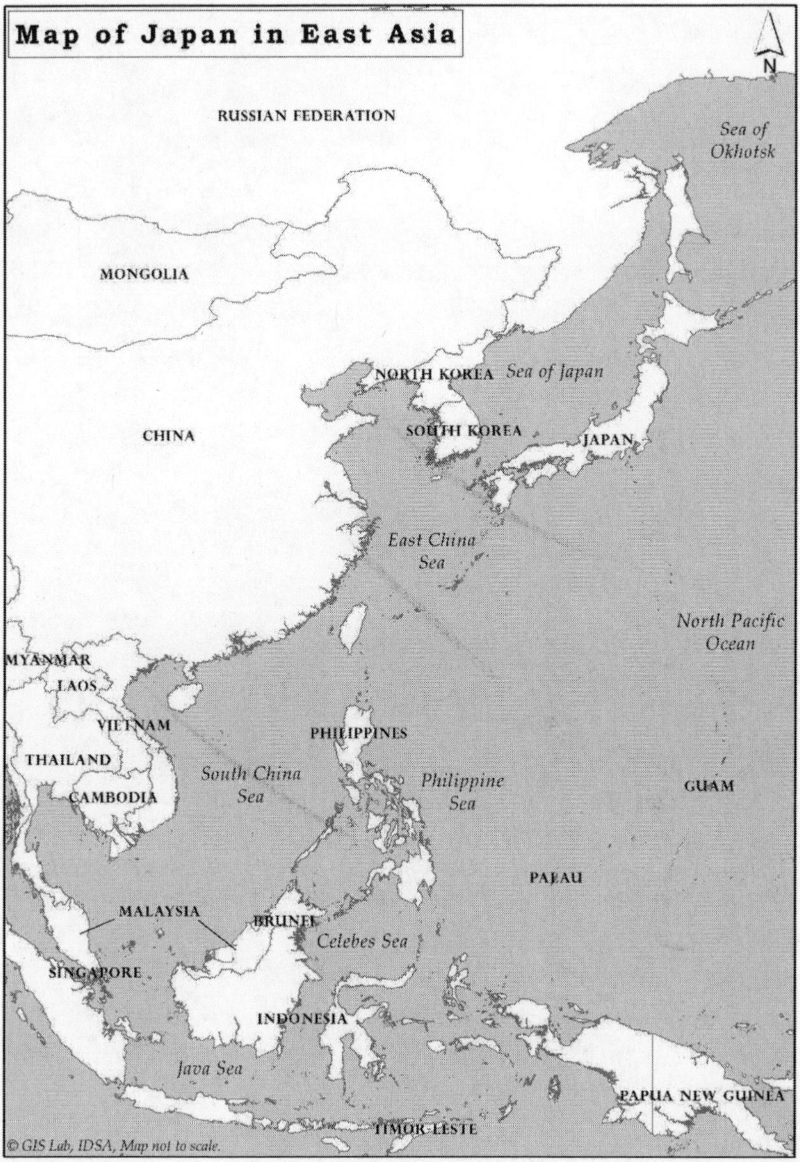

Map of Japan and Its Prefectures

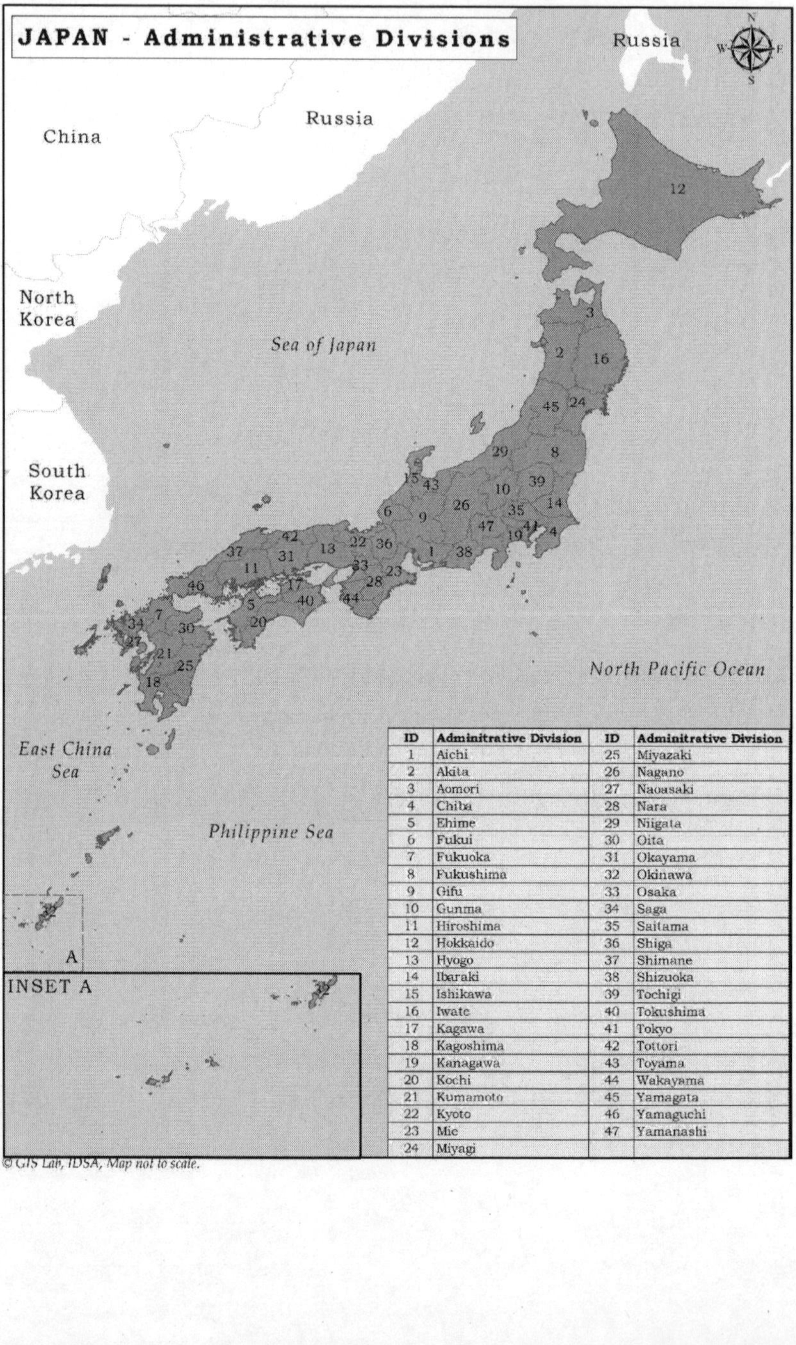

ID	Adminitrative Division	ID	Adminitrative Division
1	Aichi	25	Miyazaki
2	Akita	26	Nagano
3	Aomori	27	Naoasaki
4	Chiba	28	Nara
5	Ehime	29	Niigata
6	Fukui	30	Oita
7	Fukuoka	31	Okayama
8	Fukushima	32	Okinawa
9	Gifu	33	Osaka
10	Gunma	34	Saga
11	Hiroshima	35	Saitama
12	Hokkaido	36	Shiga
13	Hyogo	37	Shimane
14	Ibaraki	38	Shizuoka
15	Ishikawa	39	Tochigi
16	Iwate	40	Tokushima
17	Kagawa	41	Tokyo
18	Kagoshima	42	Tottori
19	Kanagawa	43	Toyama
20	Kochi	44	Wakayama
21	Kumamoto	45	Yamagata
22	Kyoto	46	Yamaguchi
23	Mie	47	Yamanashi
24	Miyagi		

© GIS Lab, IDSA, Map not to scale.

Abbreviations

ASDF	Air Self Defence Forces
ASEAN	Association of South East Asian Nations
ASW	Anti-submarine warfare
ATLA	Acquisition, Technology and Logistics Agency
CSG	Carrier Support Group
DRDO	Defence Research and Development Organisation
FY	Financial Year
GSDF	Ground Self Defence Forces
HADR	Humanitarian Assistance and Disaster Relief
IOR	Indian Ocean Region
METI	Ministry of Economy, Trade and Industry
MOFA	Ministry of Foreign Affairs
MoC	Memorandum of Cooperation
MoU	Memorandum of Understanding
MSDF	Marine Self Defence Forces
MTCR	Missile Technology Control Regime
MTDP	Mid-Term Defence Program
NSG	Nuclear Suppliers Group
ODA	Official Development Assistance
PSI	Proliferation Security Initiative
SAR	Search and Rescue
SLOCs/SLsOC	Sea Lines of Communication
SDF	Self Defence Forces
UNGA	United Nations General Assembly
UNPKO	United Nations Peace Keeping Operations
UNSC	United Nations Security Council

UNTAC	United Nations Transitional Authority in Cambodia
UNTAET	United Nations Transitional Authority in East Timor
VBBS	Visit, Board, Search and Seizure

Introduction

The visit of then Defence Minister of India, George Fernandes to Japan in January 2000 laid the basis for new dialogue on security issues between the two countries. This engagement was further promoted by the Prime Minister of Japan, Yoshiro Mori, who visited India the same year. Historically, leaders of both the countries have alluded to India and Japan being the 'pegs of security system in Asia'[1] and have introduced 'crescents' and 'arcs',[2] while laying out the vision of a 'broader Asia'.[3] The relationship stands at threshold of greater engagements with the new found chemistry between Prime Ministers Modi and Shinzo Abe.

In October 2008, the Indian and Japanese prime ministers signed the India-Japan Joint Security Declaration, asserting that the strategic partnership between the two countries would become 'an essential pillar for the future architecture of the region'.[4] However, given the meteoric rise of an aggressive China, the self-imposed constraint of strategic autonomy by India, the pacifist constitution of Japan and the declining US influence in Asia, the dynamics and prospects of this security cooperation in the mid and long term is yet to be clearly articulated. Research on the same has been little and fragmented.[5] This knowledge gap will be addressed through the project. The research will also ascertain areas that need strengthening of linkages with Japan and identify policies that the Indian establishment should adopt in order to secure its national Interests.

Despite having a number of convergences, drivers and prospects of a security architecture in Asia is hazy. India shares Japanese concerns about China as a regional hegemon and believes that a stronger partnership between the democratic nations will ensure a multi-polar Asia.[6] However, partnership with Japan in the security realm is beset with apprehensions because of Japan's security posture, which is strongly linked in an alliance with the US and a pacifist constitution, which is yet to provide unambiguous legality to its own armed forces. Therefore, the questions that need to be answered are: What strategic imperatives need to be factored in this cooperation? What are the focus areas in which the security cooperation can be enhanced? Do the cultural linkages between the two countries provide a strong foundation for security cooperation? And will this India-Japan congruence result in re-shaping the security arena of the Indo-Pacific region?

This research project aims at deepening the understanding of the security aspects in this bilateral relationship. A review of the existing literature on the subject reveals that research on India and Japan relates more to aspects of interstate relations and drivers of this relationship. The focus on security related issues has, however, been less. Authors like Rajaram Panda, in his paper 'India-Japan Relations: Dawn of a New Relationship?', published in *Indian Foreign Affairs Journal*, Vol. 9, April-June 2014, pp. 178–188, have asserted that the India-Japan relationship is in response to China's emergence as a regional hegemon and that this strategic factor has emerged as the prime driver in bilateral ties. Sourabh Gupta echoes similar views in his article 'Japan and India in a Broader Asia: Allies, Partners or Casual Friends' when he states that mutual interests of Japan and India have not been congruent. Even today, they might not be as congruent as they appear. Wellington and Antonio Henrique of University La Salle Rio de Janeiro, Rio de Janeiro, Brazil in their paper 'Japan And India: Soft Balancing as a Reaction To China's Rise', have stated that Japan and India are "getting closer" because both have a convergent focus with respect to security: China's rise. Such alliances are supported by the 'Balance of Threat' theory of Stephen M. Walt, *Alliance Formation and Balance of World Power,* International Security, No. 4 (1985): 3–43 and his *The Origin of Alliances* (Cornell University Press, Ithaca, New York, 1987). In fact, C. Raja Mohan, in 'India and the Balance of Power', *Foreign Affairs*, Vol. 85, Jul–Aug 2006 has noted, "As India starts to recognize that its political choices have global consequences, it will become less averse to choosing sides on specific issues. Alliance formation and balancing are tools in kits of all great powers—and so they are likely to be in India's as well". There have also been authors like Arpita Mathur who, in her RSIS Monograph No. 23, *India-Japan Relations: Drivers, Trends and Prospects,* argues that though Beijing's rise is one of the primary drivers catalysing India-Japan ties, New Delhi and Tokyo do not need to use the Beijing card to develop closer bilateral relations with each other as they have a number of complementarities in the regional domain as well. Similar views have been echoed by other experts on Japan.

Some scholars have alternately focused on the regional security aspects of this relationship and have highlighted as to how the security cooperation will affect the Indo-Pacific region and the world based on inter-state relations. Brahma Chellaney in his book *Asian Juggernaut: The Rise of China, India and Japan,* highlights that a process of multilateral security cooperation will undeniably help underpin Asian interests. Though competition between China and India-Japan is bound to increase, the three main players can set a model by establishing a stable political relationship based on beneficial cooperation. *India-Japan Relations in Emerging Asia* edited by Takenori Horimoto and Lalima Varma, 2013, Manohar Publishers and Distributors, New Delhi also echoes similar views with critical assessment of India-Japan relations in the context of the rapidly changing regional environment. In their book, *India and Japan—Assessing the Strategic Partnership* edited by Rajesh Basrur and Sumitha Narayan Kutty, the authors have discussed the concept of strategic partnership, the pragmatic nature of the India-Japan Strategic Partnership, and the inter-play between the drivers and constraints within the relationship. The authors have rightly brought out that India-Japan relationship carries the distinctive features of a strategic partnership and the fact that strategic partnerships are designed to help states cope with the uncertainties surrounding a system where fundamental interests are in sync, but many other interests are not.[7] These issues have been highlighted in this book through quantification of the levels of security cooperation between the two countries. However, the scope of the book by Basrur and Kutty does not encompass the basic steps that need to be taken for a robust strategic partnership and security cooperation. An attempt to touch upon the security and strategic aspects have been made by Shamshad Khan in his book, *Changing Dynamics of India-Japan Relations: Buddhism to Special Strategic Partnership,* which covers strategic and security issues as part of a chapter with two case studies. The book also focuses on the cultural, religious, political and economic dimensions of this relationship. A similar approach has been taken by Rohan Mukherjee and Anthony Yazaki in their co-edited book *Poised For Partnership—Deepening India-Japan Relations in the Asian Century.* The Security Cooperation and Strategic Partnership has been covered in Part III of this book in two chapters. It covers Japan's primary security interests and strategies, the expanding opportunities for cooperation, growing challenges and ends with certain short and long term recommendations of areas of cooperation. The recommendations are well articulated but a detailed analysis of the aspects of security cooperation and strategic partnership still eludes the readers. In addition, none of the literature available in this regard have carried out detailed research on the aspect of cooperation between the two countries in the field of peace keeping. The final aspect that needs highlighting is that there has been very little effort towards quantifying the levels of cooperation between the two countries. An attempt towards the same has been made by a Group of Experts from Foundation for National Security Research, New Delhi, to make a comparative quantitative assessment of India's Strategic Partners in their Report 'India's Strategic Partners: A Comparative Assessment', where the partnership between India and Japan has been evaluated based on consensus of the experts, on a scale of 10. But this quantification, based on a limited number of five experts, eludes the readers and scholars of the prevailing sentiments amongst a larger sample of the population of associated scholars, experts and strategists.

Therefore, the review of literature points towards the fact that the research on security cooperation between India and Japan has been fragmented and scattered in small chapters of books written on Japan. This could be because security aspects are a subset of the larger political and economic engagements undertaken and experts on the subject have yet to get into the brasstacks of enhancing security cooperation right from the tactical levels to the strategic level, holistically. The present research work, however, solely focuses on security aspects of this relationship and arrives at recommendations that will take this security relationship forward. An attempt has also been made to quantitatively assess the India-Japan Security Cooperation duly supported with statistics to arrive at the various levels of cooperation.

Keeping in mind the vastness of the subject, the scope of the study has been confined to the Indo-Pacific region. The research has been carried out with a systems approach methodology, identifying the drivers and statistically analysing the same based on data collected. The research has been carried out from an Indian researcher point of view and hence while discussing the geo-strategic imperatives, only Japanese aspects have been analysed. A SWOT analysis of the security cooperation between the two countries has been carried out to arrive at the strategies for enhancement of such cooperation.

Both primary and secondary data has been collected through available means including interactions with experts, study groups, delegates, interviews and published material. Understanding of the security environment and relations between stakeholders in overall geo-political framework through a rich picture and the process of Client, Actors, Transformation, World view, Owner and Environment (CATWOE) was carried out during the course of the research. Short term strategies that should be adopted by India to secure national interests have been derived through SWOT Analysis of stake holders.

This book has been written in four parts. Part I delves into the background of how Japan came into being and explores its historical linkages with India. The second chapter of Part I explores the role played by Japan in shaping the Independence movement in India and the India-Japan relations during the Cold War. Additionally, some important concepts that have evolved in the Indian armed forces due to the battles of the then Indian army (under the British) with Japanese troops have been highlighted. The third chapter analyses the geography and the strategic factors that shape the security posture of Japan in order to arrive at deductions, which play a very important role in defining Japan's security imperatives.

Part II covers the engagement of security aspects, which have been identified through the SWOT analyses, leading onto aspects where cooperation between India and Japan can be enhanced. Considering that maritime activities were the basis for further engagements between the two countries, Maritime Security has been covered as a separate chapter in Part II. Aspect of cooperation in UN peace keeping operations, which are largely apolitical and also form the basis for further cooperation amongst the military have also been covered in this part.

Part III presents this cooperation in a regional context and highlights the efforts to synergise India-Japan activities at the regional and global levels. This part analyses the concept of the Indo-Pacific and discusses the convergences and challenges faced by both countries in security aspects, in the region.

The final part, is an attempt at limited quantitative analyses of the India-Japan Security Cooperation, thereby establishing connect between the qualitative nature of the topic with a quantitative assessment of the level of security cooperation. This part concludes with important policy recommendations which the Government of India can take to enhance the levels of security cooperation with Japan.

The Appendices comprise of some data and the SWOT analyses table, arrived at after carrying out a Base Means Capability (BMC) analysis of India and Japan in security aspects. The BMC analysis was carried out during the course of the research. Questionnaires sent to various entities for gaining inputs and for carrying out survey have also been appended. Appendix C 'The Joint Declaration on

Security Cooperation' and Appendix D are important documents for contextualising the research work and therefore, needed to be included. These documents (Appendices C and D) are also available in open source internet and have been reproduced without any change.

Overall, the research highlights the dynamics of India-Japan security cooperation in its bilateral and regional context, provides an insight into the likely trajectory of this relationship and concludes by highlighting areas of cooperation that need attention. It is hoped that the research will be of some value to concerned functionaries in the Government of India, contemporary researchers as well as those researching on related topics in the future.

Notes

1. PM of Japan Hayato Ikeda during his visit to India in 1961 referred to India—Japan relations as: "India and Japan are natural pegs" in the security system of Asia (JICA-RI Working Paper No. 139 dated February 2017 at https://www.jica.go.jp/jica-ri/publication/workingpaper/175nbg0000054lpc-att/JICA-RI_WP_No.139.pdf, accessed on January 23, 2019).
2. Dean Acheson, speaking in the US Senate in 1950 said that the centre of US interests lay in the 'The Crescent' or semi-circle between India and Japan. These sentiments were echoed by PM Hayato Ikeda in 1961, Note 1 ibid refers (Satish Kumar (ed.) India's National Security: Annual Review 2015-16). Thereafter, H.E. Mr. Taro Aso, Minister for Foreign Affairs, in an address on 12 Mar 2007 on occasion of the 20th Anniversary of the Founding of the Japan Forum on International Relations, Inc. spoke on the "Arc of Freedom and Prosperity", wherein he alluded to the great arc encompassing countries of Europe, Central Asia and India. In December 2006, during an address to a joint session of the Japanese Parliament, then Indian Prime Minister Manmohan Singh described the need for stronger economic ties among the two Asian democracies. Emphasizing the concept of an "arc of prosperity," Mr. Singh presented India as a key factor in the development of an Asian community devoted to free trade.
3. In his 2007 address to the Indian Parliament, Japanese PM Shinzo Abe noted that Japan had "rediscovered" India in the "broader Asia" that was taking shape at the confluence of ... the Indian and Pacific Oceans (Manpreet S. Pardesi, 'Evolution of India-Japan Ties: Prospects and Limitations' in Rajesh Basrur and S.N. Kutty (eds) *India and Japan: Assessing the Strategic Partnership*, p. 31).

4. Ministry of Foreign Affairs, Japan, 'Joint Statement on the Advancement of the Strategic and Global Partnership between Japan and India', October 22, 2008 at https://www.mofa.go.jp/region/asia-paci/india/pmv0810/joint_s.html, accessed on July 9, 2018.
5. Arpita Mathur, 'India-Japan Relations Drivers, Trends and Prospects', RSIS Monograph No 23, S. Rajaratnam School of International Studies, 2012, accessed on April 2, 2016.
6. Anirudh Suri, 'India and Japan: Congruence at Last', *Asia Times Online Op-ed*, June 9, 2007.
7. Rajesh Basrur and S.N. Kutty (eds) *India and Japan: Assessing the Strategic Partnership*, p. 114.

PART I
Historical Linkages and Geo-Strategic Imperatives

1

Cultural Connections—Foundation for Security Cooperation

Abstract

Civilisations have evolved as a result of intermingling of cultures. The cultural relations may be direct which include physical contacts between differing cultures or indirect which entail an exchange of ideas, prejudices, philosophy and way of life. People to people contacts enhance trust and familiarity, which is imperative for good security relationships. India Japan cultural links, which led to the advent of Buddhism and Sanskrit in Japan, can form the foundation of a strong security relationship. This chapter attempts to trace the early evolution of Japan, the transfusion of Buddhism from India during its evolution, the resultant linkages and how this can form the foundation for a robust security relationship.

Early Japan

The Palaeolithic Period in Japan is variously dated from 30,000 to 10,000 years ago, when people lived by hunting and gathering, used fire, and made their homes either in pit-type dwellings or in caves.[1] During this period, no knowledge of pottery existed and hence this period is known as the Pre-Ceramic era. The Pre-Ceramic era was followed by two better-recorded cultures, the Jōmon (c. 10,500 to 300 BCE) and the Yayoi (c. 300 to 250 BCE).[2] The former takes its name from a type of pottery found throughout the archipelago; its discoverer, the 19th century American zoologist Edward S. Morse, called the pottery jōmon ("cord marks") to describe the patterns pressed into the clay.[3] Many scholars believe that the Jōmon people were Ainu, a people who practised a religion centred on blood-sacrifice and who survive today in small numbers in northern Japan.[4]

The early history of Japan is lost in folklore. Officially, till 1945, Japan was conceived to be founded in 660 BC by Emperor Jimmu, who was considered to be a descendant of the sun goddess, Amaterasu Omikami. In the first few centuries, Japan was inhabited by a number of tribal kingdoms or clans that were ruled by priests who also acted as chiefs. By 5th century, the Yamato clan, originally hailing from Kyushu had settled near modern Kyoto in the present day Nara prefecture (refer Map of Japan and Prefectures), and had loosely subjugated other clans dwelling in parts of Central and Western Japan, thereby laying the foundation of the modern day Japanese state.[5]

The Nara Period (AD 710–794) saw the advent of a culture that was heavily influenced by Chinese culture as exchanges between the two were common. This period also saw maintenance of historical records of events of that time. With the backing of the royal family for Buddhism (which arrived in Japan via Korea and China) a number of temples were constructed. The Heian Period (AD 794–1185), which followed the Nara period, gave rise to a culture which was different from the Chinese and can be said to have a more 'Japanese' content. This was also the time when two sets of the phonetic alphabet (*kana*) were developed partly under Indian influence, from the Chinese kanji. Society also underwent a transformation with the power passing from the kings to the warrior class, also known as the *samurai*. The title of Shogun came into being during this period, and was conferred on the Commander of the imperial armies. The Samurai introduced the *bushido* (the Way of the Samurai) which had the flair of austerity and was propagated in order to retain control over the subjugated tribal kingdoms. An interesting event of these times was the unsuccessful attempts by the Mongols under Kublai Khan to attack the Northern coast of Kyushu. Two such attempts were made in a space of one year and during both attacks, a typhoon destroyed the Mongol fleet. This divine intervention was attributed to the actions of kamikaze or Wind of the Gods.[6]

The concept of a unified Japan can be thought to have taken shape with the defeat of the Hojo clan in 1590 by the powerful samurai general Toyotomi Hideyoshi. Hideyoshi was assisted by the warlord, Tokugawa Ieyasu in his efforts and became the ruler of a unified Japan. Meanwhile, Tokugawa Ieyasu moved his base of operations to the Kanto district and began building a new regional capital in Edo or modern-day Tokyo.[7] He soon became the most influential *daimyo* (baron) and thereafter, became the Shogun in 1603. Edo was made the new capital under him and Japan was finally at peace. Under Tokugawa Ieyasu's leadership, this period, also called the Edo Period (1600–1868), was one of great cultural achievement.[8] The Meiji period commenced thereafter.

The Historical Connect with India

Buddhism spread from India far and wide across the globe through travellers, religious teachers, rulers and tradesmen. The early exchanges of Japan with India is said to have started in the 6th century AD, with the advent of Buddhism into Japan, through China and Korea.

Map 1.1: The Spread of Buddhism

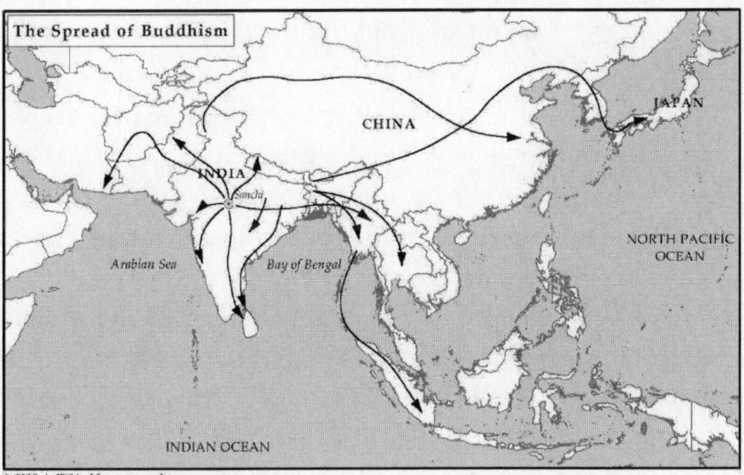

© GIS Lab, IDSA. Map not to scale.

Along with Buddhism, other aspects of Indian culture like the deities that were worshipped, the written script and certain customs also filtered into Japanese society. The ancient Japanese referred to India as the Heavenly Land (Tenjiku). Interestingly, as many as 12 Japanese deities who are revered in temples in Japan are actually Hindu deities and are regularly worshipped. These Gods came to Japan through China with Chinese names.[9] These 12 Gods are:[10]

- Bonten, 梵天 or Dai Bontenno, the God ruling Sky/Zenith, who is similar to Brahma, the creator of the Universe, with four heads overlooking each of the four directions (although shown often with one head only).
- Taishakuten, 帝釈天, the God ruling the East, who is similar to the Hindu God Indra, governing all natural forces.
- Bishamonten, 毘沙門天, the God ruling the North is actually the Hindu God Kubera, the God of Wealth.
- Katen, 火天, the God who is invoked during Shingon fire rituals and ruling the South East is similar to the fire God Agni.
- Emma or Enmaten is the God ruling the South and similar to the God of Death, Yama.
- Rasetsuten or Rasetsu, 羅刹天, is the God ruling the South West and is similar to Nirrti or Rakshasa.
- Suiten, 水天、水神、水王, ruling the West is the Hindu God Varuna, the God of water.
- Fūten/Fūjin, 風天, ruling the North West is similar to the Hindu Wind God, Vaayu.
- Ishanaten/Daijizaiten, 伊舎那天 (also known as Jizai Ten 自在天), is the diety ruling the North East and is similar to the Hindu deity Isana or Siva.
- Jiten/Chiten/Kenrochijin, 地天, ruling the downward direction or the Nadir is similar to Earth or Prithvi.
- Nitten/Dai Nittenno / 日天 is the Sun God adopted into Buddhism as a protector and is said to be a subject of Taishakuten (Indra).
- Gatten/Gakko, 月天 is the Moon who appears as a Bodhisattv in Buddhism.

Cultural linkages reached a new high between India and Japan in the 8th century AD, when an Indian monk named Bodhisena visited Japan on the invitation of the then Emperor of Japan, Shomu. Bodhisena was bestowed great honour and was accorded space in a temple called Daian-ji, from where he started teaching Sanskrit and spreading its use. He also founded the Kegon Buddhism—one of the six schools of Nara Buddhism in Japan. In 752 AD, Bodhisena was asked by the Japanese Emperor Shomuto to perform the eye opening ceremony for the giant bronze statue of the Buddha Vairocana built in Todai-ji, which is best known for its 500-tonne, 15-metre high Buddha, and is the largest bronze statue in the world.[11] In front of a huge, cosmopolitan gathering that included ambassadors from Persia, Korea, Vietnam, China and Central Asia, Bodhisena painted the pupils on the eyes of the Buddha statue, inviting the spirit in to animate the sculpture.[12] A disciple of Bodhisena went on to teach a style of dance that featured themes taken from Indian mythology, set to a musical rhythm, common in South Asia, but unknown at the time in Japan.[13] These dances became known as 'rinyugaku' and were absorbed into the local artistic oeuvre and are still preserved as Japan's traditional court dance and music.[14] Bodhisena committed himself to spread of Sanskrit in Japan. At Koyasan (Wakayame prefecture), they still have a school where Sanskrit is taught. The 47 characters of the Japanese script are said to have been devised after the pattern of the Sanskrit alphabet by the Japanese Buddhist Kobo Daishi (774–835 AD).[15] This arrangement of the Japanese syllabary based on the Sanskrit system is also attributed to the influence of Bodhisena in Japan, which, according to Riri Nakayama, "will continue as long as the Japanese language continues to exist".[16]

Even the present day Kana script of Japan is traditionally believed to have been invented by one of Japan's most significant religious figures, the Buddhist priest Kukai, who in 806 AD brought the Siddham script of India home on his return from China.[17] The Siddham script has had a profound influence on the development of the Kana script (as well as the Korean Hangul script). The Siddham script has descended from the Brāhmī script, which is also the mother script for Devanāgarī and a number of non-Indian scripts, such as certain South East Asian and Tibetan scripts. The present set of kana was codified in 1900, and rules for their usage established in 1946.[18] Extensive research carried out by the noted art-historian and filmmaker Benoy K. Behl, has revealed that Siddham is still in practice, in parts of Japan like the Koyasan (Wakayame prefecture of Japan), though it has disappeared from India. There are deep meanings in Japanese practices which take us back to early developments of philosophy in India.[19] Japan has not seen the breakdown of cultural norms, which India suffered during colonial education system.[20] The discovery of ancient Sanskrit manuscripts in old Brahmi characters preserved intact in Horyuji, the most ancient monastery extant in Japan, and some other monasteries is a pertinent point.[21] In fact the manuscripts are older than what we have in India i.e., 6th century as compared to 10th century in India.[22]

From 1868–1912, during the Meiji period, when Japan embarked upon the process of modernisation, direct exchanges commenced between India and Japan. In 1903, the India-Japan Association was inaugurated by the Meiji government. This is one of the oldest associations which laid the foundation of cultural, social and economic relations between the two countries. In the context of new emerging Asia, the Association was established to promote strong ties with India forged by spiritual sharing and understanding.[23] Over the years, the image of Japan has always been positive, more so in the early 20th century when Japan's victory over Russia was seen as an emergence of Asian countries against European powers. The immediate post-independence experience for India was no less positive, with the Tokyo tribunal, waiving of reparations, conclusion of a separate Peace Treaty, the Asian Games and extension of yen loans.[24] Japan was admired strongly in the collective Indian perception because of its post-war economic re-construction and rapid economic growth. The transformation brought in India, in the field of industrial technology and management, concepts due to the advent of Maruti-Suzuki has further enhanced Indian respect for Japanese society.

When the Allied Powers led by the United States (US) decided to draw a peace settlement for Japan, India declined to participate in the San Francisco Peace Conference held in September 1951 on the grounds that the US-drafted peace treaty failed to give due recognition to the wishes of the Japanese people.[25] Instead, India chose to enter into a bilateral peace treaty with Japan in 1952 and it was one of the first countries in Asia to open diplomatic ties with Tokyo.[26] Since then, both the countries have established diplomatic relations with each other and have enjoyed responsive relations that are based on technical and economic considerations. However, during this period, due to divergent leanings of India and Japan, the potential of the relationship could not be harnessed. Japan became a staunch ally of the US whereas India led the non-aligned countries. This conceptual divergence created an ideological barrier and resulted in both India and Japan taking diametrically opposite stands on various regional and global issues.[27] The end of the Cold War proved to be propitious for India-Japan relations since many common factors and concerns which had remained dormant for years began to manifest themselves sharply in the evolving new regional environment and the relations entered a new and positive phase after 2000.[28]

Despite the geo-political compulsions which restrained the development of cordial relations during the Cold War, both countries could quickly overcome their initial complications to come together in the 21st century. The foundations of this strategic relationship have been facilitated by the cultural linkages between India and Japan. By definition, 'Culture consists of patterns, explicit and implicit, of and for behaviour acquired and transmitted by symbols, constituting the distinctive achievements of human groups, including their embodiment in artifacts'; the essential core of culture consists of traditional (i.e., historically derived and selected) ideas and especially their attached values; culture systems may, on the one hand, be considered as products of action, on the other, as conditional elements of future action (Kroeber and Kluckhohn 1952: 181; cited by Adler 1997: 14).[29] Cultural linkages, therefore, can be termed as intangible factors such as a nation's ideas, behaviour patterns and opinions and these factors are broader than the interplay of National Interests.[30] Cultural linkages lead to enhanced understanding of each others' world view and challenges. Within the common thread of Buddhism, the pacifist outlook of Japan is well appreciated by the people of India, who themselves have maintained an outlook over centuries based on peace and tolerance. Both India and Japan share convergences on a vision of peace and shared prosperity for the world that is based on sustainable development. The global vision is underpinned by the commitment of both countries to democratic values, human rights and the rule of law. Both nations view each other as responsible nations that are capable of responding to regional and global challenges keeping in focus the strategic aspirations, interests and concerns of each other, in keeping with their strategic partnership. A strong, prosperous and dynamic India is, therefore, in the interest of Japan and vice versa.[31] The resultant bonhomie can lead onto an appreciation of the challenges that the respective societies in both countries strive to overcome. Communication and societal interaction, therefore, has the potential to become unrestricted and seamless, which can engage other aspects of governance. Security relations and strategic partnerships will also follow through, in case this platform for a deep cultural connect, is maintained.

Cultural linkages encourage cultural activities like tourism, exchange of movies, books, literature and propagating a sense of brotherhood amongst people. Indian Prime Minister Narendra Modi and his Japanese counterpart, Shinzo Abe have periodically laid stressed on the need to further expand the opportunities for tourism, youth exchange and educational collaboration between the two countries and decided to mark the year 2017 as a year of Japan-India Friendly Exchanges.[32] One of the factors to assess the extent of people to people exchanges between nations is to analyse the influx of tourists. The analyses of the number of Japanese tourists coming to India are tabulated below.[33]

Table 1.1: Japanese Tourists Visiting India (1981–2016)

Year	No. of Tourists	Total Foreign Tourists Coming To India (in millions)	% Share of Tourists	% Increase of Tourists from Last Year
1981	29032	1.28	2.27	-
1991	46655	1.68	2.78	60.70
2001	80634	2.54	3.17	72.83
2002	59709	2.38	2.51	-25.95
2003	77996	2.73	2.86	30.63
2004	96851	3.46	2.80	24.17
2005	103082	3.92	2.63	6.44
2006	119292	4.45	2.68	15.73
2007	145538	5.08	2.86	22.00
2008	145352	5.28	2.75	-0.13
2009	124756	5.17	2.41	-14.17
2010	168019	5.78	2.91	34.68
2011	193525	6.31	3.07	15.18
2012	220015	6.58	3.34	13.69
2013	220283	6.97	3.16	0.12
2014	219516	7.68	2.86	-0.35
2015	207415	8.03	2.58	-5.51
2016	208847	8.80	2.38	0.69

Source: India Tourism Statistics.

An assessment of the same reveals that though there has been an increase in the total number of tourists from Japan, the overall share of tourists has not shown a corresponding increase. The year on year percentage of tourists has even decreased in 2014 and 2015. This can be attributed to a variety of factors but it is evident that cultural connect holds a large potential for enhancement of security relations.

It is also axiomatic that cultural linkages that have been existent between India and Japan from the early 5th century to the present times have been a source of trust and bonding between people and can thus be considered as foundational pillars on which security relations and strategic partnerships can be based.[34] However, there are certain differences in traits that must be overcome as a significant gulf exists between the outlook of the Indians and Japanese, reflected even in their negotiating styles, with Indians rarely knowing when to stop negotiating and declare victory (or at least a truce), and the Japanese always wanting every last detail settled before anything can be agreed, while also seeking to build in as much control over outcomes as possible.[35] Cooperation will, thus, require a greater willingness by each side to understand the other more than superficially.[36]

Holistically, the cultural linkages play an important role in setting the stage for further enhancement in relations should other factors be ripe for an engaging arrangement. As we will also see later in this book, cultural linkages as a factor of quantitative assessment of security cooperation have been important in getting India and Japan closer to each other.

Conclusion

The universal appeal of a country's culture and its ability to establish a favourable set of rules and institutions that govern areas of international activity are critical sources of power.[37] Clearly, this suggests a rationale for states to both, nurture national cultures at home and promote these cultures abroad.[38] Both India and Japan have a long history of cultural linkages. There is a need for both nations to collaborate in order to encourage more people to people engagements. The strong but dormant bonding, and the reciprocating regard for each other bereft of historical baggage have the potential to enhance these cultural linkages and branch onto aspects related to security. In the 20th century, when both countries were undergoing transformation in their own ways, people to people engagements took on a more personalised perspective. The next chapter further analyses the events in the last century during India's struggle for independence, during the Cold War period, and during the subsequent changed security dynamics in a regional context.

Notes

1. Ancient Japan to 1185, *Encyclopaedia Britannica* at https://www.britannica.com/place /Japan/History#ref167959, accessed on January 28, 2018.
2. Ibid.
3. Ibid.
4. Facts and Details, Jomon Period (10,500 BC–300 BC) at http://factsanddetails.com/japan/cat16/sub105/item2764.html, accessed on January 28, 2018.
5. Retrieved from https://www.questia.com/library/history/asian-history/japanese-history/ancient-japan, accessed on January 28, 2018.
6. Early Japanese History, *Japan Zone* at https://www.japan-zone.com/omnibus/history1.shtml, accessed on January 28, 2018. Kamikaze was thereafter used in the Second World War to depict gallant fighters who rained from the sky on suicide missions laden with explosives, on ships.
7. Explore Japan History, Kids Web Japan at https://web-japan.org/kidsweb/explore/history/ q3.html, accessed on September 16, 2018.
8. Writing reforms in Modern Japan at https://www.japan-zone.com/omnibus/history1.shtml, accessed on January 28, 2018.
9. Krishnendu Bandopadhyay, 'Hindu Gods forgotten in India revered in Japan', *The Times of India,* January 11, 2016.
10. Pramit Pal Chaudhuri, 'India's most successful export has been the gods of Japan', *Hindustan Times,* October 27, 2010 at https://www.hindustantimes.com/world/india-s-most-successful-export-has-been-the-gods-of-japan/story-yQrh73Aprp7TH0YUBwI8NJ.html, accessed on July 31, 2018.
11. Pallavi Aiyar, 'The Indian who docked at Osaka', *The Hindu,* June 9, 2018 at https://www.thehindu.com/ society/history-and-culture/the-indian-who-docked-at-osaka/article24112221.ece, accessed on September 15, 2018.
12. Ibid.
13. Ibid.
14. Ibid.
15. Sanjeev Nayyar, China, Korea, Japan, *e-Samskriti*, March 2002at https://www.esamskriti.com/e/History/Indian-Influence-Abroad/China-Korea-Japan-3.aspx, accessed on September 17, 2018.
16. Sanjukta Das Gupta, 'Cultural Contacts between BIMSTEC Countries and Japan: An Historical Survey', CSIRD Discussion Paper: 7/2005, November 2005, pp. 5–6.
17. Jayarava, Siddham, 'The Perfect Script', *Visible Mantra* at http://www.visiblemantra.org/index.html, accessed on July 9, 2018.
18. Kana, *New World Encyclopedia* at http://www.newworldencyclopedia.org/entry/Kana, accessed on October 16, 2018.

19. Mamta Singh, Indian Culture in Japan, *The Statesman,* September 9, 2015 at https://www.thestatesman.com/supplements/indian-culture-in-japan-88931.html, accessed on September 1, 2018.
20. Ibid.
21. Sanjukta Das Gupta, note 16.
22. Ibid.
23. Event: India and Japan: Unearthing lesser-known 16th to early 20th century linkages organized by India International Centre & Mombusho Scholars Association of India, Humanities Across Borders, November 15-17, 2017 at https://humanitiesacrossborders.blog/2018/01/08/event-india-and-japan-unearthing-lesser-known-16th-to-early-20th-century-linkages/, accessed on August 1, 2018.
24. Ministry of External Affairs, Government of India, *India-Japan Relations,* July 2013 at https://mea.gov.in/Portal/ForeignRelation/India-Japan_Relations.pdf, accessed on January 29, 2018.
25. K.V. Kesavan, 'India and Japan Changing Dimensions of Partnership in the post-Cold War Period', ORF Occasional Paper #14, New Delhi, 2010.
26. Ibid.
27. Ibid.
28. Ibid.
29. Peter Naibe, 'Culture and Sustainable Development', Conference Paper, August 2014 at https://www.researchgate.net/publication/266377976_CULTURE_AND_SUSTAINABLE_DEVELOPMENT, accessed on January 25, 2019.
30. AkiraIriye,'CulturalrelationsandPolicies'atwww.americanforeignrelations.com/A-D/Cultural-Relations-and-Policies.html, accessed on September 11, 2018.
31. Ministry of External Affairs, Government of India, *India-Japan Relations,* July 2013 at https://mea.gov.in/Portal/ForeignRelation/India-Japan_Relations.pdf, accessed on January 29, 2018.
32. Anica Mann-Kapur, 'Global Lessons In Boosting Tourism—The Japanese Case Study', Yes Global Institute, December 4, 2017 at http://yesinstitute.in/2017/12/global-lessons-in-boosting-tourism-the-japanese-case-study/, accessed on September 15, 2018.
33. Ministry of Tourism, Government of India, Market Research Division, *India Tourism Statistics,* 2017.
34. Joseph Nye, in his work on 'soft power' describes 'Culture' as one of the three resources of soft power. The other two are 'Political Values' and 'Foreign Policy'.
35. Anthony Yazaki and Rohan Mukherjee (eds), 'Conclusion: Overcoming a History of Missed Opportunities', in *Poised for Partnership: Deepening*

India Japan Relations in the Asian Century, Oxford University Press, New Delhi, 2016, p. 275.

36. Ibid.
37. Christopher D. Sommerich, 'The Cultural Role of the State in Domestic and International Relations' at http://digitalcommons.unl.edu/cgi/viewcontent.cgi?article=1037& context=opentheses, accessed on September 16, 2018.
38. Ibid.

2

Linkages with Japan During India's Independence Struggle and the Second World War

Abstract

During the 20th century, the linkages with Japan saw a different hue. The centuries-old cultural links were replaced by a love-hate relationship, which was both personality driven as well as a product of the colonial rule. Whereas the likes of Netaji Subhas Chandra Bose and his followers eulogised Japan's efforts in 'ousting the Western colonial powers' from Asia, the Indian troops under the British military leadership fought the Japanese with tremendous ferocity and resilience, which matched Japanese tenacity to fight in difficult conditions. Culturally, this period saw the commencement of modern day contacts with the Japanese in terms of visits of Nobel laureate Rabindranath Tagore and Swami Vivekananda to Japan. Considering these exchanges, this chapter analyses a number of important lessons learnt during these contacts and highlights important events that have left an indelible mark on the India-Japan relations.

Introduction

Events in the 20th century had far reaching effects on the security horizon in the Indo-Pacific region. The early years witnessed the rise of an Asian power that successfully challenged a European power.

This led to a surge in admiration for Japan in India leading to a personality driven relationship with Japan especially during India's struggle for Independence. This period also saw the Indian army (under the British) fight the Japanese and draw major lessons from the battles with the Japanese. There were also certain events post the Second World War which were instrumental in shaping the environment for the run-up to deeper engagements between India and Japan in the 21st century.

A Personality Driven Relationship

In 1904–1905, the Japanese victory in the Russo-Japanese War led other Asian nations to see a promise of their own revival; they hailed both, the speed as well as content of Japan's transformation.[1] It also caught the imagination of an Asian re-surgence, of many Indians who were themselves fighting the British for independence. A large number of revolutionaries, thinkers, poets and other eminent people visited or established contacts in Japan, for avenues and opportunities to fulfil their missions. Amongst them, the great poet and thinker, Rabindranath Tagore, who later became a Nobel laureate, made a number of visits to Japan. Influence of Japan on the poet was mostly literary and spiritual, reflecting Tagore's personal bent; yet any chronicle of his relationship with Japan will surely also have to mention his discreetly expressed dismay at what he saw as signs of militant nationalism, especially during his visit in 1916.[2] It reminded him of the unthinking, belligerent chauvinism that he and others, felt had led to the outbreak of war in Europe two years earlier and did not, he believed, represent the best of Japan.[3] His expression of these feelings was not well received by most Japanese. He, however, developed a deep friendship with Japanese thinker, art historian and curator Okakura Tenshin. In the field of education, the establishment of Nippon Bhavana at Rabindranath Tagore's Visva Bharati in Santiniketan is a living testimony to the legacy of the Tagore-Okakura dialogue.[4] Other eminent personalities of that time, mostly from Bengal like Suresh Chandra Bandopadhyay, Manmatha Nath Ghosh and Hariprova Takeda were among the earliest Indians who visited Japan and have written of their experiences there.[5] Swami Vivekananda in a letter during his visit in 1893 noted that '[t]he Japanese seem now to have fully awakened themselves to the necessity of the present times ... And they are bent upon making everything they want in their own country.'[6] In another letter written on June 1901, he expressed great hope for better relations saying, "The help that Japan will give us will be with great sympathy and respect, whereas that from the West is unsympathetic and destructive.[7] Certainly it is very desirable to establish a connection between India and Japan".[8]

Reflecting on the historical relations between Japan and India in modern times, what strikes as important is the role played by two Indians, Rash Bihari Bose and Subhas Chandra Bose.[9] When Subhas Chandra Bose realised that his plan for opening a land route from Russia and Afghanistan may not succeed with German assistance, he sought Japanese assistance in challenging the British rule. With the assistance of the then Japanese Prime Minister Tojo, Bose proclaimed the formation of the Provisional Government of Free India, revived the Azad Hind Fauj (Indian National Army) and commenced his "March to Delhi". The hoisting of the flag of Free India at the Andaman and Nicobar Islands and at Mowdok (present day Bangladesh) gave India the first whiff of a possibility of a Free India.[10] Throughout the independence struggle, Japan was also home to many other revolutionary leaders like Rash Behari Bose, who fled to Japan post an unsuccessful assassination bid on then Viceroy, Lord Hardinge, and A.M. Nair who fled to escape arrest by the British in India, at the age of 18.[11] Netaji's speech at a military review parade of the Indian National Army in 1943 with slogans of '*Delhi Chalo*' and '*Give me blood and I promise you freedom*' resonated widely in the Indian minds and provided the much needed fillip to the Indian independence struggle.[12] However, everything was not rosy about the Japanese assistance and exchanges with India at that time. The Japanese occupation of the Andaman and Nicobar islands and the atrocities carried out on the local people, though least talked about, have been documented. Jayant Dasgupta, in his book, *Japanese in the Andaman and Nicobar Islands*, mentions the relationship between the Indian National Army and the Japanese forces, in that "There was no real power sharing and that Bose was merely a façade to hide Japan's imperialistic and colonial designs in South and South East Asia, the much vaunted Co-Prosperity Sphere notwithstanding".[13]

Holistically, the relationship between India and Japan till the 1930s was driven by personalities and civil societies. In the late 1930s, India started figuring in the Japanese foreign policy priorities because of its 'geo-strategic location'. India's location still remains an important factor for Japanese foreign policy priorities.[14]

Lessons Learnt During Conflicts with the Japanese

The India-Japan exchanges in the period of the 20th century till the Second World War can not only be traced from the experiences of prominent Indian personalities with their Japanese counterparts but rich and valuable lessons have also been drawn from the military conflicts of the then British Indian army and the Japanese army and from subsequent events post the Second World War.

There were numerous instances when a small number of Japanese troops were able to convincingly defeat superior numbers of their adversaries in battle. The need to come up with a strategy to counter the Japanese swift advances led military thinkers of the time to develop certain important operational concepts. These concepts then developed have been refined and are still practiced in the Indian army today. Though, this particular aspect may not have any direct bearing on the overall frame of the India-Japan security relationship, as a practitioner of warfare, it remains an obligation to highlight their important aspects, while discussing the India-Japan security relationship.

Chindits: One such concept was the evolution of the Chindit operations. Six months after the Japanese attack on the Pearl Harbor (October 1941), the Japanese Empire stretched from Manchuria in the north to New Guinea's jungle-clad Owen Stanley Range in the south, from the borders of India's Assam in the west to the Gilbert

Islands in the South Pacific.[15] In 1942, in order to halt the rapid expansion of the Japanese empire towards India's eastern parts, Brigadier General Wingate, a senior British army officer and an exponent of unconventional military thinking, presented a plan for long range penetration patrols operating behind Japanese lines to be supported by air supply. This was aimed to surprise the enemy, tie down its reserves and deceive the enemy about the main direction of attack. The first Chindits unit, the 77th Indian Infantry Brigade was formed and trained for these penetration patrols. During actual operations against the Japanese, the majority of the surviving Chindits soldiers had crossed the Chindwin River (in Myanmar) having marched around 1600 km. Only two-thirds of the original strength could return to India after the operations, the rest having been killed, taken as Prisoner of War (PoW), or having died of disease. Though the effectiveness of the patrols was debated, the last of the Chindit patrol units acted as a long range penetration patrol behind the Japanese fighting in Kohima, a battle which again had a tremendous impact on the Indian Independence Movement. The Chindit operations provided valuable lessons in air support and air supply operations. It brought out that air supply could be employed as the sole means and not just as emergency means, of supply.[16] Incidentally, presently the Indian army has a number of air maintained posts along our borders, all throughout the year. The operations also provided invaluable experience in tactical situations of infiltration and operating behind enemy lines. The brave, relentless and exhaustive operations have, thereafter, found a permanent place in the training programme of the would-be officers of the Indian armed forces in the Indian Military Academy (IMA), Dehradun and the Officers Training Academy (OTA) at Chennai. Cadets of these training institutions are made to undergo long route marches of around 40 km before they conduct tactical operations of attack and ambush in designated enemy areas. Long range patrols are also being undertaken presently along the Northern and Eastern borders and in the jungles of North East region by our soldiers as part of their security related duties.

Map 2.1: Chindits Operation 1943

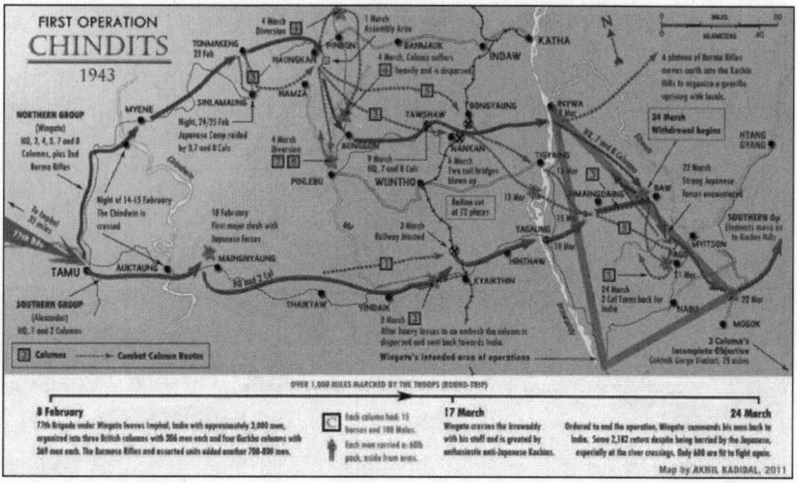

Battle of Kohima: The Battle of Kohima was another operation that influenced the way the Indian army fights wars today. This battle was part of the overall Burma Campaign of the British, which was one of the bloodiest campaigns in the Second World War where casualties reached over a hundred thousand and which culminated in the defeat of the Japanese forces.[17] By 1944, the Imperial Japanese army had a clear objective of capturing the Allied supply bases on the Imphal plains and thereafter, cutting off Allied communications to China allowing them to take over the bases for an all-out assault on British India. The Battle of Kohima in 1944 is also called the 'Stalingrad of the East', because this battle sounded the halt of the Japanese U-Go offensive and their march towards Delhi. In the Battle of Kohima, fatal casualties numbered approximately 11,000, with the British losing around 4000 soldiers. One of the greatest lessons learnt in this battle was the importance of an integrated air-land battle. The grit and determination shown by both sides is part of folklore. The tenacity to fight till 'the last man last round' was exemplified here. This battle gave Indian soldiers a belief in their own martial ability and showed that they could fight as well or better than anyone else.[18] It also highlighted the importance of air support and air supply in battles, especially in difficult jungle terrain against Japanese tactics of infiltration and encirclement. In a 2013 poll instigated by the National

Army Museum, the Battle of Kohima was awarded the title of 'Britain's Greatest Battle', beating the D-Day, Waterloo, Rorke's Drift and Aliwal (all very famous battles) to the title.[19] One of the survivors of this battle has said that there should have been a medal for the Battle of Kohima, like they have for Normandy (D-Day Landings), as it was a bigger battle than Normandy.[20]

'Despite the military defeat of Japan, and with it the INA, popular support for the INA finally precipitated British withdrawal from India,' writes author Kalyan Kumar Ghosh in his 'History of the Indian National Army' published in 1966.[21] The Commonwealth War Graves Commission currently maintains the War Cemetery in Kohima with the graves of 1,420 soldiers of the Allied forces. The cemetery is located in the same place where one of the bloodiest battles of the Burma Campaign was fought. This was the Deputy Commissioner's tennis court, which lies on the slopes of 'Garrison Hill'. The epitaph that has been carved on the memorial here, of the 2nd British Division, is famous as the Kohima Epitaph. It reads:

When you go home, tell them of us and say,
For your tomorrow, we gave our today

Author Robert Lyman, in his book *Japan's Last Bid for Victory: The Invasion of India 1944*, states that even the Japanese regard the Battle of Kohima to be their greatest defeat ever.

This Japanese connection to North East India was further strengthened when in May 2017, the Japanese Ambassador to India sought cooperation from the people in locating the mortal remains of about 70,000 Japanese soldiers in Imphal and Nagaland and declared Japan's intention of building a war museum at Maibam Lokpa Ching in Manipur's Bishenpur district.[22] The Japanese Ambassador to India, Kenji Hiramatsu, took a delegation of 38 Japanese companies based in Delhi to Imphal, Manipur in May 2017, to encourage investments in the region. The visit was organised particularly to mark the commemoration of the 73rd Anniversary of the Battle of Kohima, fought between the Japanese army and the Allied Forces in 1944. The ambassador in his speech on the occasion pledged to invest and develop the region to help it overcome the devastating effects of the war. Japan is particularly keen to invest in Assam, Manipur and Nagaland, states with which it shares a "historic emotional link".[23] Speaking at the fourth Northeast Connectivity Summit in Kohima from September 22 to 23, 2017, Kenko Sone, Minister, Economic Affairs, Embassy of Japan stated, 'India's North East region is situated at a strategically and economically important juncture between India and Southeast Asia as well as within the BIMSTEC (Bay of Bengal) community'.[24] Japan has undertaken works on road connectivity, energy projects, water supply and sanitation, forest resources management, Japanese language education and post-war reconciliation, which aimed to build a deeper understanding of the actions of the Japanese forces in the region during the Second World War.[25]

Kohima Epitaph

Source: https://en.wikipedia.org/wiki/Battle_of_Kohima#/media/File:Kohima_War_Cemetery,_Kohima,_Nagaland_(89).jpeg. Author: By PP Yoonus - Own work, CC BY-SA 3.0, https://commons.wikimedia.org/w/index.php?curid=30220677

The Tokyo Tribunal: The Tokyo Tribunal is the third event which stands out as part of the India-Japan exchanges post Second World War and has had an everlasting influence in the India Japan relations. Post Second World War, the allies set up a tribunal to try the military and political leaders of Japan and Germany as war criminals. Eleven judges were selected by the International Military Tribunal for the Far East (IMTFE) and called to Tokyo to deliberate upon the fate of 28 leaders of Japan (for Germany, the trials were called Nuremberg Trials). The trials, which began in May 1946, lasted for two and half years. Post the completion of the hearings in 1948, the judges discussed their opinions on the entire proceedings for days. The Japanese remember with great praise, the dissent registered by Justice Radha Binod Pal of India who differed from the rest of the jury in his verdict. In a long dissent note, Pal wrote that 'in colonizing parts of Asia, Japan had merely aped the Western powers and that the charges of crimes against peace and humanity were a sham employment of legal process for the satisfaction of a thirst for revenge.'[26]

Justice Radha Binod Pal believed that the international community at the time did not possess the level of detached impartiality or sophistication to declare war a crime.[27] In the conclusion to his dissent, he quoted the following lines by Jefferson Davis (these lines are also engraved on the memorial of Justice Radha Binod Pal):

> *When Time shall have softened passion and prejudice, when Reason shall have stripped the mask from misrepresentation, then Justice, holding evenly her scales, will require much of past censure and praise to change places.*[28]

These three important events contributed a lot to India-Japan connections during India's Independence struggle and the period post the Second World War. Once India became independent, it expressed support for Japanese interests; its delegation at the Far Eastern Commission, for example, was sympathetic to Japanese concerns about rebuilding their nation and encouraging Japanese industry and finance. In 1949, the Indian delegation stopped pressing the question in the Commission regarding its share of reparations from Japan and proposed halting the reparations altogether, noting that the burden of making such payments told heavily on the living standards of the Japanese people.[29]

Conclusion

Though the chapter is selective in highlighting the exchanges between India and Japan in the 20th century, it emphasizes that these influences need to be nurtured and in the present context, furthered, for meaningful engagement amongst the people and militaries of both the countries. The stand taken by India in waiving off the reparations and thereafter signing a separate peace treaty with Japan in 1952, terming the US drafted peace treaty as not according to the wishes of the Japanese people, was seen in a positive light in Japan. However, this positive orientation could not be sustained due to different ideological positions taken by both countries during the Cold War. It was only after the end of the Cold War, with a change in security dynamics in the region that India Japan ties have seen an enhancement. This has been possible due to a number of drivers that have been discussed later in this book. However, before we get onto the drivers, it is imperative to understand the impact that geography, geo-political and geo-strategic considerations have, in addition to the religious and cultural background as detailed above, on the security outlook of a nation like Japan. The same has been expounded in the next chapter.

Notes

1. P.G. Rajamohan, Dil Bahadur Rahut and Jabin T. Jacob, 'Changing Paradigm of Indo-Japan Relations: Opportunities and Challenges', Indian Council for Research on International Economic Relations, Working Paper No. 212, April 2008.
2. Editorial, Rabindranath Tagore and Japan, *The Japan Times*, September 7, 2003 at https://www.japantimes.co.jp/opinion/2003/09/07/editorials/rabindranath-tagore-and-japan/#.W5_ttc4zbIW, accessed on September 17, 2017.

3. Ibid.
4. 'Event: India and Japan: Unearthing lesser-known 16th to early 20th century' linkages organized by India International Centre & Mombusho Scholars Association of India, *Humanities Across Borders,* November 15–17, 2017 at https://humanitiesacrossborders.blog/2018/01/08/event-india-and-japan-unearthing-lesser-known-16th-to-early-20th-century-linkages/, accessed on August 1, 2018.
5. India-Japan Relations, *YKBD* at https://www.ykbd.org/india-japan-relations/, accessed on October 17, 2018.
6. P.G. Rajamohan, Dil Bahadur Rahut and Jabin T. Jacob, note 1.
7. Ibid.
8. Ibid.
9. Embassy of Japan lecture on "Two Boses: Ras Behari Bose And Subhas Chandra Bose by Prof. Krishna Bose, Chairperson, Netaji Research Bureau and Prof. Nobuko Nagasaki, Professor, University of Ryukoku" at https://www.in.emb-japan.go.jp/Friendship_Year2007/Lecture-Nov.html
10. Maj Gen Shah Nawaz Khan, 'My *Memories of INA and its Netaji*', Raj Kumar Publications, Delhi: 1946 at https://www.japantimes.co.jp/news/2011/08/14/national/history/japans-unsung-role-in-indias-struggle-for-independence/#.Wr8PtS5ubIU, accessed on January 29, 2018.
11. Jon Mitchell, 'Japan's unsung role in India's struggle for independence', *The Japan Times*, August 14, 2011 at https://www.japantimes.co.jp/news/2011/08/14/national/history/japans-unsung-role-in-indias-struggle-for-independence/#.Wr8PtS5ubIU, accessed on January 29, 2018.
12. Netaji Subhas Chandra Bose, To Delhi, To Delhi, Speech at a Military Review of the Indian national Army, July 5, 1943 at https://www.scribd.com/doc/19855244/Speech-of-Subhas-Chandra-Bose, accessed on September 17, 2018. Netaji Subhas Chandra Bose gave many memorable speeches and some of them are documented here.
13. Jayant Dasgupta, *Japanese in the Andaman and Nicobar Islands, Red Sun over Black Water*, Manas Publications, New Delhi, p. 75.
14. Shamshad A. Khan, *Changing Dynamics of India-Japan Relations, Buddhism to Special Strategic Partnerships*, Pentagon Press, New Delhi, 2107, p. 36.
15. 'Japan's Territorial Expansion 1931-1942', *Stratfor World View,* December 8, 2015 at https://worldview.stratfor.com/article/japans-territorial-expansion-1931-1942, accessed on September 20, 2018.
16. Lieut Colonel P. W. Mead R.A., 'The Chindit Operations of 1944', *Royal United Services Institution Journal,* Volume 100, 1955 - Issue 598, September 11, 2009, pp. 250–262.
17. Jack Griffiths, 'History of War', *History of War Magazine,* July 3, 2015

at https://www.historyanswers.co.uk/history-of-war/commemorate-the-200th-anniversary-of-waterloo-in-issue-19-of-history-of-war/, accessed on July 3, 2015.

18. Gardiner Harris, 'A Largely Indian Victory in World War II: Mostly Forgotten in India', *Asia Pacific,* June 21, 2014 at https://www.nytimes.com/2014/06/22/world/asia/a-largely-indian-victory-in-world-war-ii-mostly-forgotten-in-india.html, accessed on March 30, 2018.
19. Jasper Copping, Second World War Clashes Named as 'Greatest British Battle' *The Telegraph,* April 20, 2013 at https://www.telegraph.co.uk/history/10008053/Second-World-War-clashes-named-as-Greatest-British-Battle.html, accessed on March 30, 2018.
20. Jonathan Owen, 'Battle of Kohima: Survivor of one of WWII's bloodiest battles on why he is flying to Tokyo to meet his former foes', *Independent,* November 6, 2015 at https://www.independent.co.uk/news/world/asia/battle-of-kohima-survivor-of-one-of-wwiis-bloodiest-battles-on-why-he-is-flying-to-tokyo-to-meet-his-a6724651.html, accessed on September 21, 2018.
21. Rakesh Krishnan Simha, 'Japan's INA gambit and the Raj's demise', *Tehelka.com*, August 8, 2014 at http://www.tehelka.com/2014/07/japan-indian-national-army-subhas-chandra-bose-british-rule/, accessed on March 30, 2018.
22. 'Japan to build war museum in Manipur', *Business Standard,* May 21, 2017.
23. Dipanjan Roy Chaudhury, 'Japan teams up with India for Northeast, to extend Rs 2,239-crore loans', *Economic Times Bureau,* September 18, 2017 at https://economictimes.indiatimes.com/news/economy/infrastructure/japan-teams-up-with-india-for-northeast-to-extend-rs-2239-crore-loans/articleshow/60703906.cms, accessed on March 30, 2018.
24. Kallol Bhattacherjee, 'Japan keen on friendship with Northeast', *The Hindu,* September 24, 2017 at http://www.thehindu.com/news/international/japan-keen-on-friendship-with-northeast/article19747834.ece, accessed on April 30, 2018.
25. Ibid.
26. Sanchari Pal, Irrfan Khan's 'Tokyo Trial' Tells the Intriguing Story of a Forgotten Indian Judge Honoured in Japan, *The Better India*, April 1, 2017 at https://www.thebetterindia.com/94017/judge-radhabinod-pal-tokyo-trial-irrfan-khan-india-japan/ accessed on April 30, 2018.
27. Ibid.
28. Ibid.
29. P.G. Rajamohan, Dil Bahadur Rahut and Jabin T. Jacob, note 1.

3

Geography and Strategic Factors Shaping Security of Japan

Abstract

The geography of Japan has had a profound effect on public outlook towards security. The Japanese sometimes refer to their national character as reflecting an island nation mentality pointing towards a self-contained society. The external environment around Japan also impacts security, thereby defining its strategic behaviour. Internal factors such as demography and a pacifist Constitution *also play an important role in the strategic choices made by Japan. Deductions from the interplay of these factors assist in understanding the overall security posture adopted and the future strategic options available to Japan.*

Introduction

Geography is an important factor that shapes the security posture of a nation. Geography also influences national character and culture to a large extent. The very geography of being an island nation necessitates Japan to be a maritime nation. The Japanese sometimes refer to their national character as reflecting an island nation mentality pointing towards the sense of being a self-contained society with a unique culture.[1] This chapter initially carries out a geo-strategic analysis of Japan, in terms of its security challenges. In the course of this analysis, Japan's relations with its neighbours including its position in the regional security matrix has been factored. Thereafter, the factors of US-Japan relations, demography, Japan's pacifist Constitution and the status of the SDF have been considered in order to deduce the security imperatives of Japan.

Map 3.1: Early Maritime Routes of Japanese Sailors and Pirates

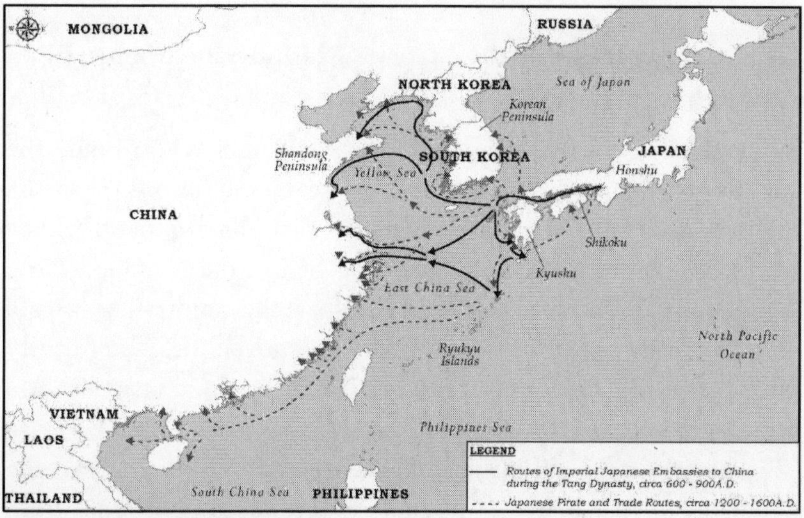

Source: GIS Lab, Manohar Parrikar IDSA.

Maritime Geography

The Japanese archipelago extends roughly 1860 miles from Southern Okinawa to northernmost tip of Hokkaido, approximately 26 degrees to 46 degrees North latitude. Japan is surrounded by the Sea of Japan and the East China Sea in the West, the Pacific Ocean in the South and East and the Sea of Okhotsk in the North (Refer Map of Japan in East Asia). The warm northward bound Pacific Ocean currents meet the cold southward bound Okhotsk current to produce great fishing grounds along Japan, which has a coastline of more than 18,400 miles with no inland point more than 93 miles from the sea.[2] The sea has, resultantly, played the most important role right from Japan's early human habitation, its economic and cultural contacts with the Chinese and the Koreans, the advent of Buddhism, and in thwarting foreign invasions, notable among them being the attempted invasion by the Mongolians in the late 13 century and destruction of the Mongolian force by the Kamikaze (divine wind). The map below indicates the early maritime activities of Japanese sailors and pirates with China and neighbouring countries.

Geo-Strategic Imperatives of Japan's Maritime Environment: An Analysis

Being geographically insulated due to waters all around, the islands of Japan did not see large scale migrations post the migration of 300 BC, which brought the Yamato people. The earlier inhabitants 'the Ainu' were pushed to the Northern Parts of Japan by the Yamato people. Therefore, the country has largely seen homogeneity as well as linguistic and cultural uniformity over the years. Resultantly, separatism and ethnic struggles are largely unheard of, in Japan.

This geographical insulation has also made Japan one of the countries in Asia that did not face the scourge of colonisation. In fact, when Japan faced the threat of giving in to the Western influences, it sealed itself off for three centuries during the Tokugawa rule from 1600 to 1868, the commencement of the Meiji Restoration. During the Meiji rule, again the geographical identity enabled thriving of unadulterated nationalism and also pursuing the Western developments that they thought was important for the progress of the nation. Once the economy and military was strong, this separate geographical location again enabled Japan to fan out in the search for resources to build *the Greater Asia Co-prosperity Sphere.*[3]

A brief analysis of the maritime areas around Japan will provide a better understanding of the security issues confronting Japan For the sake of analysis, the areas around Japan have been divided into areas close to territorial Japan, areas not adjoining but critical to Japan and areas depicting global security aspirations.

Areas Close to Territorial Japan

The immediate areas around Japan comprising of the East China Sea, the Sea of Japan and the Sea of Okhstok can be construed as the areas having an immediate security influence on Japan and constitute the Inner Security Ring (refer Map of Japan in East Asia for details). The Sea of Japan lying to the West connects Japan to the Koreas and Russia and the East China Sea connects Japan to China. These water bodies have been the main source of contact with China and Korea over centuries. Currently, the major security issue in this region is the missile and nuclear development programme of North Korea. Though North Korea has been striving to develop long range and intercontinental ballistic missiles, Japan faces a security threat even from the short and medium range missiles from North Korea. North Korea, in 2017, tested a large number of missiles in order to gain the capability to hit the US mainland, which it considers its arch enemy. Details of missile tests carried out by North Korea are given in Table 3.1.

As regards the nuclear tests, North Korea has conducted six tests till now, the first being in 2006, then 2009, thereafter 2013, twice in 2016, and the most recent nuclear test in 2017. North Korea presents an immediate threat due to its dogged pursuance of trying to attain nuclear capability through any means and its cultivated animosity for Japan.

Japan-China Relations: Historically, Japan has been deeply influenced by Chinese culture, art, architecture, language and religion. It was only during the Meiji period that Japan looked westwards and gradually inculcated Western influence in Japanese culture. The Japanese aggression in the early 20th century and the war atrocities committed by their military have been the cause of strained relations between China and Japan. Currently, China views Japan as not having atoned adequately for its war crimes, whereas Japan views the aggressive rise of China and efforts at changing the status quo as major hurdles in good relations between them.

Table 3.1: Missile Tests of North Korea in 2017[4]

Date	Missiles Launched in 2017(Towards Sea of Japan)	Target Range	Remarks
11 Feb	KN-15 (Solid Fuel)	500 km	1st successful solid fuel missile
05 Mar	Five Extended Range Scud Missiles (Solid Fuel)	965 km	One crashed after take-off
21 Mar			Exploded within seconds of launch
04 Apr	KN-17 (liquid fuel)	55 km	Inflight failure
15 Apr	KN-17(liquid fuel)		Exploded shortly after take-off
28 Apr	KN-17(liquid fuel)		Broke-up mid air after 34 km
14 May	Hwasong-12 (First successful launch)	700 km	Alt-2000 km. Speculation of new type of missile
21 Mar	KN-15 (solid fuel)	500 km	
28 May	Scud (Short Range)	430 km	
04 July	KN-14 (ICBM)	930 km	
28 July	KN-14 (Second ICBM)	1000 km	Fell inside EEZ of Japan (88 nautical miles West of Japan); 3700 km in space
25 Aug	3 x SRBM		Two in-flight failures; One blew up on ignition
28 Aug	Hwasong-12	2680 km	Broke up at end of flight
15 Sep	Ballistic Missile	3700 km	Flew over Hokkaido for 17 minutes. Landed in the Pacific Ocean
28 Nov	Hwasong-15 missile	1000 km east into the Sea of Japan.	Rocket had a potential range of 13000 km (enabling it to reach mainland US) and reached a height of 4,500 km. The rocket broke up on re-entry into atmosphere.

Source: Data collected by the author from various sources.

Post the US-China ping-pong diplomacy in 1971 and resulting better diplomatic relations, Japan also stepped up diplomatic activity. The September 1972 visit to Beijing of Japan's newly elected Prime Minister, Tanaka Kakuei, culminated in the signing of a historic joint statement that ended nearly 80 years of enmity and friction between the two countries.[5] In this statement, Tokyo recognised the Beijing regime as the sole legal government of China, respecting China's position that Taiwan was an inalienable part of the territory of the People's Republic of China and for its part China waived its demand for war indemnities from Japan.[6] The enactment of the Treaty of Peace and Friendship between Japan and China on 23 October 1978 during culmination of the historic meeting in Tokyo between China's then-paramount leader, Deng Xiaoping, and Japan's then-prime minister, Takeo Fukuda resulted in ending almost a century of enmity heralding a new era of relations.[7] The Sino-Japanese relations further strengthened in the subsequent decades both due to economic concerns as well as security concerns to limit the Soviet influence in the region.

Thereafter, Japan became a major source of capital, technology, and equipment for China's modernisation drive.[8] Bilateral trade between the two countries increased exponentially and Japan became China's largest creditor, accounting for nearly half of the estimated US$ 30 billion in credit lined up from 1979 to 1983.[9] Despite the number of issues that caused frictions between the two countries like the visit of the Japanese leaders to the Yasukuni Shrine and the softening of war atrocities in Japanese textbooks, the economic aid continued. Since 1979, Japan's ODA to China has played a very important role in China's social and economic development.[10] From that time to the present, China has altogether obtained approximately ¥3.4 trillion loans as well as other types of technical cooperation assistance and grant aid.[11] In the early years of the 21st century, Japan reduced the amount of aid to China due to a variety of reasons. The recent rise of China and its ever-increasing military spending has become a source of concern for Japan. Whereas the true military expenditure of China is considered to be more than the officially projected figures, Japan has, till 2017, traditionally restricted its military expenditure to less than 1 per cent of the GDP. A comparison of the military expenditure figures is tabulated in Table 3.2.

Table 3.2: Comparison of Military Expenditure of China and Japan 2009–2018 (billion US dollars)

Year	2009	2010	2011	2012	2013	2014	2015	2016	2017	2018
China	105.64	115.71	137.98	157.39	179.88	200.77	214.09	216.03	227.83	250.00
Japan	51.47	54.66	60.76	60.01	49.02	46.89	42.11	46.48	45.39	46.62

Source: The World Bank Data at https://data.worldbank.org/indicator/MS.MIL.XPND.CD?end=2018&locations=JP&start=2009&view=chart.

The Senkaku Islands (Diaoyu Islands) Dispute: Both China and Japan stake territorial claims over the Senkaku islands, which are a rocky outcrop comprising of five small islands and three rocks jutting out from the sea and are uninhabited. These islands are also claimed by Taiwan. The Senkaku islands lie approximately 170 km from Taiwan as well as the nearest Japanese islands and approximately 330 km from the Chinese mainland.[12] Simmering tensions between China and Japan in the East China Sea came to a head on September 11, 2012 when the Japanese government purchased three of the disputed Senkaku islands, which were claimed by both China and Japan but administered by Japan, from private owners.[13] The islands are presently under Japanese control but a number of encroachments into the waters of these islands by the Chinese are recorded by the Japanese. The yearly details of Chinese ships entering Japan's waters as taken from the Ministry of Foreign Affairs, Japan website is tabulated in Table 3.3.

Additionally, the exploration and commercialisation of undersea resources has also come under dispute due to claims and counter-claims regarding the median line in the sea with China and the allegations of trespassing into each other's maritime domains. Japanese have recorded an increase in Chinese activity in waters and airspace around Japan. Resultantly, the number of scrambles by Japanese Air Self Defence Forces (ASDF) against Chinese incursions has intensified over the years and is depicted graphically.

Table 3.3: Chinese Encroachments Recorded by the Japanese Government

Year	No. of Chinese Vessels Identified within Japan's Territorial Seas	No. of Chinese Vessels Identified within Japan's Contiguous Zone
2012 (Sep onwards)	68	407
2013	188	819
2014	96	729
2015	95	709
2016	130	752
2017	108	696
2018 (Till August)	58	389

Source: Data from Ministry of Foreign Affairs, Japan Website.

Figure 3.1: Year-wise Scrambles by the ASDF against Chinese Aircrafts (2007–2016)

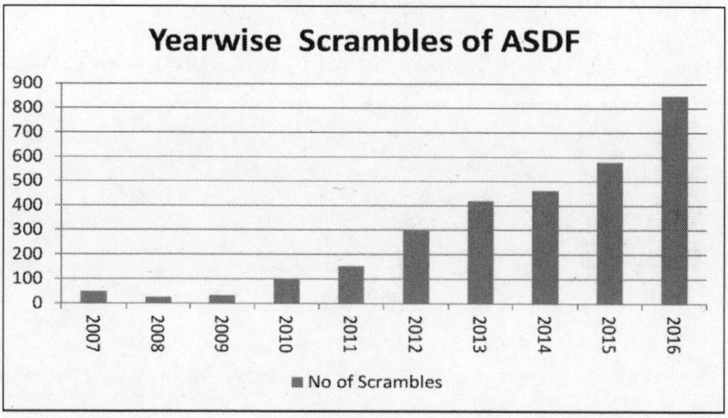

Source: Defence of Japan 2017 published by the Ministry of Defense, Japan.

On September 7, 2010, while contesting respective claims over the Senkaku islands, a Chinese fishing trawler collided with Japanese Coast Guard patrol boats in disputed waters near the islands. The captain of the ship was apprehended by the Japanese and subsequently released after a few days. This led to objections from China, which also levied an embargo on the export of Rare Earth Metals (REM) to Japan. China exports more than 90 per cent of the world's REMs and presently has a monopoly over the rare earth metals market.[14] Japan is the world's largest importer of REMs. The fact that embargo of such strategic resources can be implemented, reinforced Japanese fears of their security vulnerabilities being exploited by the Chinese.

Air Defence Identification Zone (ADIZ): In November 2013, the Chinese Ministry of National Defence declared the establishment of an ADIZ, which considerably overlapped the existing ADIZs from Japan, South Korea and Taiwan. Significantly, the promulgated ADIZ also covered the Senkaku Islands. Chinese authorities outlined the identification rules applicable to aircrafts flying over East China Sea, which included reporting of flight plans, maintaining radio communications and keeping the transponders on. A vague warning against non-cooperative aircrafts was also mentioned.[15] Though initially objected to and challenged by the US, Japan, Taiwan and South Korea, all countries subsequently relented and asked their civil flights to follow the identification rules.

Map 3.2: ADIZ of China, Japan, South Korea and Taiwan

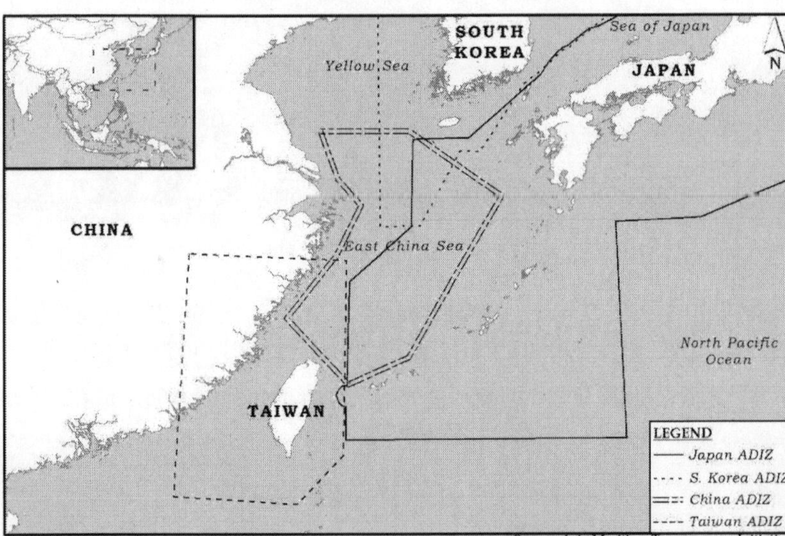

© GIS LAB, IDSA, Map not to scale. Source: Asia Maritime Transparency Initiative

The ADIZ promulgated by the Chinese is being viewed as another aspect of the aggressive actions by the Chinese challenging the present security equilibrium and coercively attempting to establish ownership on the global commons or on territories belonging to other countries. Similarly, the attempts to explore marine resources and underwater hydrocarbon resources is being seen by Japan as part of the aggressive designs of China, aggravating the security threat.

Kuril Islands (Northern Territories): The dispute between Russia and Japan over the Southern Kuril Islands represents one of the longest standing territorial disputes in East Asia and concerns possession of the four southernmost islands in the chain, Etorofu, Kunashiri, Shikotan, and Habomai.[16] After the Russo-Japanese War in 1904–1905, based on the Treaty of Portsmouth, the Southern half of the Sakhalin Island was given to the Japanese along with the Kuril Islands. This boundary dispensation remained stable till the Second World War. However, a few days before the Japanese capitulation in the Second World War, Russia attacked and occupied the entire island of Sakhalin and the Southern Kuril Islands (which are called Northern Territories, in Japan). Presently, under the control of Russia, the issue is yet to be resolved. Incidentally, no peace treaty exists between Russia and Japan post the Second World War, these four islands being in the eye of the storm. Efforts at resolution between the premiers of the two countries are underway. However, Russia has recently commenced militarisation of some of these islands. It was reported in February 2018 that the Russian Air Force had taken control of a civilian airport on Iturup Island (the Etorofu Island as per the Japanese), paving the way for further militarisation and the deployment of Russian warplanes.[17] Russia has cited the US-Japan security alliance and the deployment of US troops in Japan as one of the main reasons as hindrance to the talks for resolution. At the Eastern Economic Forum in Vladivostok, President Putin during his meeting with Prime Minister Abe remarked that both countries should sign the peace treaty without any pre-conditions. This points towards a continuation of this vexed issue without resolution for some more time to come.[18]

Fig 3.2: Japan's Energy Imports

Japan Fossil Fuel Imports

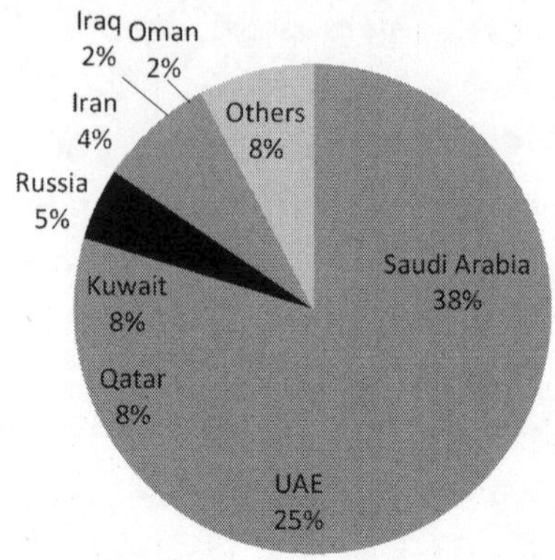

Japan LNG (Natural Gas) Imports

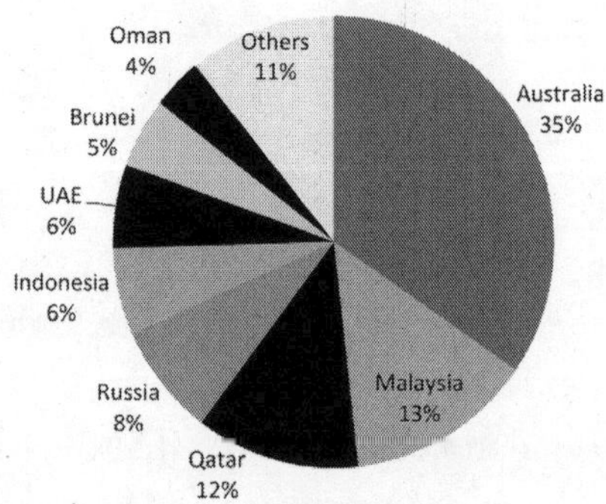

Japan Coal Imports

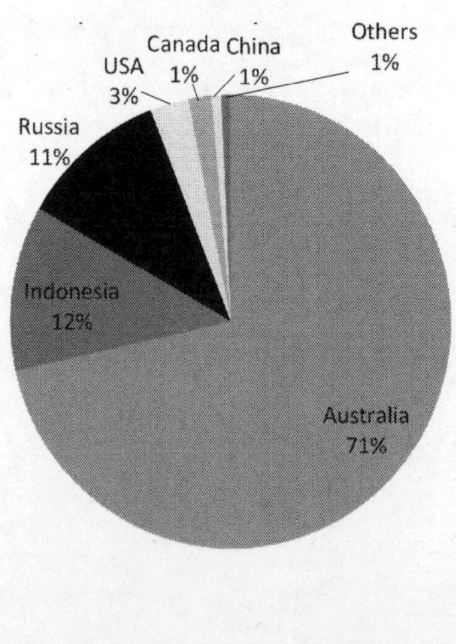

Areas Critical to Japan

The Outer Security Ring constitutes those areas which do not have a direct bearing on Japan's territorial sovereignty but have critical security implications. The South China Sea and the SLOCs in the IOR form a part of this ring. The South China Sea, and the SLOCs through it, can be termed as the lifeline of Japan. In 2013, the Chinese declared that a major part of the South China Sea lies within their self-proclaimed nine dash line (which includes the Sprately and the Paracel island groups). With more than 90 per cent of the trade of Japan sailing into the South China Sea, these declarations and the construction of artificial islands by China in the South China Sea have posed a major security threat to the life-line of Japan. Lately, there have been reports of military assets being deployed in these islands of the South China Sea by China. Japan, being poor in natural resources such as oil and natural gas is heavily dependent on the SLsOC The energy self-sufficiency ratio of Japan in 2014 was 6 per cent which was low compared to even other OECD countries.[19] Japanese crude oil and LNG imports as depicted in the pie charts below, show that major supply routes have to cross the South China Sea to reach Japan.

Japan also has major trade relations with littorals of the South China Sea and a number of industrial bases in countries of this region. Japanese direct investment in Southeast Asia in the first half of 2013 reached almost US$ 6 billion. Japanese banks have lent a record amount into the region, and Japanese corporate acquisitions in Southeast Asia have already increased manifold.[20]

Japan, therefore, needs to ensure that its own influence in this region does not become subservient to Chinese influence. Cooperation with littorals of the South China Sea is paramount. It also needs to mitigate the growing Chinese influence through capability enhancement of these countries. Japanese involvement in the security of the Malacca Straits is a prime example of the security concerns in the Outer Security Ring.

Areas Depicting Global Security Aspirations

This security circle comprises of the global aspirations of Japan. It ranges from the establishment of the base at Djibouti, the anti-piracy activities of the MSDF, participation in the US led Proliferation Security Initiative (PSI), enhancing the maritime reach of the MSDF, and building a capability of force projection.

Japan SDF Base, Djibouti: This Self-Defence Force Base at Ambouli, Djibouti (ジブチ共和国における自衛隊拠点 (jibuchi-kyouwakokuni-okeru-jieitaikyoten)) is a military base operated by the Japan Self-Defence Forces (JSDF). Djibouti hosts military bases of the US, France, Japan, Italy and China. Consequent to Japan's Diet (Parliament) passing the 'Anti-piracy Measures Law' in 2009, the Japan Maritime Self-Defence Force MSDF commenced anti-piracy operations and deployed two destroyers (JS Sazanami and JS Samidare (DD-106) and two JMSDF P-3 Orion patrol aircrafts in Djibouti, which began patrols in June 2009. In 2011, the JMSDF established its own base at Djibouti with a command headquarters, boarding facilities and parking apron, at a cost of ¥ 4.7 billion (US$ 40 million) with around 180 troops. The assets in the Japanese base have since been enhanced and Japan is currently expanding the base by further leasing three hectares of land to the east of the present 30-acre base. The base, Japan's first long-term, large-scale overseas outpost since World War II, also acts as a counterweight to what Tokyo sees as growing Chinese influence in the region.[21] It also provides Japan a foothold in Africa and along the critical SLOCs through which its energy requirements are met. During the inter clan clashes at Juba, South Sudan in July 2016, where one Japanese engineering company and staff officers were deployed, Japan had three C-130 aircrafts ready to airlift Japanese troops and other Japanese citizens, in case of need.

Japan and the IOR: Japan is heavily reliant on the IOR for energy and raw material imports. Trade with this region has skyrocketed to US$ 225 billion (2014 figures), a figure that dwarfs Japanese trade with the EU as the IOR grew into a bustling ring of growing economies, with a dense web of trade.[22] Ninety per cent of Japan's oil requirements come from the Persian Gulf and have to pass through the Indian Ocean.[23] In an effort to protect its SLOCs and also match up with the Chinese push for infrastructure development in the IOR, Japan is currently constructing or renovating eight major port construction or renovation projects at Seychelles, Madagascar, Mozambique, Kenya, Oman, India, Bangladesh and Indonesia.[24]

The disintegration of the USSR removed one of the main incentives of hosting US bases on Japanese soil. Shifting US focus onto the Middle East, the gradual decline of US influence in East Asia and the 1996 Shining Path incident in Peru pointed to the erosion of the strong dependence of Japan on the US and the necessity to protect its own interests abroad. In addition, the expansion of the Chinese influence in the Indo-Pacific region has triggered the need for a more pro-active maritime strategy by Japan. These developments have led to the Japanese commencing their look-out for 'friends elsewhere'.

Anti-Piracy Activities: Japan is also a part of the Combined Task Force (CTF)-151, a multinational task force, which operates in the Gulf of Aden and off the Eastern coast of Somalia. Japanese ships also contribute to the safety of navigation in the Malacca Straits through hydrographic survey and production of navigational charts, installation and maintenance of aids to navigation, clearance of navigable channels, donation of an oil skimming vessel and buoy tenders, tide and current observation, and other technical assistance to Indonesia, Singapore and Malaysia.[25]

US-Japan Security Alliance

Forged in the wake of World War II, the US-Japan security alliance has served as one of the region's most important military relationships and as an anchor of the US security role in Asia.[26] Both nations consider this alliance to be a cornerstone for peace and stability in East Asia. Article 5 of the Japan-US Security treaty states, "Each Party recognizes that an armed attack against either Party in the territories under the administration of Japan would be dangerous to its own peace and safety and declares that it would act to meet the common danger in accordance with its constitutional provisions and processes ..."[27] This translates into an understanding that disputed areas like the Senkaku Islands are also covered under this treaty.[28]

Another article, Article 6 of the Treaty states, "For the purpose of contributing to the security of Japan and the maintenance of international peace and security in the Far East, the United States of America is granted the use by its land, air and naval forces of facilities and areas in Japan".[29] Resultantly, the presence of US troops and other military assets in Japan has been guaranteed under this arrangement.

This has resulted in the US inadvertently becoming a resident power superimposed in the region. This is not acceptable to other powers in the region who themselves would like to wield influence and hence, feel constrained by the US presence. Development of new challenges and threats have provided an opportunity to the US to further shore up military capability of its allies as well as introduce technologically superior weapons systems and equipment that will serve their strategic interests of dominating the region. The stationing of the Terminally High Altitude Air Defence (THAAD) System in South Korea and possibly Japan, and the opposition by China and Russia should be seen in this context.

Another implication of this treaty is that the US nuclear umbrella extends to the territory of Japan. Despite the three Non-Nuclear Principles outlined in 1967 by then Prime Minister of Japan Eisaku Sato, namely, teneting no possession, production or introduction of nuclear weapons, Japan which ardently proposes a nuclear free world, is itself content with the nuclear protection of a nuclear power.

Incidentally, the military presence of US Forces Japan (USFJ) stationed in Japan not only contributes to the defence of Japan, but also functions as deterrence and enhances US response capabilities to address contingencies in the Indo-Pacific region as it also serves as a core element of the Japan-US security arrangement.[30] An important aspect in this regard is the Freedom of Navigation patrols carried out by US warships in the South China Sea. These patrols are carried out to emphasize that the South China Sea is part of the global commons and cannot be claimed to be a part of the blue territory of China.

Additionally, this security arrangement also forms the basis of the foreign policy of Japan. Forces of both countries are also working towards laying down the foundations of addressing other challenges such as piracy, maritime terrorism and proliferation of weapons of mass destruction. Another aspect of this relationship is the collaboration between the two countries in science and technology for over 25 years in areas such as new energy technologies, supercomputing, and critical materials, which is currently in progress and has been extended up to the year 2024.[31]

This alliance was strengthened in 2015 through the release of the revised US-Japan Defence Guidelines, which provide for new and expanded forms of security-oriented cooperation.[32] In January 2016 the United States and Japan signed a new five-year package of host nation support for US forces stationed in Japan.[33]

The Japan-US security arrangements, complemented by the alliances established between the US and other countries such as the Republic of Korea, Australia, Thailand and the Philippines as also by friendly relations developed with other countries, play an important role in the security dynamics of the Indo-Pacific region. However, the unpredictability of the Trump regime is forcing Japan to commence making alternate security arrangements. The Abe cabinet had no real warning of the announcement made by South Korean officials on March 8, 2018 that Trump had agreed to meet with North Korean leader Kim Jong-un.[34] Abe's readiness to run to Washington to patch up and paper over these and other shocks barely disguises the seething frustration in Tokyo with its erstwhile ally.[35] The growing outreach of Japan towards China and Russia can be considered as one of the outcomes of these developments.

Holistically speaking, though re-energising the US-Japan security alliance and revising the US-Japan defence guidelines are positive developments, unless there is de-escalation of tensions between Japan and China, and Japan and the two Koreas, peace and stability in the Indo-Pacific are likely to remain remote possibilities.[36]

Demography

Demography has acquired a great significance in the social discourse in Japan and has influenced Japan's outlook towards social aspects, security dynamics and the prevalent international order. Japan is currently the world's oldest country and set to become older. In 2050, the government of Japan estimates that 40 per cent of Japan's population will be over 65 years of age.[37] In the last few decades, the country's social security budget has increased by 15 per cent. While five decades ago there were 12 workers for every retiree, there will be an equal 1:1 ratio in the next 50 years.[38] With its ageing population and the inherent aversion to immigrants, Japan has started relying on artificial intelligence and robots to make up for the falling numbers.

2017 is the 37th year in a row that the population of children in Japan has continued to drop. About 941,000 Japanese children were born in 2017, which is the lowest number since the country started recording its births in 1899.[39] The population pyramid of Japan shows a bulge at the age of late 1960s and a population growth currently has a negative growth rate of minus 0.7 per cent.[40]

Figure 3.3: Population Pyramid of Japan (2016)

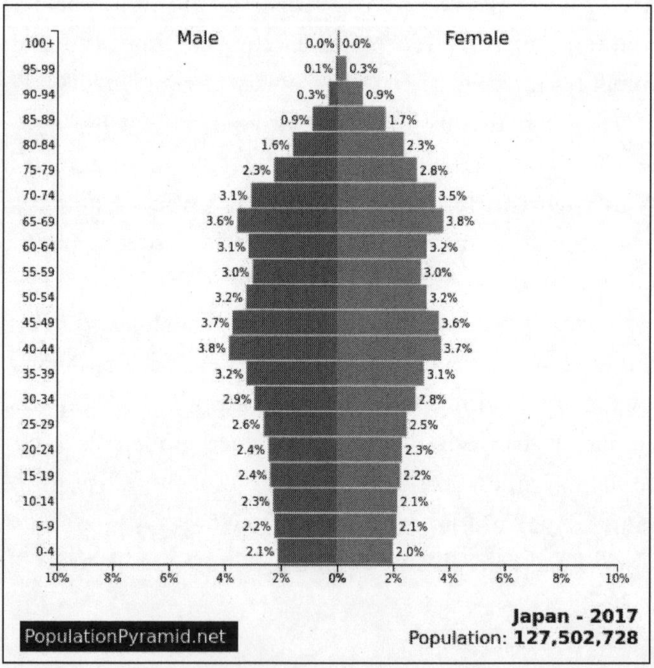

Source: Populationpyramid.net available at https://www.populationpyramid.net/japan/2019/.

As per the Japan External Trade Organisation (JETRO) White Paper on Global Trade and Investment Report 2017, which compares the working-age population as a percentage of the total population with other major advanced countries, the ratio of Japan's working-age population is declining at a rapid rate. As of 1990, Japan's working-age population had been at the high level of 69.7 per cent; by 2015, it had dropped to 60.8 per cent, already below the levels of the US (66.3 per cent), Germany (65.9 per cent), UK (64.5 per cent), and France (62.4 per cent). Japan's working-age population will continue to decline in number, and is forecast to hit 51.3 per cent in 2050 with a further widening gap with other major advanced countries.[41]

One important area where this has affected Japan is the aspect of recruitment for the SDF. Amid a rock bottom birth rate, the number of Japanese aged 18 to 26, which is the core of the recruitment pool for the SDF, has shrunk to 11 million from 17 million in 1994 and is forecast to shrink to 7.8 million over the next 30 years.[42] Despite the depleting population figures, the Japanese do not encourage foreigners and migrant human resource to fill in for the depleting population. The overall proportion of foreigners as compared to the population of Japan is very less (1.89 per cent). The population of foreigners and the year-on-year per cent change is tabulated as shown.

Table 3.4: Population of Foreigners in Japan by Nationality

Country	Population	% of Registered Foreign Population	Year on Year % Change
China	695,522	29.2	4.5
South Korea	453,096	19.0	-1.0
Philippines	243,662	10.2	6.1
Vietnam	199,990	8.4	36.1
Brazil	180,923	7.6	4.3
Nepal	67,470	2.8	23.2
USA	53,705	2.3	2.7
Taiwan	52,768	2.2	8.3
Peru	47,647	2.0	5.0
Thailand	47,647	2.0	5.0
Others	340,299	14.3	9.9

Source: Survey of the Ministry of Justice, Japan 2016.

The tabulation above reveals that even out of the foreigners present in Japan, India does not figure in the top ten countries in the overall strength of foreigners living in Japan.[43]

The demographic issue has started ringing the alarm bells and Japan is slowly changing its outlook towards migrants by bringing in legislations and making efforts at changing the public outlook towards migrant workforce. On June 15, 2018, the Council on Economic and Fiscal Policy, which is chaired by Prime Minister Shinzo Abe, decided to introduce a new visa for non-professional foreign labourers.[44] Under the new policy, the government plans to create a new five-year visa category, through which Japan would receive 500,000 low-skilled labourers by 2025, with the newcomers expected to work in five sectors that have been suffering from an acute labour shortage: nursing care, lodging, agriculture, construction and shipbuilding.[45] With the huge human resource and skilled personnel available in India, as well as the growth in the number of Japanese language and industrial training institutes, there is scope for more and more Indians to shift focus towards Japan for work and living. This represents an opportunity for Indians. With increased focus on technology and manufacturing, it also represents a greater opportunity to security related technology, manufacture and trade between the two countries.

The Japanese Constitution

Both the Preamble and Article 9 of the Japanese Constitution express the principle of pacifism. The Preamble of the Constitution proclaims: "We, the Japanese people ... resolved that never again shall we be visited with the horrors of war through the action of government...."[46]

Article 9 of Japan's Constitution reads as follows:

1. Aspiring sincerely to an international peace based on justice and order, the Japanese people forever renounce war as a sovereign right of the nation and the threat or use of force as a means of settling international disputes.

2. In order to accomplish the aim of the preceding paragraph, land, sea and air forces, as well as other war potential, will never be maintained. The right of belligerency of the state will not be recognised.[47]

Though the Constitution was imposed upon Japan, it also came to reflect the views of most Japanese people.[48] Though the Constitution was re-interpreted in 1954, to allow the formation of forces for self-defence, it barred Japan from sending forces abroad, even for UN peace keeping activities for the next four decades. Meanwhile, US pressure on Japan to contribute more towards the overall security effort put in by the Americans, continued. Over time, certain restrictions were eased out, but Japan still remained constrained by Constitutional interpretation that barred any exercise of the right to collective self-defence.[49]

In 2016, the Legislation for Peace and Security took effect, which allows Japan to contribute more proactively to the peace and stability of the international community under the policy of "Proactive Contribution to Peace" based on the principle of international cooperation.[50] The Legislation for Peace and Security consists of the Act for the Development of the Legislation for Peace and Security (which bundles together a host of partial amendments to existing laws), and the newly enacted International Peace Support Act.[51] This legislation has allowed Japan to take a more nuanced view of the security environment surrounding it, with greater powers to the SDF to use weapons under certain conditions. Recently, PM Shinzo Abe has reiterated his determination to amend Article 9 of the Constitution in order to legalise the SDF. The Constitutional revision process is long and needs to go through a process of public referendum as well. A Kyodo News public opinion poll conducted in the first week of October 2018, after the Cabinet reshuffle, found that 48.7 per cent of respondents in public are opposed to Abe's attempts to allow the LDP to move forward and amend the Constitution, while 36.4 per cent supported such moves.[52]

However, the language of Article 9, renouncing war as a sovereign right of the nation, the undefined legal status of the SDF and the non-participation of SDF in any scene of combat activity has inhibited the Japanese defence policy to this moment. The re-election of Japanese PM Shinzo Abe as the party leader of the Liberal Democratic Party(LDP) in the elections held in September 2018 gives a fillip to the possibility of instituting the first ever amendment to the Japanese Constitution. The revision PM Shinzo Abe is proposing is referred to as "kaken", meaning adding something to the Constitution.[53] The LDP seeks to keep the current two paragraphs of Article 9 and add a paragraph to give explicit legal standing to the SDF.[54] Any nation that has security relations with Japan needs to understand the restrictions imposed by the Pacifist Constitution and work through it.

The Japanese Self-Defence Forces

Article 9 of the Japanese Constitution written under the auspices of the US forbade Japan from maintaining a military. The US forces agreed to guarantee the security of Japan in return for stationing the US forces in Japan. In the 1950s, when the US troops stationed in Japan had to move out to participate in the Korean War, the void so created needed to be filled. A constitutional interpretation of Article 9 granting Japan the inherent right of self-defence and the possession of the minimum armed strength needed to exercise that right, led to the raising of a force of 75,000 personnel, urged by the US. These forces were initially named the National Police Reserve in 1950, and was later renamed as National Safety Force in 1952 (post-merger of the National Police Reserve and the Maritime Guard [created as an organisation of the Japanese Coast Guard in April 1952]). Based on an agreement between political parties in 1953, it was decided to develop a long term programme to establish defence capabilities and transform the National Safety Force into a SDF. Accordingly, the SDF was assigned the mission of defending Japan against direct invasion. To avoid the appearance of a revival of militarism, Japan's leaders emphasized constitutional guarantees of civilian control of the government as well as the armed forces, and used non-military terms for the organisation and functions of the forces wherein the overall organisation was called the Defense Agency (rather than the Ministry of Defense) and the terms Ground Self-Defense Force (GSDF), the Maritime Self-Defense Force (MSDF), and the Air Self-Defense Force (ASDF) were used instead of the army, navy, and air force.[55]

The SDF has since been the mainstay of protection of the sovereignty of Japan and has played a major role in disaster relief operations throughout the years. Under the NDPG promulgated in 2014, Japan's future defence forces are planned to be developed based on the concept of a Dynamic Joint Defense Force capable of acting as an effective deterrent to and responding to security challenges to Japan. The forces are also expected to fulfil the role of stabilisation of the Asia-Pacific Region and contribute towards the improvement of the Global Security Environment.

In adherence to Constitutional provisions, the SDF has been denied the possession and employment of offensive weapons, which are capable of projecting military force other than for the defence of own territories. However, considering the increasingly severe security environment in the region, the SDF currently possesses the F-35 aircrafts, helicopter carriers, armoured tanks and an Amphibious Rapid Deployment Brigade, to name a few of the assets, that have the capability to project military force anywhere in the world. Presently, as per Global Fire Power rankings, Japan stands 8th in the overall Military Strength rankings. With the Legislations for Peace and Security 2015 in place, the SDF can participate in limited collective security when an armed attack against Japan occurs or when an armed attack against a foreign country that is in a close relationship with Japan occurs ... (subject to the three new conditions under which use of force is permitted by the Constitution, are satisfied).[56]

So where does the SDF stand today? Equipment and technology wise, the SDF is one of the foremost militaries, especially the navy (MSDF), which is among the five strongest navies in the world. However, the SDF is not equipped to deal with security threats on foreign soil. Their concepts, operational art and tactics do not mention offensive strategies and the SDF as a whole lacks expeditionary capability (capability to carry out offensive posturing away from own shores).

Deductions

In the realm of security, the following geo-strategic imperatives emerge from the analyses above:

- As a society, the Japanese social set up is homogenous and well knit. The society never had to face a migration influx since 300 BC. Resultantly, the society at large looks at migration with disdain. Considering the demographic profile, this aspect has a profound implication on security and related issues.
- The demand for resources will always be the foremost priority for a resource-scarce Japan. There will always be a motive to reach out to resource rich regions whether it is in the form of Greater Asia Co-prosperity Sphere; bilateral agreements with resource rich countries; Asia-Africa Growth Corridor (AAGC) type partnerships; or cooperation in the Belt and Road Initiative (BRI).
- Sea Lines of Communications (SLOCs) are Japan's lifeline and their safety and security is paramount.
- Being spread over a vast area of 1860 miles, Japan's security imperative to protect the sovereignty of its island territories is an absolute must.
- Considering the scarce resources available on land, Tokyo's desire to explore undersea energy and mineral resources in its immediate territorial waters and the resulting need to provide security for those assets, are also an absolute imperative.
- The maritime space in East Asia is crowded. It has become further complicated with claims and counter claims on the small islands/shoals and water bodies, by many stake holders. Cooperation rather than competition and conflict will ensure that peace and security prevails in its vicinity. Only then can it focus on nation building.

- The East Asian neighbourhood is wary of Japan's past and still views nationalist activity in Japan with a suspicion reminiscent of the Japanese invasions and atrocities in the early 20th century. Security imperatives, however, force Japan to enhance its military strength to be able to address future security threats and challenges. The security imperatives and external perceptions need to be balanced.
- Cooperation in the maritime space also points towards capacity building of other littorals to increase influence as well as to ensure that no external influence can overshadow the Japanese presence. It, therefore, needs to understand and ensure capability building in the littoral states.
- Public opinion and the Constitution prohibit use of force to settle international disputes. The SDF can be employed only for defensive purposes and certain support activities. Offensive posturing, an expeditionary offensive capability of the forces, the development of a risk-taking mentality and contingency war planning are not the attributes that will be exhibited by the SDF.
- Demographic imperatives shape the need for economic outreach, acceptance of immigrants and development of alternate technologies for coping with the crisis.

These strategic imperatives have shaped the Japanese security landscape for some time now and will remain relevant in any security discourse of Japan. Any security engagement with Japan will entail a detailed understanding of these imperatives.

Conclusion

The analysis of the strategic imperatives provide a better and clearer understanding of the domestic politics of Japan, which in turn influence foreign policy and security relations with other countries. Importance of public opinion in a democracy cannot be underestimated and hence, the internal dynamics of the society such as culture, demographics, outlook towards military force and understanding of the security picture are very important aspects that have been elucidated in this chapter. The security treaty with the US; the Chinese presence in the South China Sea; the missile and nuclear threat from North Korea; and other security challenges need to be factored when seeking security cooperation with Japan.

Notes

1. Victoria Lyon Bestor and Theodore C. Bestor, 'Japan and the Sea', *Education about Asia,* 19(2), Fall, 2014 at https://scholar.harvard.edu/files/bestor/files/bestor_2014_eaa.pdf, accessed on October 3, 2017.
2. Ibid.
3. The concept of Greater Asia Co-prosperity Sphere was mooted by the Japanese Imperial military to create a sphere of influence in Asia free from the Western colonial influence under Japan, in a bid to gain control over the natural resources of this region.
4. Retrieved from various Internet sites.
5. Ronald E. Dolan and Robert L. Worden (eds), *Japan: A Country Study,* Washington: GPO for the Library of Congress, 1994 at http://countrystudies.us/japan/, accessed on September 23, 2018.
6. Ibid.
7. Cary Huang, 'China And Japan Are Still Best Of Frenemies, 40 Years On From Treaty Of Peace And Friendship', *South China Morning Post,* September 23, 2018 at https://www.scmp.com/week-asia/opinion/article/2165253/china-and-japan-are-still-best-frenemies-40-years-treaty-peace-and, accessed on September 23, 2018.
8. Victoria Lyon Bestor and Theodore C. Bestor, note 1.
9. Ibid.
10. Zhigang Wu, 'Research on Japan's ODA to China and its Contribution to China's Development', at https://www.cc.kyoto-su.ac.jp/project/orc/econ-public/china/documents/WUDP28.pdf, accessed on September 24, 2018.
11. Ibid.
12. Japanese Coast Guard Brochure at http://www.kaiho.mlit.go.jp/e/english.pdf, accessed on September 25, 2018.
13. Lyle J Morris, 'The New "Normal" in the East China Sea', *The RAND Blog Commentary,* February 27, 2017 at https://www.rand.org/blog/2017/02/the-new-normal-in-the-east-china-sea.html, accessed on September 25, 2018.
14. Sriparna Pathak, 'Japan-China relations strained over rare earths find', *Asia Times,* April 1, 2018 at http://www.atimes.com/japan-china-relations-backdrop-rare-earths/, accessed on September 24, 2018.
15. Michael Green, Kathleen Hicks, Zack Cooper, Jpohn Schaus and Jake Douglas, 'Counter-Coercion Series: East China Sea Air Defence

Identification Zone', *Asia Maritime Transparency Initiative*, June 13, 2018 at https://amti.csis.org/counter-co-east-china-sea-adiz/ accessed on July 3, 2018.

16. Dmitry Gorenburg, 'The Southern Kuril Islands Dispute', *PONARS Eurasia Policy Memo No. 226* September 2012, CNA Strategic Studies/ Harvard University. The Russian names for the first two islands are Iturup and Kunashir.
17. Lara Southgate, 'An old dispute re-emerges as Russia militarises Kuril Islands, Global Risk Insights', March 16, 2018 at https://globalriskinsights.com/2018/03/japan-russia-dispute-northern-territories/, accessed on September 16, 2018.
18. Fyodor Lukyanov, Russia-Japan—peace can wait, *Nikkei Asian Review,* dated 19 September 2018, available at https://asia.nikkei.com/Opinion/ Russia-Japan-peace-can-wait, accessed on September 21, 2018.
19. 'Japans Energy, Ministry of Economy, Trade and Industry Agency for Natural Resources and Energy' at http://www.enecho.meti.go.jp/en/ category/brochures/pdf/japan_energy_2016.pdf, accessed on April 29, 2018.
20. 'Abenomics encourages Japanese firms to invest—abroad' at http://www.scmp.com/business/economy/article/1318151/abenomics-encourages-japanese-firms-invest-abroad, accessed on April 29, 2018.
21. Staff Report, 'Japan to expand SDF base in tiny but strategically important Djibouti', *The Japan Times*, November 19, 2017 at https://www.japantimes.co.jp/news/ 2017/11/19/national/japan-expand-sdf-base-tiny-strategically-important-djibouti/#.Wz36V9IzbIU, accessed on July 5, 2018.
22. Peter Wyckoff, 'Making Waves: Japan and the Indian Ocean Region', *Stimson*, May 1, 2017 at https://www.stimson.org/content/making-waves-japan-and-indian-ocean-region#_ednref15, accessed on July 6, 2018.
23. Rajaram Panda, IDSA reply for the Ask the Expert Column, *Institute for Defence Studies and Analyses* at https://idsa.in/askanexpert/ HowmuchJapannationalinteresteffecttheIndianocean, accessed on September 25, 2018.
24. Ibid.
25. Cooperation and Contributions Toward Littoral States Donation of Revolving Fund for combating oil spill from ships (1981) Source: MLIT 2014, Jebat 41(2), December 2014.
26. Beina Xu, 'The US-Japan Security Alliance, Council of Foreign Relations', July 1, 2014 at https://www.cfr.org/backgrounder/us-japan-security-alliance, accessed on September 29, 2018.
27. 'Japan-US Security Treaty', Ministry of Foreign Affairs of Japan at https://www.mofa.go.jp/region/ n-america/us/q&a/ref/1.html, accessed on September 29, 2018.

28. Ankit Panda, 'Mattis: Senkakus Covered Under US-Japan Security Treaty', *The Diplomat*, February 6, 2017 at https://thediplomat.com/2017/02/mattis-senkakus-covered-under-us-japan-security-treaty/, accessed on September 29, 2017.
29. Victoria Lyon Bestor and Theodore C. Bestor, note 2.
30. Defence of Japan 2017.
31. Extension of the Agreement between Japan and the US on Cooperation in Research and Development in Science and Technology, Ministry of Foreign Affairs, Japan.
32. Victoria Lyon Bestor and Theodore C. Bestor, note 1.
33. Ibid.
34. Editorial Japan, Peak Japan, *East Asia Forum,* September 3, 2018 at http://www.eastasiaforum.org/2018/09/03/peak-japan/#more-144152, accessed on September 29, 2018.
35. Ibid.
36. Titli Basu, 'US-Japan Security Alliance: Standing the Test of Time', Institute for Defence Studies and Analyses, May 29, 2015 at https://idsa.in/issuebrief/USJapanSecurityAlliance_tbasu_290515, accessed on September 29, 2018.
37. 'Japan Population 2018', *World Population Review* at http://worldpopulationreview.com/ countries/japan-population/, accessed on October 11, 2018.
38. Ibid.
39. Siobhán O'Grady, There have never been so few children in Japan (at least, not since they started counting), The Washington Post, May 4, 2018 at https://www.washingtonpost. com/news/worldviews/wp/2018/05/04/there-have-never-been-so-few-children-in-japan-at-least-not-since-they-started-counting/?noredirect=on&utm_term=.2a0a7eef181d, accessed on May 4, 2018.
40. Figures are as per the Statistic Bureau of Japan at https://countrydigest.org/japan-population/, accessed on April 17, 2018.
41. JETRO, white Paper on Global Trade and Investment Report 2017 Chapter 3, E-commerce and foreign human resources as a new overseas business model at https://www.jetro.go.jp/ext_images/en/reports/white_paper/trade_invest_2017_overview.pdf, accessed on June 30, 2018.
42. '"Unless We Replace With Robots": Few Takers For Military Jobs In Japan', NDTV World Reuters, September 19, 2018 at https://www.ndtv.com/world-news/military-recruiters-struggle-as-applicant-pool-dries-up-in-ageing-japan-1919088, accessed on September 21, 2018.
43. 'What are the most popular places for foreigners to live in Japan?', *Japan Times*, July 7, 2017 at https://resources.realestate.co.jp/living/what-are-the-most-popular-places-for-foreigners-to-live-in-japan/, accessed on April 16, 2018.

44. Takehiro Masutomo, 'Japan's Open to Foreign Workers. Just Don't Call Them Immigrants', *South China Morning Post,* June 30, 2018 at https://www.scmp.com/week-asia/business/article/2152880/ japans-open-foreign-workers-just-dont-call-them-immigrants, accessed on September 21, 2018.
45. Ibid.
46. The Constitution of Japan.
47. Ibid.
48. Daniel Sneider, 'Evolution or New Doctrine?Japanese Security Policy in the era of Collctive Self-Defence' in *Japan's Relations in Asia*, James D.J. Brown and Jeff Kingston (eds), Routledge, London and New York, 2018, p. 36.
49. Ibid., p. 40.
50. Ministry of Foreign Affairs, Japan, *Japan's Legislation for Peace and Security , Seamless Responses for Peace and Security of Japan and the International Community*, Government of Japan, March 2016.
51. Defence of Japan 2016, Ministry of Defence, Japan.
52. Kyoo Staff Report, LDP to present draft for revising Japan's pacifist Constitution to Diet without consulting Komeito, *The Japan Times,* October 5, 2018 at https://www.japantimes.co.jp/news/2018/10/05/national/politics-diplomacy/ldp-present-draft-revising-japans-pacifist-constitution-diet-without-consulting-komeito/#.W77JW2gzbIU, accessed on October 11, 2018.
53. Jeffrey W. Hornung, 'Giving Japan a military', *The Japan Times,* June 13, 2017 at https://www.japantimes.co.jp/opinion/2017/06/13/commentary/japan-commentary/giving-japan-military/#.W79qimgzbIU, accessed on October 11, 2018.
54. Jeffrey W. Hornung, 'Abe versus Japan's "invisible hand"', *The Japan Times,* October 3, 2018 at https://www.japantimes.co.jp/opinion/2018/10/03/commentary/japan-commentary/abe-versus-japans-invisible-hand/#.W77Q8WgzbIU, accessed on October 11, 2018.
55. 'Japan Defence Agency, Japan's Self Defence Forces' at https://fas.org/irp/world/japan/jda.htm, accessed on October 11, 2018.
56. The "three new conditions" are as follows: "(1) When an armed attack against Japan has occurred, or when an armed attack against a foreign country that is in a close relationship with Japan occurs and as a result threatens Japan's survival and poses a clear danger to fundamentally overturn people's right to life, liberty and pursuit of happiness; (2) When there is no appropriate means available to repel the attack and ensure Japan's survival and protect its people; (3) Use of force to the minimum extent necessary". These conditions are to be interpreted as conditions under which the use of force is permitted by the Constitution.

PART II
Security Cooperation

4

Maturing India-Japan Security Cooperation

"My friends, where exactly do we now stand historically and geographically? To answer this question, I would like to quote here the title of a book authored by the Mughal prince Dara Shikoh in 1655. We are now at a point at which the Confluence of the Two Seas is coming into being".[1]

Abstract

India-Japan Security Cooperation signed in Oct 2008 lays down the basis for cooperation between the two countries in security aspects. A number of engagements have taken place in the last decade that has pushed the trajectory of this security cooperation to a higher plane. The strategies for enhancing cooperation have been arrived at by analysing the strengths and weaknesses of India in security aspects and the opportunities and threats presented by Japan, through a SWOT analysis. The strategies so obtained will, if implemented, contribute towards enhancing this security cooperation in the short term.

Background

Post-Independence, India became a staunch proponent of non-alignment and refused to be a part of either the NATO or the Warsaw camp. However, due to geo-political and security imperatives, there was a visible inclination towards USSR. Japan, on the other hand, signed the 1952 security agreement and aligned itself with the US and was perceived by India, to be more of a client state than an independent nation.[2] Relations between both countries were, thus, at an all-time low during the Cold War. However, trade continued between the two countries. Iron ore from India was instrumental in rebuilding Japan immediately after the Second World War. Yen loans by Japan to India were also a regular feature during this period. Enhanced economic engagements commenced with the opening-up of India in the early 1990s, but the nuclear tests in 1998 by India marred the relations and Japan imposed strong economic sanctions against India. It was only at the beginning of the 21st century that Japan and India resolved to take their bilateral relationship to a qualitatively new level. Both countries realised that the international situation, characterised by inter-dependence and the advent of globalisation, offered fresh opportunities to both countries for enhanced engagement for mutual benefit. The foundation for this was laid in August 2000, when the two Prime Ministers, Mr. Yoshiro Mori and Mr Atal Behari Vajpayee, agreed to establish the "Global Partnership in the 21st Century". Till 2000, Japan looked at India only through the economic lens. As J.N. Dixit states in his book, 'My South Block Years' (published 1997) "*Japan's interests in India is primarily economic. In other spheres, India does not form a primary focus of attention yet*".

The shift from economic to strategic interests was a result of the changing security dynamics in the region. Rise of China and simultaneous waning of the US influence were undoubtedly the most important reason for the two countries getting closer. Enhanced Chinese military modernisation, increased territorial claims in East Asia and increasing influence of China in countries of the Indo-Pacific region was a matter of concern for India, Japan and other like-minded countries. In addition, domestic compulsions of low growth rate of economy, ageing population and India's outreach to the East were significant in convergence of strategic interests of both the countries. Historical connections between the countries, democracy and India's adherence to international norms accentuated this convergence.

As the strategic component of the relationship became pronounced, engagements at all levels were encouraged, which resulted in the signing of the Declaration of India Japan Security Cooperation in October 2008.[3] Signing this security declaration, both nations pledged to work towards a comprehensive basis for deepening the security cooperation with the following elements:[4]

- Information exchange and policy coordination on regional and global affairs.
- Bilateral cooperation within multilateral frameworks in Asia (in particular the East Asia Summit, the ASEAN Regional Forum and the ReCAAP processes).
- Defence cooperation including Coast Guards.
- Safety of transport.
- Terrorism.
- Peacekeeping and peace building.
- Disaster management.
- Disarmament and non-proliferation.

The Security Cooperation concretised the engagement process through consultations, dialogues, staff talks, exchanges and cooperation between appropriate agencies.[5] A decade has passed since the security cooperation was signed. A number of developments have taken place since then, many in the realm of security. The National Defence Program Guidelines 2014 (which will remain effective till 2023) as well as the first National Security Strategy (NSS) also adopted in 2014, attaches importance to India for its security and diplomatic policies. Japan's enunciation in the new defence guidelines that it will strengthen its relationship with India in a broad range of fields, is reflective of the fact that it did not want to limit its security cooperation to maritime field only, as was envisioned in the NDPG adopted before 2010.[6]

This chapter traces the security related developments in a bilateral context, taking into consideration the progress made so far; it highlights areas that hold potential; and specifies specific measures that need to be taken for robust security cooperation.

SWOT Analysis[7]

In order to arrive at the areas of cooperation in the security realm, a SWOT analysis has been carried out. The SWOT analysis is based on continuous research over a prolonged period of security related aspects between Japan and India. The Strengths (S), Weaknesses (W), Opportunities (O) and Threats (T) of security cooperation between Japan and India have been identified and tabulated. The Strengths are then matched with the Opportunities that can be exploited in the context of the cooperation between the two nations. These are the SO Strategies. Similarly, what Strengths can be used to mitigate the Threats that have been envisaged, are drawn as ST Strategies. Weaknesses that have been observed in the context of India–Japan security cooperation can be overcome through the opportunities that this relationship provides and these are drawn as WO Strategies. Lastly, there are certain Weaknesses that need to be hidden till the Threats are mitigated or the weaknesses are overcome. These are the WT strategies. A summary of the same is as under:

- SO Strategies - Utilise Strengths to Exploit Opportunities.
- ST Strategies - Utilise Strengths to Mitigate Threats.
- WO Strategies - Exploit Opportunities to Overcome Weaknesses.
- WT Strategies - Hide Weaknesses till Threats Mitigated.

SWOT Analysis provides short and mid-term strategies that need to be adopted to enhance the security cooperation. The strategies have been analysed. Details of the SWOT analysis have been placed at *Appendix A*. The SWOT analyses have also facilitated identification of aspects that demand attention for enhancement of security cooperation and formation of relevant policy recommendations/ strategies. The evolved strategies have been passed through an *Environment*, *Values* and *Resources* (EVR) funnel to check whether the prevailing security *Environment*, the *Values* of the people concerned and the *Resources* available to the two countries permit implementation of such strategies before analysing them here in this chapter and before suggesting pragmatic recommendations which are covered in Chapter 8. The symbolic figure explains the process:

Figure 4.1: Symbolic Depiction of the SWOT Analyses and Evolution of Strategies

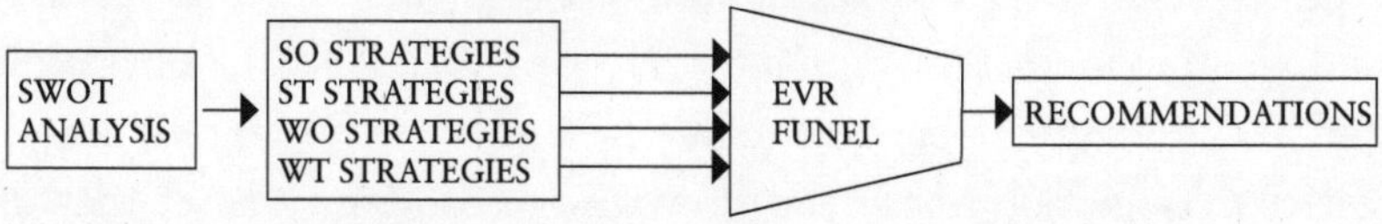

Source: Prepared by the author based on the process of SWOT analysis.

The strategies that have evolved from the SWOT analysis (refer Appendix B for further details), their status and avenues for cooperation have been analysed hereafter.

Strengthen Defence Equipment and Technology Cooperation (WO Strategy: W6O2O10): As a pacifist state, Japan never looked at sale of defence technology as a means of proactively contributing to peace. However, during the formulation of the National Security Strategy (NSS) and drafting of the National Defence Program Guidelines (NDPG) and the Medium Term Defence Program (MTDP) for the Japanese Fiscal Year 2014 to 2018, it was realised that cooperation amongst the industry, government and academia for a defence build-up and proactively utilising commercially available dual use technologies was imperative. Accentuating this very thought, the 'Ministry of Defence (MoD) Strategy on Defence Production and Technology Bases' released in June 2014 states that there is a need for strategically implementing defence R&D based on Japan's comparative advantages.[8]

On April 1, 2014, the Japanese Government, in accordance with the NSS that was adopted on December 17, 2013, promulgated the "Three Principles of Transfer of Defence Equipment and Technology" as the new principles related to transfer of defence equipment and technology to other countries, which replaced "the Three Principles on Arms Exports and their Related Policy Guidelines".[9] This policy document as well as the white paper on "Strategy on Defence Production and Technology Bases" state, "MoD will take necessary measures under the government's leadership to proactively and strategically promote defence equipment and technology cooperation such as international joint development and production".[10] On December 12, 2015, the agreement concerning the Transfer of Defence Equipment and Technology was signed between the Indian and the Japanese Government.[11] However, Defence Cooperation and Technology has been an area where the progress for enhanced security cooperation has been slow. Concerns about the security of technology, high costs and customised Indian requirements have been the main issues.

Both countries, however, aspire to have integrated, enmeshed and mutually beneficial defence cooperation. This is evident from the willingness on the part of Japan to part with latest technology as regards the US-2 amphibious planes. A Joint Working Group is still looking into the possibilities of continuing with the proposed procurement of 12 US-2 amphibious aircraft at the proposed cost of US$ 13 billion. Lately, ShinMaya Industries and manufacturers of the US-2, have signed a MoU with India's Mahindra Group to set up maintenance, repair and overhaul of services for the US-2 amphibious aircraft in India during the Def Expo Defence Exhibition in Chennai in April 2018.[12] As per the fact sheet circulated by the Ministry of Foreign Affairs, Japan, the US-2 ShinMaya aircraft cooperation seeks to concurrently advance the aeronautics industry including maintenance, repair and overhaul, and the parts manufacturing of US-2 in India.[13] The US-2 may also be permitted to be exported to third countries under mutual agreement.[14] Such interactions are an indication of the trust and faith that the two countries have been able to build over the years.

Another area where superior Japanese technology has manifested itself is the production of Soryu submarines. The combination of long-endurance stealth, sensors, modern torpedoes and missiles makes the Soryu class an effective hunter-killer and probably one of the best submarines in the world.[15] While placing a tender for building six contemporary conventional submarines as part of Project 75I, the Japanese submarines were also under consideration by the Indian navy. The Request For Information (RFI) entailed construction of four out of the six submarines in Indian shipyards with Transfer of Technology (ToT) and certain design changes to cater to specific Indian requirements.[16] The Japanese fear that their superior Soryu class submarine technology will be compromised due to proliferation through ToT and customisation as per Indian requirements. Additionally, a 'Make in India' initiative will involve the Indian industry, which does not have a very high credibility of timely deliveries, which in turn would affect Japanese credibility.[17] Japan reportedly has not subscribed to the Indian bid for procurement. However, being one of the most powerful conventional submarines in the world, their induction will be a potent force in the IOR and have a high deterrent value. Incidentally, in October 2018, the 11th Japanese MSDF Soryu submarine, JS Oryu, was launched, which is the first Soryu submarine to utilise lithium-ion batteries in place of the erstwhile lead acid batteries. This launch has given the Japanese submarines an additional functional advantage of stealth and long range in operations.[18] Currently, Japan is exploring technologies for unmanned underwater communications, underwater vehicles and underwater wireless power-transmission methods for submarines. These technologies can leap-frog Indian technological threshold to a higher plane.[19]

In the overall context, it is imperative that we look for complementarities in a broad sense and not look towards a single deal only. A case in point is the requirement of light tanks by India for its northern mountainous borders, some being in the high altitude regions. During the Doklam standoff at the northern borders along the Line of Actual Control, China publicised photos of its homegrown light tank, Xinqingtan, which is equipped with a 105 millimetres main gun and a 1,000-horse-power engine for high altitude and mountain warfare, in Tibet.[20] The Indian Army which is also on the look-out for light tanks can look at Japanese manufacturers of armoured vehicles like the Mitsubishi Heavy Industries, which possesses advanced tank engine technology that may suit the qualitative requirements of the Indian army under the 'Make in India' programme. The indigenous tank engines for Indian heavy tanks T-90 and T-72 developed by DRDO in July 2018 exhibits that India has adequate expertise in absorbing imported tank engine technology. Additionally, it may be wiser to look at the purchase or manufacture of smaller equipment, subsystems and components such as lithium-ion batteries, image sensors, carbon-fibre aircraft components which are of dual-use and can be particularly useful for India's own weapons development efforts.[21] Such components/sub systems are crucial to tide over the lack of technological expertise and do not grab unwanted media attention, thereby facilitating smooth transactions.[22] Recently, Maruti's Japanese partner Suzuki Motor Corp decided to set up a plant for Lithium ion batteries at Hansalpur in Gujarat in partnership with Densho and Toshiba and will start production by 2020.[23]

Craft Collaborations and Commence Joint Productions (SO Strategy: S1O2): In addition to defence procurements and technology transfers, the need for enhancing interactions between governments, defence industries, scientists and engineers so that equipment collaboration and dual use technology sharing is encouraged has been recognised by political leaders of both nations and they have encouraged intensified engagements during the defence ministerial meetings held in 2018. When compared with joint research projects of Japan with other countries like the USA, UK and Australia, India still needs to make a beginning. A case in point can be a co-development strategy for fighter aircrafts. Both India and Japan are on the look-out for the latest fighter aircrafts. The huge time lag for development and high costs involved make it challenging for either country to follow the project unilaterally. Ballistic Missile Defence is another area where both the countries are looking towards other nations of the world for armament and technology. Co-development in such areas holds potential. Development of surveillance systems, radars and strategic electronics for communications can also be part of a collaborative effort by India and Japan. These can be on similar lines as the joint research projects and joint development projects being carried out by Japan with other countries as per the Table 4.1.

Table 4.1: Research Projects and Joint Development Projects of Japan

Country	Date	Research Projects and Joint Development*
US	Since 1992	25 Joint Research Projects 01 Joint Development Project
UK	July 2013	04 Joint Research Projects • Joint research on chemical and biological protection technology • Technology information on air-to-air missile seeker technology for joint research • Co-operative research project on the feasibility of a joint new air-to-air missile. • Joint research on personnel vulnerability evaluation (PVE) (R&D of personal equipment) • Joint preliminary study on potential collaborative opportunities for future combat air system (FCAS)/future fighters.
Australia	July 2014	01 Joint Research Project • Joint research in the field of marine hydrodynamics. • Exploration of potential cooperation opportunities in the F-35 programme(sought).
France	January 2017	Both France and Japan seek to cooperate in the field of unmanned underwater vehicle (UUV) for mine detection
India	December 2015	Establishment of JWG for procurement of US-2. MRO agreement concluded with Mahindra Ltd

*Source: Defence of Japan 2017.

The initial steps towards joint research are being taken. An Indo-Japanese joint call for proposal under the India-Japan Cooperative Science Programme (IJCSP) was issued by the Department of Science and Technology (DST), Ministry of Science & Technology, Government of India, New Delhi and the Japan Society for the Promotion of Science (JSPS) for inviting Indian and Japanese scientists to submit their proposals for joint research projects and joint workshops in various areas like Fundamental Sciences, Materials and System Engineering, Natural Systems, Astronomy, Space, Earth System and Sciences and Mathematics and Computational Science.[24] After judicious assessment based on scientific strength, technical aspects, project objectives and national priorities of both the countries, India and Japan have jointly decided to support the 28 proposals (23 joint research projects and five workshops).[25] Still in the formative stages, this initiative has the potential to evolve into joint manufacturing and applications in many fields including security realms.

Another issue pertaining to collaborations and joint production is the aspect of defence procurements. The current focus of Indian defence procurements is on 'Make in India'; Japanese firms should collaborate with the Indian defence industry to make inroads into the defence markets. New players find the Indian defence procurement system time consuming and effort intensive. Moreover, they are not well conversant with the intricacies of the Defence Procurement Procedure (DPP), thereby leading to their elimination in defence bids. A case in point is the procurement case of K-9 Thunder artillery gun from South Korea. The trial equipment was a piece of functional equipment, which was in-service in the Korean army. Efforts to get the artillery gun back into South Korea after their trials in India did not materialise due to the DPP provisions of keeping the trial equipment until all negotiations are over. Such issues lead to a general exasperation, which hinders subsequent participation in defence procurements. Japan should, therefore, acquaint itself with the latest provisions of the DPP and seek amendments to the same, should some of these provisions go against its established norms. As an alternate course, Japan can also take advantage of the strategic partnership with India to maintain progress of government to government defence sales, where normal procurement procedures seem to be time consuming. The Japanese Defence Attaches posted to New Delhi can play an active and important role in this regard. Organising Defence Expos and ensuring participation of indigenous defence industries of both countries is another constructive step in this regard.

Enhance Engagement between ATLA and DRDO (S5O9): The defence ministers of India and Japan in their defence ministerial talks in September 2017 have hailed the productive engagement between the Acquisition, Technology and Logistics Agency (ATLA) and the Defence Research and Development Organisation (DRDO). Similarly, the first ever meeting on defence industry cooperation held by ATLA and the Department of Defence Production (DDP) in Tokyo, witnessed significant participation of government entities and companies of both countries.[26] They expressed their expectation that such meetings will lead both countries to future defence equipment and technology cooperation and enhance interaction between governments and industries of both countries.[27] ATLA and DRDO, in their engagements, have also agreed to initiate discussions for collaboration in research in the areas of Artificial Intelligence (AI) and Robotics (*to collaborate in the development of military grade robotics and artificial intelligence (S11O11)*).

AI and Robotics have arrived in a big way affecting many aspects of our lives. It was the defeat of the South Korean world champion of the game of 'Go' by the Google computer programme *Alpha Go*, which reinforced the opinion that AI could be used as a tool that could surpass the human mind. Though the US is currently a world leader in employing AI especially in defence aspects, China is trying a fast catch up. "There should be no doubt that the Chinese military is chasing transformative AI technologies", said retired PLA Maj Gen Xu Guangyu, now a senior researcher at the China Arms Control and Disarmament Association, a government-supported think tank. He further informed, "China will not ignore or let slip by any dual-use technology, or any technology at all, that might improve the ability of the military to fight, (improve) awareness, or (improve) ability to attack".

Taking note of the development of AI in the world, leaders of Japan and India emphasized the need to initiate technical discussions for future research collaboration in the area of Unmanned Ground Vehicles and Robotics. The India-Japan Joint Statement in September 2017 during the visit of PM Shinzo Abe to India noted the commencement of technical discussions between ATLA of Japan and DRDO of India. India and Japan have promised to enhance strategic ties by increased cooperation in the sectors of defence, robotics and AI in the coming years.

In an ambitious defence project, the government has started work on incorporating AI to enhance op preparedness of the armed forces in a significant way that would include equipping them with unmanned tanks, vessels, aerial vehicles and robotic weaponry.[28] The potential of cooperation in this field is boundless with applications in the armed forces in terms of tactical augmented reality systems, mine detecting vehicles, miniature UAVs, pilotless helicopters and "swarm intelligence". Artificial Intelligence (AI) powered robots can negotiate hazardous terrains, perform remote surgery, and execute surveillance and strike missions.[29] Robotic soldiers can be made to man inhospitable terrain under inclement weather conditions. The Centre for Artificial Intelligence and Research (CAIR) of India has brought out the RoboSen—a mobile robot system targeted at patrolling, reconnaissance and surveillance, capable of autonomous navigation in semi structured environments with obstacle avoidance capability and continuous video feedback.[30] CAIR is also developing man portable Unmanned Ground Vehicle (UGV) for low intensity conflicts and surveillance in the urban scenario; wall climbing and flapping wing robot, walking robot with four and six legs for logistics support, and Network Traffic Analysis (NETRA) which can monitor internet traffic.[31] Autonomously controlled equipment like drone swarms that are fleets of low-cost quad copters having a shared 'brain' can be used for surveillance as well as attacking opponents. Such weapons as well as cyber weapons can also be developed by AI. As President Putin stated, "Artificial intelligence is the future ... It comes with colossal opportunities, but also threats that are difficult to predict. Whoever becomes the leader in this sphere will become the ruler of the world".[32]

Asian enterprises, especially those in India and China, are fast adopting AI to reinvent their business models and perceive AI as a complete disruptive force.[33] Led by China (from 31 per cent to 61 per cent) and India (from 29 per cent to 69 per cent), the investment and adoption in Asia has jumped significantly between 2016 and 2017 as government-backed AI is fuelling innovation in existing technology firms, start ups and academic communities.[34] The first blue print on

AI released by the government think tank Niti Aayog in Jun 2018, titled "*National Strategy for Artificial Intelligence*", declares India as the AI "garage for the emerging and developing economies". Though the Indian focus is on the social sector, its spillover effects on security related aspects cannot be negated. With the US as the global leader and China as the rising challenger, India and Japan need to collaborate so as not to be left behind. The question that needs to be answered is whether or not Japan will share their expertise with Indian companies for collaborative research or does it look towards Indian market only for its business interests.

Though personal and consumer robotics in India is still at its nascent stage, use of industrial and surgical robots are coming up in a big way. The passion to use robots in India for specialised precision jobs is on the rise. In India, an estimated 700 robotic-assisted surgeries are carried out each month by over 50 surgical robots. According to Vattikuti Foundation, India has the potential to be the second largest surgical robot market by 2020.[35] Therefore, there is an imperative need to pursue a coordinated policy for robotics and exploit the huge IT talent pool available. The Indian government and industry needs to reach out to other countries for such collaborations. Japan, in these respects, is an ideal partner, whose robotics companies have a long and distinguished pedigree and are also at the very edge of startling new innovations.[36] Japanese companies such as Fanuc, Yaskawa Electric, and Kawasaki Heavy Industries make up for 50 per cent of the global market in the factory and industrial robotics space.[37] A report published in METI stated that Japan should achieve a Robot Revolution by having three pillars. First, by Japan becoming the robot innovation hub in the world. Second, by utilisation and dissemination of robots across Japan, aiming to achieve a society with the highest level of robot utilisation in the world and to realise in daily life that robots exist all over Japan; and third by development of the Robot Revolution, standardising Japan's robot technologies, and disseminating Japan`s Robot approach to broader fields globally.[38] Japanese analysts see that its citizen's passion towards Robots could spark a revolution for new industrial revolution worldwide.[39] Presently in Japan, the favourite subjects of study for young students in colleges are Mechatronics and Robots, and one can find almost everyone attempting to make some or the other robotic tool. Overall, with a high degree of acceptability towards robots and a huge collaboration potential with India, Japanese companies also have a vested interest in building better technological relations with India, especially in this field.[40] Collaborations and cooperation in this field will also be facilitated by a deeper understanding of each other's security needs.

The study titled "Advance artificial intelligence for growth: Leveraging AI & Robotics for India's Economic Transformation", jointly conducted by The Associated Chambers of Commerce and Industry of India (ASSOCHAM) and multinational professional services firm PricewaterhouseCoopers (PwC) has noted that exchanging best practices and learnings from prior initiatives, creating an ecosystem that is supportive of research, innovation and commercialisation of applications, and revision of secondary school and university curricula to inculcate interest in AI will help create an enabling environment for AI-led growth.[41] It also suggests that the government should act as a catalyst in furthering growth by opening training centres focused on equipping young individuals with high-end skills in the field of analytics and Machine Learning, which in turn, could be tied in with inviting data-driven global enterprises to set up their centres of excellence in India.[42] These measures will create the environment for seamless transition of AI into defence related functions.

Conduct Joint Training and Exercises between Armed Forces (SO Strategy S9,O3,O14): Utilisation of training facilities and sharing of combat experience are areas of cooperation, which can be easily explored by both India and Japan. Japan's geography dictates that SDF will have to operate domestically in different types of terrain. Comprising of 6,852 islands, Japan stretches 3,000 km North East to South West. The SDF has to operate in a variedly changing land-form as 73 per cent of Japan is mountainous and each of the main islands has a mountain range passing through it. The highest mountain, Mount Fuji, is 3,776 m (12,388 ft) high. In addition, since the mountains are densely covered by forests, the overall forest cover rate of Japan is 68.55 per cent. Therefore, the SDF needs to prepare itself to fight in varied terrain like mountainous and jungle terrain inside the country. To cater for out of area contingency operations, such as the SDF deployment in Iraq (though for non-combat employment) from 2003 to 2008, they will require to be trained to operate in terrain not found in Japan viz. the desert terrain. This challenge can be mitigated by the experience of the Indian Army, which has a long experience of conducting military operations in various terrains. The Indian Army can offer valuable expertise and training assistance to the SDF.[43] Japan should utilise the various institutes of expertise for varied terrain like the High Altitude Warfare School (HAWS), the Counter Insurgency and Jungle Warfare School (CIJW) School and the Desert Battle School (DBS) for training the SDF. Training of the SDF in these centres should be in sub-unit combat groups of a platoon or a company for realistic training under the supervision of experienced instructors.

The raising of an Amphibious Rapid Deployment Brigade (ARDB) by Japan also provides opportunities for co-training and joint exercises *(SO Strategy-S9O15)*. The amphibious brigade was raised for quick reaction to threats to the sovereignty of Japan's island territories. The brigade, roughly comprising of 2,100 troops, was declared operational in April 2018. Though in its nascent stage presently, the unit is modelled on the US Marine Corps. The commander of this brigade, Major General Shinichi Aoki admits that the formation is still 'less than perfect' and there is a need to continue training so that the mandate given by the public can be fulfilled.[44]

Correspondingly, India with its island territories and long coastline also has an amphibious brigade for out of area contingencies (OOAC). In order to acquire enhanced capabilities, the INS Jalashva, formerly USS Trenton, was acquired from the US, thereby providing the platform to execute battle drills for such contingencies. Drills and manoeuvres of the amphibious brigade are conducted along with the annual naval exercises in India. The 2017 annual navy exercises named Theatre Level Readiness and Operational Exercise (TROPEX 17) was conducted in Jan-Feb 2017 and saw participation of over 45 ships, including the aircraft carrier INS Vikramaditya, five submarines, 50 naval aircrafts, 11 ships from the Coast Guard, troops from the army and 20 aircraft from the air force including Su 30s, Jaguars and AWACS.[45] Such exercises provide an apt-opportunity to test the joint combat capability of the navy, army, air force and coast guard.[46] With both the countries evolving their amphibious doctrines, joint amphibious exercises as part of the larger theatre level exercises will go a long way in enhancing interoperability, honing drills and imparting realistic training. India already has the experience of participating in bilateral amphibious exercise, Exercise Habu Nag along with the US, off the coast of Okinawa (Japan) in 2010. A trilateral format of such nature between the US, Japan and India can also be thought of.

Offer Indian Experience to Mitigate Terrorism Threats during Olympics (S2S9O18): In addition to training for combat situations, the impending 2020 Tokyo Olympics will necessitate training Japanese SDF and police in urban insurgency. The rich Counter Insurgency (CI) and Counter terrorism (CT) experience of Indian armed forces thus needs to be exploited by the SDF. Training of Japanese dog squads as well as participation of Indian dog squads can be another area of mutual cooperation. Both countries should also conduct joint research and development to come out with technological breakthroughs in anti-terrorist operations such as scanning items and personnel, identification in a crowd, mass surveillance, close combat weapons and armaments, electronic eavesdropping on terrorist communication channels, jamming and intelligence sharing. The web between terrorism, transnational organised crime, money-laundering, and illegal arms trafficking makes a strong case for functional counter-terror approaches, mechanisms, and strategies.[47]

This convergence on terrorism should not be limited to the Tokyo Olympics itself. Both countries have been victims of terrorism. The gruesome killing of two Japanese by the ISIS in 2015 and the death of seven Japanese citizens in the Bangladesh café siege in July 2016 shook the Japanese government and further strengthened its resolve to fight terrorism.[48] Internally also, Japan is wary of the activities of the terrorist group Aum Shinrikyo (AUM), the Japanese doomsday cult, which carried out the sarin attack in the crowded Tokyo subway in March 1995. The former leader of Aum Shinrikyo, was executed on July, 6 2018 alongside six other members of the cult. India too has been a victim of terrorism in all its forms with a number of attacks all across the country for a number of decades. External support from Pakistan to terrorists in India has seen the Indian armed forces in perpetual CI and CT operations since the 1990s. With both countries bearing the brunt of terrorism, India and Japan need to cooperate more, in order to meet this challenge. In their Joint Statement in September 2017, both countries called upon all countries of the world to work towards rooting out terrorist safe havens and infrastructure, disrupting terrorist networks and financing channels and halting cross-border movement of terrorists.[49] Both countries were explicit in naming Pakistan based perpetrators of terror attacks, including Jaish-e-Mohammad, Al-Qaida, Lakshar-e-Taiba, the ISIS, and their affiliates. In their Action Plan for Advancing Security Cooperation between India and Japan of December 2009 (Appendix D refers), both nations have devised arrangements for intelligence exchanges and have agreed to cooperate in technical aspects of counter terrorism by establishing a Joint Working Group (JWG) on CT. This initiative has been led by the Ministry of External Affairs (MEA) of India and Ministry of Foreign Affairs (MOFA) of Japan, in consonance with the participation of concerned government agencies. The 4th India-Japan Joint Working Group on Counter Terrorism was held in November 2015. The Financial Intelligence Units (FIUs) of both nations have also agreed to set up appropriate information exchange framework to check money laundering and terrorist financing.[50] Recently, Japan has decided to set up a Counter Terrorism Unit-Japan within the foreign ministry, headed up by the office of Prime Minister Shinzo Abe and comprising defence ministry officials and the National Police Agency (NPA), along with the Cabinet Intelligence and Research Office, known to be Japan's equivalent of the CIA.[51]

Exercises and training are also being planned to enhance integration on issues related to terrorism. The Indian army and the GSDF are planning on a Counter Terrorist and Counter Insurgency exercise in order to gain from the rich experience of India and share standard operating procedures (SOP) in combating this menace.[52] Though the contours of the joint exercise are yet to be spelt, it could include profiling of weapons and equipment, communication systems and procedures, synergy in intelligence gathering, sharing, surveillance and optimal use of force against the identified terrorist targets.[53] Japan has long supported the Indian position that all countries need to ensure that their territories are not used to launch terrorist attacks on other countries.[54] It has joined India in calling out Pakistan to bring to justice the perpetrators of terrorist attacks, including those of the November 2008 terrorist attack in Mumbai and the 2016 terrorist attack in Pathankot.[55] In the course of the upcoming exercises between the Indian army and Japan's GSDF, the focus should be on attaining a higher degree of cohesion and synergy ensured through regular series of joint manoeuvres simulating likely terrorist threat scenarios that may confront the two nations in future.[56] There is, hence, a need for putting in place a coordinated crisis response system and upgrade the tactical abilities of anti-terrorist forces of India and Japan.[57]

Enhance Official Interactions and Exchanges between Armed Forces (SO Strategy-S9, O3, O14): Strong linkages between the armed forces will enhance mutual understanding of security needs and emulation of the best practices of each other. Staff talks and visits by senior commanders of the two armies and air forces that are conducted periodically in order to enhance cooperation between the two Services and ensure exchanges at the functional level, are only in the initial stages of implementation. Interactions and dialogues are imperative for robust defence cooperation between nations. The Action Plan to advance India-Japan security cooperation of

December 2009 (refer Appendix C) has instituted certain interactions between the authorities of both countries as under:[58]

- 'Regular meetings between the Ministers of Defence.
- Annual Defence Policy Dialogue at the level of Defence Secretary/ Administrative Vice-Minister of Defence.
- Annual Military-to-Military Talks between Joint Secretary, MOD of India, and Deputy Director General, MOD of Japan.
- Regular reciprocal visits between Service Chiefs of both sides.
- Regular Service to Service Staff Talks of the Army, Navy and Air force.
- In addition, the Action Plan also mentions annual bilateral naval exercises, to enhance cooperation and core ability for maritime operation and disaster relief, multilateral Naval Exercises, when possible, Passing Exercise (PASSEX) during ship visits and participation as observers in major army and air force exercise'.[59]

Table 4.2: The Defence Exchanges between India and Japan in the Last Three Years (2014–2017)

High-level talks between heads of state and defence	09
High-level talks between heads of defence departments/directorates	07
Regular discussions between defence ministry representatives	09
Visits by high level official dignitaries (ministers and above)	28
Unit-level exchanges (Naval Exercises, Participation in Fleet review, exchange of experts, aircraft crew and other units).	14

Source: Defence of Japan 2016.

The Indian Air Force (IAF) and the Japan Air Self Defence Force (JASDF) commenced their inaugural Air Staff Talks, only in 2016. In the Defence Ministerial talks of September 2017, the leaders expressed their desire to explore opportunities that would increase the cooperation between the air forces of both countries through regular visits of their aircrafts to each other's air bases. Interactions between the corresponding services of the armed forces need to be strengthened with scheduled exercises, discussions, visits and subscription to training courses in each other's military training institutions at tactical and operational levels. The state of student exchange in respective training institutions at the tactical and operational levels is abysmally low. As compared to many other countries, only four military students imbibed training in 2016 and only one in 2017. The details of the number of newly accepted students by Japan in FY 2016 for some countries vis-à-vis India for the year 2016 are as under:

Table 4.3: Number of Newly Accepted Students by Japan in FY 2016[60]

	US	Thailand	South Korea	Myanmar	Vietnam	Pakistan	India
National Institute for Defense Studies	2	1	0	0	0	0	0
National Defense Academy	8	5	1	3	8	0	1
Ground Self Defense Force (Staff College etc)	3	1	3	2	1	4	0
Maritime Self Defense Force (Staff College, etc.)	0	2	2	1	0	0	1
Air Self-Defense Force (Staff College, etc.)	1	2	3	2	0	0	0
Joint Staff College	2	2	3	3	1	0	1
Total	**16**	**13**	**12**	**11**	**10**	**4**	**3**

Source: Defence of Japan 2016.

Exchange Expert Manpower Pool to Collaborate in IT; Deepen Cyber Security Cooperation (ST Strategy: S10T8): The cyber security domain also presents an enhanced scope of mutual cooperation. The second Cyber Security Dialogue between India and Japan was held in New Delhi in August 2017. Areas of discussion included domestic cyber policy landscape, cyber threats and mitigation, mechanism on bilateral cooperation and possible cooperation at various international fora such as the ARF Inter-Sessional Meeting on Security.[61] Both sides shared the view that they will deepen the dialogues at various levels including through the India-Japan Cyber

Dialogue.[62] The promising sign in this field is that as compared to the first dialogue that was held in 2012, the delegation of both sides included various other agencies like the National Centre of Incident Readiness and Strategy for Cyberspace (NISC), the Cabinet Intelligence and Research Office and the Japanese Computer Emergency Research Team/Coordination Centre (CERT/CC). The Indian delegation comprised personnel of the MEA, the Ministry of Electronics and IT, the DoT, the National Critical Infrastructure Protection Centre and the National Investigation Agency in 2017.[63] The Joint Statement released at the end of the Joint Working Group conference for Comprehensive Cooperation Framework for Information and Communication Technologies (ICT) stated that both sides prioritised areas of Green ICT, Cyber Security Cooperation and ICT for Disaster Management for detailed deliberations with a view to start working on the implementation of these joint projects.[64] The spirit of cooperation was highlighted again when Japan's Minister of Economy Trade and Industry Hiroshige Seko, during his meeting in May 2018 with Mr Ravi Shankar, Minister for Electronics and IT emphasized, "Japan is the centre for hardware and India is the centre for software and hence both countries should collaborate more in the field of cyber security".

However, due to the demographic decline, the domestic IT talent pool is also reducing and Japan is currently in dire need of talent from foreign countries to plug the void and resuscitate its economy. Japan is expected to face a shortage of 600,000 positions for IT engineers.[65] Striving to avoid another lost decade, it is facing the toughest employment market for employers—the market for top talent and it is looking for the solution abroad.[66] Currently, there are an estimated 132,060 IT professional opportunities unfilled, with another 60,000 more positions to be added by 2020 and therefore, to fix this labour deficit, Japan's government and businesses have been fast at work to develop these human resources domestically.[67] In addition, Japan is also looking towards countries like India to get skilled human resource. As stated by Tokyo Governor Yoichi Masuzoe at a press conference in June 2014, "We [Japan] have to import many intelligent people from abroad, we badly need young talented persons".[68] Major opportunities for Indian IT experts exist in the fields of automation, manufacturing, digital services, block chain, artificial intelligence, data analytics and IoT, all of which have security related aspects as spinoffs. Initiatives like Project Indian Institutes of Technology (PIITs) programme have been initiated by Japanese companies to attract Indian talent. The IIT interns who have joined Japanese companies have already impressed the Japanese with their talent.[69]

However, to ensure a steady stream of talent from India to Japan, Japan needs to overcome its restrictions of language skills, red tapism and long delays in recruitment. It also needs to change the manner in which foreign workers are looked at in Japanese society, and the privileges and rights they have. As per the Global Competitiveness Index Report (World Economic Forum) of 2017–18, the rankings of Japan and India in the capacity to attract and retain talent as shown below indicate that Tokyo will need to take effective measures to retain talent from New Delhi.

Table 4.4: Comparison of Global Competitiveness Rankings 2017–18

	India (Rank out of 137 countries)	**Japan (Rank out of 137 countries)**
Capacity to Attract Talent	19	73
Capacity to Retain Talent	24	44

Source: World Economic Forum.

Certain measures are being taken by the Abe government to attract skilled workers from foreign countries like the proposals of grant of permanent visas. Moreover, Japanese students should also come and join IITs in India and gain from the high standards of engineering studies. This will build a common pool of talent that can collaborate to evolve new technologies and products. The industry should support cooperation of the two countries that share the same values on democracy and the rule of law, and champion innovative technology and cyber threat intelligence to prevent cyber-attacks.[70]

It is also important to have the industry involved in their cyber security collaboration to protect critical infrastructure and share cyber threat intelligence to make cyber-attacks cost-prohibitive to attackers.[71] Overall, through the framework of the cyber security discussions, both countries should apportion adequate resources for cyber security, create bilateral mechanisms for information sharing on cyber threats and countering techniques, develop robust, realistic joint training and exercises as well as collectively ensure protection of civilian critical infrastructure.

A Japanese researcher while giving his views at an Indian think tank stated that high end confidential technology and systems are not available for foreigners to work on, in Japan.[72] Such restrictions in the name of security of information and technology will have to be done away with, if credible talent is to be attracted on a permanent basis. Despite the call by leaders of both countries for deeper engagement in this field, the progress has been rather slow.

Engage in HADR at Bilateral and Regional Levels (SO Strategy-S7O6): Humanitarian and Disaster Relief (HADR) is one of the areas where countries can cooperate spontaneously because of the non-aggressive nature of activity and universal acceptance of mutual assistance, thereby developing trust and confidence. This is one of those areas where countries collaborate, conduct demonstrations and exercises before moving onto to more sensitive areas of national interest. For Japan and India, the field of HADR can thus be one strong pillar of security cooperation.

Japan has historically been a nation that has been repeatedly affected by natural disasters. Natural disasters in Japan include floods, cyclones, typhoons, earthquakes, tsunamis, and volcanic eruptions. Located in the highly volatile and seismic zone also called the 'Ring of Fire', Japan experiences more than 100,000 earthquakes every year, including some earthquakes that are too feeble for people to feel. According to the Seismology Society of Japan, out of the 100,000 quakes a year, 1,000 to 1,500 exceed 1 on the 7-level Japanese seismic intensity scale, meaning they are strong enough for people to notice.[73] In terms of the open-ended magnitude scale, records show that over the past century there has been an average of one magnitude-7 or greater quake almost every year.[74] Also cyclones, typhoons and volcanic eruptions are a regular feature in Japan. Likewise, India with its vast area, geographical diversity and different climatic conditions also has its share of natural disasters causing massive losses to life and property. Droughts, floods, cyclones, avalanches, earthquakes, landslides and snowstorms pose the greatest threats.

An intense engagement in the field of HADR is, therefore, natural. The Action Plan for the Advancement of Security Cooperation of December 2009 between Japan and India (Appendix D refers) has given out following measures that need to be taken:

- "Jointly develop maps and risk areas for various disasters like the Tsunami, earthquake prone areas, flood basins groundwater mapping and so on. Dialogue between National Disaster Management Authorities (NDMA) of India and Cabinet Office of Japan through Asian Disaster Reduction Centre (ADRC) for sharing information on disaster prevention and preparedness.
- Participation in each other's HADR exercises to take note of best practices, different technologies and approaches to handle/ mitigate disasters.
- Capacity building through the Workshop on Water-related Disaster management conducted by the International Centre for Water Hazard and Risk Management (ICHARM) of Japan.
- Sharing experience in landslide disaster prevention between National Institute for Land and Infrastructure Management (NILIM), Public Works Research Institute (PWRI) of Japan and National Institute of Disaster Management (NIDM) of India.
- Capacity Building for disaster management and sharing Japanese experience on disaster relief through training programmes conducted by Japan International Cooperation Agency (JICA).
- Participation as observers in Japan's nationwide disaster management drill.
- Sharing of disaster-related information between Japan Aerospace Exploration Agency (JAXA) and Indian Space Research Organisation (ISRO) through the "Sentinel Asia" process.[75]

Most of these measures mentioned above, are in various phases of implementation and progress. HADR has been one of the important roles of the SDF. It was upgraded from one of the secondary roles to a primary role of the SDF in 2014. In India also, the armed forces have been playing a very primary role in disaster management along with the National Disaster Management Authority (NDMA). Sharing of best practices, sharing of earth quake resistant building technology, data and statistical analysis, early warning mechanisms and capacity development to deal with disaster situations are some of the areas where cooperation can be enhanced. Likely areas of collaboration could include Data and Statistical support and analysis, capacity development, Climate Change Mitigation and Adaptation Action, knowledge management and information sharing among others. The National Institute of Disaster Management (Ministry of Home Affairs, Govt. of India) has signed an MoC with National Institute of Land and Infrastructure Management (NILIM) and an MoU with Public Works Research Institute (PWRI), Japan to undertake joint activities in the field of landslides and related management of disasters.[76] The bilateral collaboration is to strengthen the comprehensive strategy for landslides studies, prevention, mitigation, preparedness and management in India through cooperation between relevant organisations/experts of the two countries, i.e. Japan and India.[77] The areas of mutual cooperation include:

- "Development of Early Warning system related to landslide including real time monitoring.
- Development of pragmatic model for slope stability analysis to understand failure of mechanism in different geo-environmental conditions.
- Training and Capacity building and dissemination of technologies to the potential users for implementation."[78]

HADR exercises are generally held on a multilateral format wherein stake holders practise various drills, procedures and ways to cooperate with each other pooling resources for the common cause. The Indian air force held its first HADR exercise named

'Samvedna' in association with South Asian Region nations off the coast of Kerala from March 12–17, 2018 with an objective to galvanise all stakeholders in synergising a unified HADR effort.[79] During the India-Japan Annual Defence Ministerial Dialogue held at Tokyo in September 2017, it was agreed that the Japan Ground Self Defence Force (JGSDF) would invite Indian Armed Forces personnel to participate in the HADR exercise conducted by JGSDF as observers.[80] The authorities dealing in disaster management, therefore, need to engage more often to arrive at quick response to any disaster. The need to utilise all resources at hand is also imperative to ensure that the rescue and relief operations are conducted smoothly and swiftly.

In the case of the Great East Japan Earthquake in 2011 as well as the Tsunami and the Fukushima nuclear disaster, satellite observation by remote sensing satellites assisted damage assessment and provision of rescue and relief. In this context, Japan and India can expand the scope of international space cooperation for disaster management by including a pre-disaster phase of efforts, thereby mitigating future risks of natural disasters.[81] As leading space faring nations, Japan and India can also contribute to the capacity building in the Indo-Pacific region for the use of space technology in disaster management.[82] Post the tsunami, in the Indian Ocean, India has deployed a tsunami monitoring and alert system, which is benefitting other IOR rim countries. Advancements in space technology, launch of satellites, monitoring the IOR and upgradations in the early warning systems of institutions like the Indian Meteorological Department (IMD), the Indian Institute of Tropical Meteorology (IITM) facilitate the monitoring, tracking and relaying of timely warnings about impending hazards of natural disasters like cyclones, heavy concentrated rainfall, droughts, tsunami, etc. Japan too, with one of the most technologically advanced tsunami warning systems, has honed its drills and procedures to mitigate risks of disasters and has contributed immensely to the capacity building of disaster prone countries. Both countries can cooperate to assist regional countries with prior warning of natural disasters and provide resources during the disaster phase and the reconstruction phase. In addition to cooperating in Asia, both countries can share their experiences and expertise in assisting African countries deal with disaster relief through the forum of the Asia Africa Growth Corridor (AAGC). Under the AAGC, both India and Japan should seek to focus on Africa's development challenges and opportunities with emphasis on human security, environment and natural resource preservation, risk management, governance, as well as inclusive growth through collaborative partnerships.[83]

Collaborate for Enhanced Connectivity through Infrastructure Development (WO Strategy W4O13): Assistance in infrastructure development to India by Japan has been in the form of Official Development Assistance (ODA), and has contributed in a big way towards infrastructure growth in India. Japanese ODA has increased over the years and presently, India is the largest ODA recipient, which is an indication of its growing importance to Japan.[84] A detail of the ODA received over the years by India from Japan is as shown in Table 4.5.

The Japan International Cooperation Agency (JICA) in accordance with the Development Cooperation Charter (development cooperation activities guidelines approved by the Japanese Cabinet in 2015) provides bilateral aid in the form of Technical Cooperation, Japanese ODA Loans and Grant Aid. The ODA loans are being used for infrastructure and social developmental activities throughout the country, but the developmental activities being undertaken in the North East region are of particular significance. The remoteness of the area, its rough terrain, the young mountains and an ongoing insurgency have precluded major infrastructural activity in this region. In August 2017, the JICA actively participated in the first meeting of the Japan-India Coordination Forum (JICF) for Development of North-Eastern Region. Road networks, power infrastructure,

Table 4.5: Japanese ODA to India, 2000-2015[85]
(in 100 million yen)

Fiscal year	ODA Loan	Grant Aid	Technical Cooperation
2000	189.26	18.29	9.03
2001	659.59	14.34	10.15
2002	1,112.39	9.10	9.60
2003	1,250.04	17.44	10.34
2004	1,344.66	29.89	9.67
2005	1,554.58	21.09	8.36
2006	1,848.93	5.96	13.17
2007	2,251.30	3.97	12.31
2008	2,360.47	4.28	11.79
2009	2,182.17	3.81	18.55
2010	2,035.66	11.58	22.12
2011	2898.37	2.78	34.69
2012	3531.06	1.04	33.01
2013	3650.59	16.62	43.62
2014	1186.43	2.17	44.86
2015	3664.78	1.58	50.97
2016	3713.45	1.10	159.50

Source: Knowledge Report 2017, FICCI, India and Ministry of Foreign Affairs website.

tourism, handicrafts and handlooms, organic farming, food processing, disaster management, bamboo and sheries were the areas for which the Ministry of Development of North Eastern Region was keen to get external assistance.[86] Providing fillip to development activities through ODA loans and to India's Act East Policy, an MoC was signed on September 14, 2017 during the visit of PM Shinzo Abe to India to establish the India-Japan Act East Forum. This forum will facilitate Japanese ODA for the development of the North-East. Its first meeting was co-chaired by then Foreign Secretary Dr S. Jaishankar and the Japanese Ambassador to India Mr Kenji Hiramatsu.[87]

JICA is currently assisting in the widening, paving and other improvement on National Highways 51 and 54 through the North East Road Network Connectivity Improvement Project (Phase 1) by providing an ODA loan of up to ¥ 67.17 billion.[88] The

Phase 2 of this project encompasses building four new bypasses on National Highway 54 of Mizoram State and improving the existing National Highway 40 of the state of Meghalaya in North East India, an area bordering Bangladesh, Bhutan and Myanmar.[89] The highway improvement will strengthen connectivity in the North East region and usher in fresh development activity. The security spinoff of such activity is that good connectivity assists faster transportation of troops and supplies. Enhanced connectivity also facilitates movement of troops during times of need and assists side stepping of forces for prompt positioning at the point of application. The overall mobilisation time for troops from their peace locations to forward areas will reduce greatly, thereby assisting in early posturing and enhanced security deployments in these areas.

Speaking at a seminar held on promotion of Intra-Regional Connectivity in North-Eastern Regions (NER) of India on December 5, 2017, Mr Takema Sakamoto, Chief Representative JICA India Office mentioned, 'JICA is keen to support the sustainable development of NER. The development of NER is very important because it will uplift the standard of living of citizens in these regions, will lead to the balanced development of India and will act as a gateway between India and neighbouring countries'.[90]

The other significant area where Japanese ODA assistance has been sought is a project in the Andaman and Nicobar Islands. The objective of the project is to augment power generation capacity and to stabilise power supply by replacing and renovating diesel generators and relevant facilities.[91] Interestingly, this will be the first time that India will be accepting foreign infrastructure assistance on the strategically important islands. Provided the momentum of security cooperation is maintained, India and Japan have a unique opportunity to upgrade the islands into a security hub for the monitoring and surveillance of the critical areas around. The Japanese willingness to assist India in such infrastructure development as well as the Indian initiative to make these critical security sensitive areas available to the Japanese indicate the high degree of trust and convergence in the strategic and security affairs of both the countries.

Harness Complementary Developments in Space Technology for regional and bilateral Advantage (SO Strategy S6O8): The September 2017 visit of Japanese Prime Minister Shinzo Abe to Gujarat for the annual bilateral summit, gave a boost to bilateral space cooperation. Team Indus, a Bengaluru-based private aerospace company and Japanese startup Hakuto (meaning Rabbit in Japanese) had joined hands with ISRO to launch India's first private spacecraft to moon in March 2018.[92] Team Indus and Hakuto were two of the five teams selected by Google Lunar XPRIZE to compete for launching a rover on the moon, make it move 500 metres and send back hi-definition pictures of the lunar surface. The plan was to utilise the PSLV-XL to carry the Indian rover ECA and the Japanese rover Sorato to an orbit 800 km above the surface of the earth. Though the effort seems to have run into problems, this could lay the frame work for future collaboration of sorts for efforts at space exploration.[93] Had the effort been successful, it would have been the first time private entities from two countries would have undertaken a robotic space exploration mission.

The Japan Aerospace Exploration Agency (JAXA) was born through the merger of three institutions, namely the Institute of Space and Astronautical Science (ISAS), the National Aerospace Laboratory of Japan (NAL) and the National Space Development Agency of Japan (NASDA).[94] It was designated as a core performance agency to support the Japanese government's overall aerospace development and utilisation.[95] Historically, Japanese space activities commenced in the 1950s with the development of a "pencil" solid-propellant fuel rocket by Professor Hideo Itokawa which was only 23 cm in length.[96] Japan's first satellite Osumi on the L-4S rocket was launched successfully by the ISAS IN 1970. Post the Cold War, Japan's outlook towards security and space underwent a change and the importance of use of space assets in order to ensure national security was appreciated. Responding to the launch of North Korea's Taepodong missile in 1998 in particular, the Japanese government decided to introduce an Information Gathering Satellite (IGS) in order to enhance Japan's surveillance capabilities with the first two IGS satellites being launched in 2003.[97] Japan currently has accomplished many of world-class space missions, especially in the fields of lunar and asteroid exploration.[98] Japan also has good experience in X-ray astronomy, has been an important partner in International Space Station (ISS) programme and recently agreed with the United States in extending its operation through 2024.[99]

Likewise, India's achievement in its space programme has also been extraordinary. India has launched more than 140 missions, which include 82 satellites, has had successful space exploration missions (MOM & ASTROSAT), satellite navigation (IRNSS & GAGAN), satellite communication (13 satellites and 240 transponders), earth observation (11 Low Earth Orbit and three Geostationary satellites) in orbit with an independent access to space through a reliable and operational PSLV launch vehicle, and a proven operational indigenous geostationary launch vehicle, GSLV, incorporating an indigenously developed cryogenic upper stage.[100] India today has end to end capabilities in space; the country builds and launches its own heavy duty rockets; designs and fabricates some of the most sophisticated satellites.[101]

In space policy aspects, both countries share common orientations. Space applications in both countries include remote sensing, navigation, surveillance, communications, meteorology, early warning and management of disaster, as well as a host of other applications. Space activities which have developed in civilian aspects have now commenced into security realms keeping national security in mind.

In the joint statement on India and Japan Vision 2025: Special Strategic and Global Partnership Working Together for Peace and Prosperity of the Indo-Pacific Region and the World, issued on December 12, 2015, Prime Minister Narendra Modi and Prime Minister Shinzo Abe shared the view that imperatives of a stronger bilateral strategic partnership require deep and broad-based cooperation and concrete actions in many fields including space.[102]

Japan's 2015 Basic Plan for Space places greater emphasis on the security aspect of space activities than ever before.[103] Similarly, after the anti-satellite test of China in January 2007, India too has come to terms with the likely militarisation of space and has included security aspects in space activities. ISRO has launched several space assets potentially contributing to national security in India, which include RISAT-2, GSAT-7, CARTOSAT-series, and IRNSS.[104] In the security domain, the major areas of cooperation could be maritime security, earth observation applications, satellite communications, synthetic aperture radars, sensor systems in hyper-spectral domain, disaster management, and manned space exploration. In addition to the above, joint space missions hold immense potential. The joint missions would include joint manufacture of satellites, collaborative launches, joint space missions and complementing space capabilities of each other for respective goods.[105] A possible area of cooperation can be identified between the recently established NavIC GPS system of India and the Quasi-Zenith Satellite System (QZSS) of Japan, to have an expanded coverage in the Indo-Pacific.[106] Collaboration in satellite positioning will also bring the two nation's industries and space agencies together, apart from bringing a commonality of applications in maritime and terrestrial navigation and even among security applications.[107]

Japan has a lot of experience in space missions through participation in the International Space Station Mission, planetary exploration missions such as Kagurya (lunar exploration) and Hayabusa (asteroid sample return mission). Collaboration with India will foster regional cooperation. In fact, JAXA and ISRO have signed a MoU to promote collaboration in space field in November 2016 and an Implementation Arrangement (IA) concerning joint study of Lunar Polar Exploration.[108] The joint study will include possible mission objectives and operation concepts, and both agencies will work out the plan targeting the end of JFY 2018.[109]

Utilise Space Technology to Enhance Maritime Domain Awareness (SO Strategy Sj1O2): The Indo-Pacific expanse is vast and its critical sea lines of communication need constant monitoring due to the prevalence of traditional and non-traditional maritime threats.

India and Japan can share resources and information pertaining to the maritime domain. This will assist in painting a holistic maritime picture of threats posed by various nations at sea as well as combat non-traditional threats of piracy, terrorism, trafficking, armed robbery, smuggling, WMD proliferation, illegal fishing, pollution and other unlawful acts at sea. MDA can be further enhanced through collaborative use of satellites, promoted through information sharing by the use of a number of earth observation satellites (both optical and radar) like the ALOS-2 (Advanced Land Observing Satellite-2; SAR mission)/Daichi-2[110] of Japan and the RESOURCESAT2A of India.[111] Additionally, as Japan cooperates with the US on MDA, this collaboration gets strengthened as a trilateral effort with a scope of establishing a regional grid over the Indo-Pacific once other space faring nations join in.

It has been reported that JAXA of Japan, CNES of France and DLR of Germany are working together on Hayabusa 2/MASCOT on a mission to asteroid Ryugu.[112] Such international missions hold promise of cooperation for India also. Similarly, India and France are working together on a constellation of satellites for maritime awareness and are planning to launch eight to ten maritime surveillance satellites focusing on the IOR.[113] A contribution from Japan can not only enhance the timeframe by which such a system can be in place but also increase the swath of the surveillance grid by encompassing the entire Indo-Pacific region.

Space and HADR: As already brought out while analysing HADR issues, space based assets are of great assistance in disaster management. Both nations being prone to disasters like earthquakes, volcanoes, floods, forest fires, etc., can make collaborative use of space based systems to aid rescue work and mitigate risks. Remote sensing, GIS applications and climate change related applications are other areas which have huge potential for cooperation. With the rapid rise in use of outer space by various nations, the presence of space debris through a space situational awareness picture can also be shared between India and Japan, thereby complementing the individual efforts of both countries.

Lastly, there is a requirement to regulate space through policies and legal frameworks. This would require a coordinated effort of industry, experts and researchers of both sides. Cooperation in this aspect at the bilateral and multilateral levels will facilitate promotion of a regionally and globally acceptable policy, ensure standardisation in use of space, avoid 'unfair' competition or restriction for space technology, institute voluntary codes of conduct and diminish the threats of space militarisation.[114] Cooperation in space between Japan and India will not only benefit the two countries but also reach out to many other nations in the region for the collective good. Employment of satellites by India for use by SAARC nations is a living example in this regard.[115]

Conclusion

Important aspects affecting security cooperation have been discussed in this chapter. Maritime aspects and UN peacekeeping activities have been covered separately. What remains to be seen is the degree of openness and trust that the two nations can build so that there is optimum sharing of technology and information. This cooperation cannot reach its optimum potential by giving mere 'vision statements' and rhetoric. It remains to be seen as to how much the public display of closeness between leaders of both countries actually translate to implementation on ground. Cooperation in maritime issues, which is the bedrock of the security cooperation between India and Japan has been discussed in the next chapter.

Notes

1. "Confluence of the Two Seas" Speech by H.E. Mr. Shinzo Abe, Prime Minister of Japan at the Parliament of the Republic of India dated, August 22, 2007 at https://www.mofa.go.jp/region/asia-paci/pmv0708/speech-2.html, accessed on September 26, 2018.
2. Dr K.V. Kesavan, India and Japan Changing Dimensions of Partnership in the post-Cold War Period, ORF Occasional Paper #4, May 2010 at https://www.orfonline.org/wp-content/uploads/2010/11/OccasionalPaper_14.pdf, accessed on July 19, 2010.
3. Text of the Security Declaration has been appended as Appendix A.

4. Ministry of Foreign Affairs Japan, 'Joint Declaration on Security Cooperation between Japan and India' at http://www.mofa.go.jp/region/asia-paci/india/pmv0810/joint_d.html, accessed on March 25, 2018.
5. 'Joint Declaration on Security Cooperation between Japan and India' at Ministry of Foreign Affairs, Japan at http://www.mofa.go.jp/region/asia-paci/india/pmv0810/joint_d.html.
6. Shamshad A. Khan, *Changing Dynamics of India-Japan Relations: Buddhism to Special Strategic Partnership,* Pentagon Press, New Delhi, p. 79.
7. For a detailed SWOT analysis, please refer Appendix B of this book.
8. Ministry of Defense, Japan, *Defense Technology Strategy—Towards Delivering Superior Defense Equipment and to Secure Technological Superiority*, August 2016 at http://www.mod.go.jp/atla/en/policy/pdf/defense_technology_strategy.pdf, accessed on May 1, 2018.
9. Ministry of Foreign Affairs of Japan, Press Release, 'The Three Principles on Transfer of Defense Equipment and Technology', April 1, 2014 at http://www.mofa.go.jp/press/release/press22e_000010.html , accessed on May 1, 2018.
10. Ministry of Foreign Affairs, Japan, *Three Principles on Transfer of Defense Equipment and Technology*, April 1, 2014. A provisional translation of the text of the principles is available as Appendix C of the monograph and at http://www.mofa.go.jp/press/release/press22e_000010.html.
11. For full details of the text of the Agreement, please visit Ministry of Foreign Affairs, Japan at http://www.mofa.go.jp/files/000117470.pdf.
12. Mike Yeo, 'Japan eyes Franco-German maritime patrol aircraft requirement despite export setbacks', Defence News, April 26, 2018 at https://www.defensenews.com/industry/2018/04/25/japan-eyes-franco-german-maritime-patrol-aircraft-requirement-despite-export-setbacks/ accessed on April 26, 2018.
13. Ibid.
14. Rohit Srivastava, 'When will the Navy get the US-2', *SP Naval Forces*, Feb-Mar 2018, 13(1).
15. Kyle Mizokami, 'Why China Fears Japan's Super Stealth Soryu-Class Submarines-The best submarine in the world?', *The National Interest*, May 6, 2017 at https://nationalinterest.org/blog/the-buzz/why-china-fears-japans-super-stealth-soryu-class-submarines-20547, accessed on July 19, 2018.
16. In addition to specific design changes, Indian navy would have had to look at the short shelf life of 20 years of the submarine, its cost and its relatively short operating range of 6,100 nautical miles, which though suitable for Japan would require changes in the Indian context. Japan, takes an iterative approach to submarine construction, with a new submarine class

introduced roughly every 20 years that builds upon previous ones. The current class, Soryu, builds upon the older Oyashio class, and the two classes form the entirety of the present Japanese fleet.

17. Abhijit Singh, 'India-Japan defence ties are soaring but high-profile deals unlikely', *Business Standard*, September 30, 2017 at http://www.business-standard.com/article/economy-policy/india-japan-defence-ties-are-soaring-but-high-profile-deals-unlikely-117092000307_1.html, accessed on March 25, 2018.
18. Kenji Asada, 'Japan's silent submarines extend range with new batteries', *Nikkei Asian Review*, October 5, 2018 at https://asia.nikkei.com/Economy/Trade-War/Japan-s-silent-submarines-extend-range-with-new-batteries, accessed on October 8, 2018.
19. Mike Yeo, note 12.
20. Gabriel Dominguez, 'London and Samuel Cranny-Evans, China confirms conducting trials of new light battle tank in Tibet', *IHS Jane's Defence Weekly*, London June 30, 2017 at http://www.janes.com/article/71940/china-confirms-conducting-trials-of-new-light-battle-tank-in-tibet, accessed on June 16, 2018.
21. Sameer Patil, 'India Balances Asian Security With Japan—Analysis', *Eurasia Review,* December 22, 2015 at http://www.eurasiareview.com/22122015-india-balances-asian-security-with-japan-analysis/, accessed on July 20, 2018.
22. Discussion of the researcher with Col Vivek Chadha (Retd), Research Fellow, IDSA.
23. Pankaj Doval, 'Suzuki to Start Electric Car Battery Plant in Gujarat through JV', *The Times of India,* September 14, 2017 at https://timesofindia.indiatimes.com/auto/miscellaneous/suzuki-to-start-electric-car-battery-plant-in-gujarat-through-jv/articleshow/60513810.cms, accessed on September 26, 2018.
24. Call for Proposals, 'India-Japan Cooperative Science Programme (IJCSP) 2018', Department of Science and Technology, Government of India at http://www.dst.gov.in/sites/default/files/For%20Website%20DST-JSPS%20Call%20for%20proposals.pdf, accessed on September 26, 2018.
25. Department of Science and Technology, Government of India, 2017, Result - Indo-Japanese joint call for proposal under India-Japan Cooperative Science Programme (IJCSP) at http://www.dst.gov.in/prize/result-indo-japanese-joint-call-proposal-under-india-japan-cooperative-science-programme-ijcsp, accessed on June 16, 2018.
26. Press Information Bureau, Government of India, Joint Press Statement on 'The India-Japan Annual Defence Ministerial Dialogue', September 6, 2017 at http://pib.nic.in/newsite/pmreleases.aspx?mincode=33 accessed on June 20, 2018.

27. Ibid.
28. India Working on Unmanned Tanks, Vessels, Robotic Weaponry for Future Wars, *The Deccan Chronicle,* May 20, 2018 at https://www.deccanchronicle.com/nation/current-affairs/200518/india-working-on-unmanned-tanks-vessels-robotic-weaponry-for-future.html, accessed on September 27, 2018.
29. Lt. General P.C. Katoch (Retd), 'Artificial Intelligence in Defence', *SP's Aviation* February 5, 2018 at http://www.sps-aviation.com/experts-speak/?id=265&h=Artificial-Intelligence-in-Defence, accessed on July 20, 2018.
30. Ibid.
31. Ibid.
32. James Vincent, Putin says the nation that leads in AI 'will be the ruler of the world', The Verge, September 4, 2017 at https://www.theverge.com/2017/9/4/16251226/russia-ai-putin-rule-the-world, accessed on June 17, 2018.
33. India, China lead Artificial Intelligence investment, adoption in Asia, says report, IANS, February 21, 2018 at http://www.financialexpress.com/industry/technology/india-china-lead-artificial-intelligence-investment-adoption-in-asia-says-report/1073765/, accessed on September 27, 2018.
34. Ibid.
35. India can become second largest market for robotic surgery: Vattikuti Foundation, *Economic Times*, Healthworld, November 19, 2017 at https://health.economictimes.indiatimes.com/news/medical-devices/india-can-become-second-largest-market-for-robotic-surgery-vattikuti-foundation/61713706, accessed on June 17, 2018.
36. R. Shashank Reddy, Transforming Indo-Japan Relations through Robots, Carnegie India, December 7, 2017 at https://carnegieindia.org/2017/12/07/transforming-indo-japan-relations-through-robots-pub-74968, accessed on June 15, 2018.
37. Ibid.
38. Japan's vision to be robotics super-power: India's role and benefit *The Financial Express,* March 23, 2015 at https://www.financialexpress.com/industry/japans-vision-to-be-robotics-super-power-indias-role-and-benefit/56470/, accessed on September 27, 2018.
39. Ibid.
40. Ibid.
41. The Associated Chambers of Commerce & Industry of India, Government must drive cross-border collaboration with countries leading in AI research, suggests ASSOCHAM-PwC Study, June 17, 2018 at http://www.assocham.org/newsdetail.php?id=6863, accessed on October 12, 2018.
42. Ibid.

43. Inputs based on an interaction with Defence Attaché of Japan to India.
44. Japanese Self-Defense Forces launch 1st amphibious fighting unit, Kyodo News, April 7, 2018 at https://english.kyodonews.net/news/2018/04/2f3bb80eb01b-japan-holds-kick-off-ceremony-for-1st-full-fledged-amphibious-force.html, accessed on July 9, 2018.
45. Press Information Bureau, Government of India, Ministry of Defence Indian Navy Concludes Theatre Level Exercise Tropex 2017, February 26, 2017 at http://pib.nic.in/newsite/PrintRelease.aspx?relid=158689, accessed on June 18, 2018.
46. Ibid.
47. Monika Chansoria, 'Japan-India Joint Counter-Terrorism Mechanism the Need of the Hour', Japan Forward, October 5, 2017 at https://japan-forward.com/japan-india-joint-counter-terrorism-mechanism-the-need-of-the-hour/, accessed on June 15, 2018.
48. Reiji Yoshida, Ayako Mie and Jesse Johnson, 'Seven Japanese among hostages killed during Dhaka siege: Suga', *The Japan Times*, July 2, 2016 at https://www.japantimes.co.jp/news/2016/07/02/ national/seven-japanese-among-hostages-killed-during-dhaka-siege-suga/#.W1HnftIzbIU, accessed on July 20, 2018.
49. Ministry of External Affairs, 'Toward a Free, Open and Prosperous Indo-Pacific', India-Japan Joint Statement during visit of Prime Minister of Japan to India, September 14, 2017.
50. Ministry of Foreign Affairs, Japan, 'Action Plan to advance Security Cooperation based on the Joint Declaration on Security Cooperation between Japan and India', December 29, 2009 at https://www.mofa.go.jp/region/asia-paci/india/pmv0912/action.html, accessed on June 7, 2018.
51. Xinhua, Asia and Pacific Edition, 'Japan launches anti-terrorism intelligence unit', December 8, 2015 at http://www.xinhuanet.com/english/2015-12/08/c_134897032.htm.
52. Author's Interview with Defence Attaché of Japan in India.
53. Monika Chansoria, 'Japan-India Joint Counter-Terrorism Mechanism the Need of the Hour', Japan Forward, October 5, 2017 at https://japan-forward.com/japan-india-joint-counter-terrorism-mechanism-the-need-of-the-hour/, accessed on June 15, 2018.
54. Ibid.
55. Ibid.
56. Ibid.
57. Ibid.
58. Refer Appendix D for details of the Action Plan.
59. Ministry of Foreign Affairs, Japan, Action Plan to advance Security Cooperation based on the Joint Declaration on Security Cooperation

between Japan and India, December 29, 2009 at https://www.mofa.go.jp/region/asia-paci/india/pmv0912/action.html, accessed on June 7, 2018.

60. Compiled from the Defence of Japan 2016.
61. MEA Press Release August 18, 2017, Second India—Japan Cyber Dialogue, New Delhi at http://mea.gov.in/press-releases.htm?dtl/28869/Joint_Press_ReleaseSecond_JapanIndia_Cyber_Dialogue, accessed on February 21, 2018.
62. Ibid.
63. Highlighting Japan-India CyberSecurity Cooperation in the "Confluence of the Two Seas", Mihoko Matsubara, September 25, 2017 at https://researchcenter.paloaltonetworks.com/2017/09/cso-highlighting-japan-india-cybersecurity-cooperation-confluence-two-seas/.
64. Press Information Bureau, Government of India, Ministry of Communications, December 10, 2014, 19:28 IST India and Japan Release Joint Statement on Cooperation for Information and Communication Technologies (ICT) at http://pib.nic.in/newsite/PrintRelease.aspx?relid=113046.
65. Panos Mourdoukoutas, 'Japan Tries To Recruit IT Engineers From India, But It Won't Work', *Forbes*, June 30, 2017 at https://www.forbes.com/sites/panosmourdoukoutas/2017/06/30/japan-tries-to-recruit-it-engineers-from-india-but-it-wont-work/#710561bc5247, accessed on October 12, 2018.
66. Panos Mordoukoutas, 'Tokyo Badly Needs Young Talented People—Where Will They Come From?', *Forbes,* June 7, 2014 at https://www.forbes.com/sites/panosmourdoukoutas/2014/06/07/tokyo-badly-needs-young-talented-people-where-will-they-come-from/#6380d93a5f50, accessed June 16, 2018. .
67. Ibid.
68. Ibid.
69. 'Foreign IT workers seen as solution to industry shortage', *The Japan Times*, June 30, 2017 at https://www.japantimes.co.jp/news/2017/06/30/national/foreign-workers-seen-solution-industry-shortage/#.WyS9ZNR97Gh, accessed on June 16, 2018.
70. Ibid.
71. Ibid.
72. Prof Motohiro Tsuchiya, while speaking on Japan's Cyber Security Strategy in IDSA in February 2017.
73. Jun Hongo, 'Getting a handle on earthquakes', *The Japan Times,* April 24, 2004 at https://www.japantimes.co.jp/news/2007/04/24/reference/getting-a-handle-on-earthquakes/#.W6zm884zbIU, accessed on September 27, 2018.
74. Ibid.

75. Ministry of Foreign Affairs, Japan, 'Action Plan to advance Security Cooperation based on the Joint Declaration on Security Cooperation between Japan and India', December 29, 2009 at https://www.mofa.go.jp/region/asia-paci/india/pmv0912/action.html, accessed on June 7, 2018.
76. National Institute of Disaster management, Ministry of Home Affairs at http://nidm.gov.in/recent4.asp, accessed on September 27, 2018.
77. Ibid.
78. 'A Brief Note on Joint Indo Japanese Training cum Field Workshop on Landslides and Disaster Management' held during February 13–17, 2012 at https://reliefweb.int/sites/reliefweb.int/files/resources/PDF_164.pdf.
79. Multilateral HADR Air Force exercise from March 12-17, *The Economic Times*, March 10, 2018 at https://economictimes.indiatimes.com/news/defence/multilateral-hadr-air-force-exercise-from-march-12-17/articleshow/63244964.cms, accessed on June 20, 2018.
80. Press Information Bureau, Government of India, Joint Press Statement on The India-Japan Annual Defence Ministerial Dialogue, September 6, 2017 at http://pib.nic.in/newsite/pmreleases.aspx?mincode=33, accessed on June 20, 2018.
81. Specifics of Space Cooperation Potential Between Japan and India Yuichiro Nagaia, Mukund Kadursrinivas Raob, Hideaki Shiroyamac, K.R. Sridhara Murthid, Motoko Uchitomie at the 67th International Astronautical Congress (IAC), Guadalajara, Mexico, September 26–30, 2016 at http://www.nias.res.in/sites/default/files/2016-MukundRao-67th-Internat-Astronautical-Congress-1.pdf, accessed on February 2, 2018.
82. Ibid.
83. Rajeev Issar, 'Cooperation in Disaster and Climate Risk Management in AAGC', Research and Information System for Developing Countries (RIS) Discussion Paper #222 January 2018 at file:///C:/Users/IDSA/Downloads/DP%20222%20Rajeev%20Issar.pdf, accessed on June 21, 2018.
84. Lalima Varma, 'Japan's Official Development Assistance to India-A Critical Appraisal', *SAGE Journal,* January 19, 2010 at https://doi.org/10.1177/097492840906500302, accessed on August 6, 2018.
85. Ministry of Foreign Affairs Japan, 'Overview of Japan's ODA to India' at http://www. mofa.go.jp/policy/oda/region/sw_asia/india_o.pdf, accessed on July 21, 2018.
86. Newsletter from JICA India Office, Issue No. 38, July-September 2017 at https://www.jica.go.jp /india/english/office/others/c8h0vm000001l2ap-att/issue38.pdf.
87. 'Launch of India-Japan Act East Forum', December 5, 2017 at http://www.mea.gov.in/press-releases.htm?dtl/29154/Launch_of_IndiaJapan_Act_East_Forum.

88. Press Release, JICA Continues to Invest in Improving Transitability by Extending ODA Loan of Approximately INR 2,500 crore for the North East Road Connectivity Project at https://www.jica.go.jp/india/english/office/topics/press180402_05.html, accessed on September 27, 2018.
89. Ibid.
90. Newsletter from JICA INDIA OFFICE, October-December 2017, Issue no. 39, July-September 2017 at https://www.jica.go.jp/india/english/office/others/c8h0vm000001l2ap-att/issue39.pdf, accessed on April 7, 2018.
91. 'Information Disclosure under New Guidelines', Japan International Cooperation Agency at https://www.jica.go.jp/english/our_work/social_environmental/id/asia/south/india/c8h0vm00009t9ejx.htmld, accessed on October 12, 2018.
92. Dipanjan Roy Chaudhury, 'Japanese Prime Minister Shinzo Abe visit to boost Indo-Japan space cooperation', *The Economic Times,* September 12, 2017 at https//economictimes.indiatimes.com/articleshow/60471730.cms?utm_source=contentofinterest&utm_medium=text&utm_campaign=cppst, accessed on July 21, 2018.
93. Team Indus' moon mission dream dashed, News Today, January 25, 2018 at https://www.newstodaynet.com/index.php/2018/01/25/teamindus-moon-mission-dream-dashed/
94. Official website of Japan Aerospace Exploration Agency at http://global.jaxa.jp /about/jaxa/index.html, accessed on February 2, 2018.
95. Ibid.
96. Obituary: Hideo Itokawa, James Kirkup, March 19, 1999 at https://www.independent.co.uk/arts-entertainment/obituary-hideo-itokawa-1081504.html.
97. See, note 81.
98. Ibid.
99. Ibid.
100. Ministry of Foreign Affairs, note 5.
101. Pallava Bagla, 'Reaching for the skies—India's space technology at its best', Ministry of External Affairs, January 26, 2014 at http://mea.gov.in/articles-in-indian-media.htm?dtl/22778/Reaching+for+the+skies++Indias+space+technology+at+its+best
102. Ministry of External Affairs, Joint Statement on India and Japan Vision 2025: Special Strategic and Global Partnership Working Together for Peace and Prosperity of the Indo-Pacific Region and the World (December 12, 2015) at http://www.mea.gov.in/bilateral-documents.htm?dtl/26176/Joint_Statement_on_India_and_Japan_Vision_2025_Special_Strategic_and_Global_Partnership_Working_Together_for_Peace_and_Prosperity_of_the_IndoPacific_Region, accessed on May 4, 2019.
103. See, note 81.

104. Ibid.

105. Ibid.

106. Office of National Space Policy, Cabinet Office, Japan, New Basic Plan on Space Policy, February 26, 2015, envisages the establishment and operationalisation of a seven satellite constellation of QZSS(Quasi-Zenith Satellite System) which will be a successor to the MICHIBIKI (the first QZSS) around 2023.

107. See, note 81.

108. Website of Japan Aerospace Exploration Agency (JAXA Signs Implementation Arrangement (IA) with ISRO concerning joint study of Joint Lunar Polar Exploration, December 6, 2017 (JST) at http://global.jaxa.jp/press/2017/12/20171206_isro.html, accessed on May 4, 2018.

109. Ibid.

110. ALOS-2, eoPortal Directory at https://directory.eoportal.org/web/eoportal/satellite-missions/a/alos-2

111. Department of Space, ISRO, RESOURCESAT2A at https://www.isro.gov.in/Spacecraft/resourcesat-2a

112. Japan space probe launches new robot onto asteroid, *The Economic Times,* October 3, 2018 at https://economictimes.indiatimes.com/news/science/japan-space-probe-launches-new-robot-onto-asteroid/articleshow/66050846.cms, accessed on October 12, 2018.

113. India, France Plan Maritime Surveillance Satellites: French Agency Chief, NDTV at https://www.ndtv.com/india-news/india-france-plan-maritime-surveillance-satellites-french-agency-chief-1917307, accessed on October 12, 2018.

114. See, note 81.

115. D.S. Madhumathi, 'India launches satellite to help South Asian nations', *The Hindu,* May 5, 2017 at http://www.thehindu.com/sci-tech/science/india-launches-south-asia-satellite/article 18391277.ece, accessed on May 10, 2018.

5

Maritime Security Cooperation

Abstract

Maritime Security Cooperation is one of the aspects, which has drawn India and Japan together especially after the MV Alondro Rainbow incident in 1999. Cooperation between the coast guards and the navy has flourished over the years. Post 2015, the permanent participation of Japan in the Malabar Exercises has brought the navies of all three participating countries, India, Japan and the US, closer to each other in terms of interoperability and better understanding of one another's capabilities. Security of SLsOC is important as major trade of both countries pass through these important lines of communication and through the major choke points. The participation of both India and Japan in global and regional forums in combating traditional and non-traditional threats is important and needs to be integrated further, especially in South East Asia. Internal security of the Andaman and Nicobar Islands is an aspect that can be enhanced through Japanese assistance by defence equipment and technology cooperation. In addition, capacity development of littorals in the Indian Ocean Region and the West Pacific as well as ship building are potential areas of cooperation.

Introduction

The Indian Ocean has been the centre of seafaring activity from very old times. Emphasizing that the ancient Hindu kingdoms possessed requisite skills for constructing robust and durable ocean-going ships as well as could accurately navigate in open seas with the help of magnetic compass, Sardar KM Panikkar states, "Millenniums before Columbus sailed the Atlantic and Magellan crossed the Pacific, the Indian Ocean had become a thoroughfare of commercial and cultural traffic".[1] In the present times, this ocean has become the sea bridge between the hydrocarbon and resource rich West Asia and Africa, and the energy hungry economies lying to its East. The Indian Ocean converges into the narrow Malacca Strait before opening up towards the East into the Pacific Ocean. The SLsOC from the Indian Ocean cross over to the Malacca Strait and move across the South China Sea to South Korea, Japan and other vibrant economies. Considering the dependence of the countries in the Indo-Pacific on these important SLsOC for resources and energy as imports and manufactured goods as exports, maritime security has gained prominence for stakeholders in this region.

Maritime security can be defined as comprising of a collection of all the issues that pertain to the seas, and have a bearing on national security. These include, inter-alia, seaborne trade and infrastructure for its pursuit, management of sea resources, environmental issues, and employment of naval forces.[2] In this chapter, the maritime security cooperation between India and Japan is being viewed from a military standpoint and related economic, commercial and infrastructural aspects have not been dwelt upon, in detail.

Maritime security of the ships plying in the waters of the Indian Ocean and the West Pacific was a shared responsibility, which did not evoke much concern till the late nineties. The vulnerabilities of Japanese trade assets in the Indo-Pacific region were highlighted when in 1999, the Japanese ship, Alondro Rainbow was hijacked off the coast of Indonesia by pirates. Subsequently, the pirates were captured and the ship released due to a joint effort of the Indian coast guard and the Indian navy. This drew Japanese attention towards the geo-strategic importance of India in the maritime domain.

Map 5.1: Map of the Alondra Incident

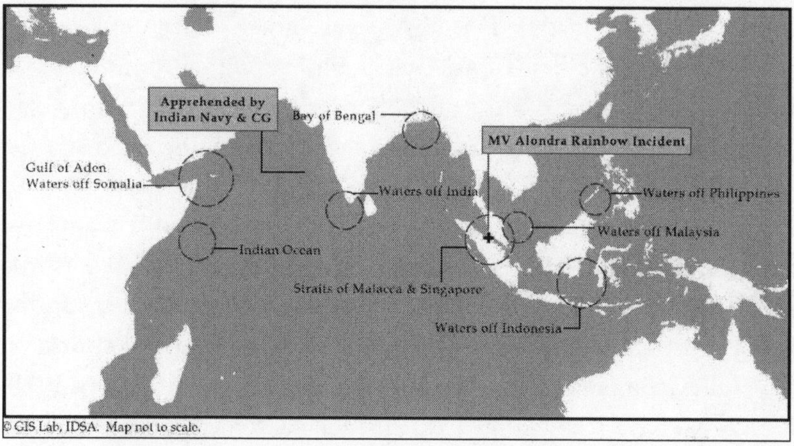

Source: Data compiled by Author from various sources. Prepared by GIS Lab, Manohar Parrikar-IDSA.

Engagement between Coast Guards of India and Japan

As a result of the enhanced engagement between the two countries thereafter, the coast guards of India and Japan signed a MoC for establishing a cooperative relationship in 2006 in order to combat crime at sea and develop regional co-operation.[3] The Action Plan to advance security cooperation based on the Joint Declaration on Security Cooperation between Japan and India of December 2009 (Appendix D refers) lays down that "the two Coast Guards will continue to promote cooperation to ensure maritime safety, maritime security and to protect marine environment through joint exercise and meetings according to the Memorandum on Cooperation between them".[4] Based on the MoC, regular biannual exercises, 'Sahyog Kaijin' was instituted. The 15th edition of the Sahyog Kaijin was held off the coast of Chennai in 2016.Coast guard cooperation has graduated from carrying out Search and Rescue (SAR), sharing of information and exchange of technical assistance to sharing of best management practices, personnel exchange along with a large number of visits and regular staff talks.

Director General Rajendra Singh, PTM, TM, Director General Indian Coast Guard led a high level Indian delegation, which participated in the first Coast Guard Global Summit jointly hosted by the Japan Coast Guard and Nippon Foundation, in Tokyo in September 2017. The International legal framework for SAR, the implementation of effective SAR systems, and the need for and benefit of international and interregional cooperation for effective SAR on a global basis were amongst the issues discussed in the summit. Officials from more than 30 countries participated in the summit to discuss inter-regional cooperation and collaboration beyond existing bilateral and regional framework.[5] In January 2018, a SAR exercise was conducted off the coast of Chennai. As many as nine ships and eight aircrafts of the Indian coast guard along with Japanese coast guard ship 'Tsugaru' with helo (helicopter pad on the deck of a ship) participated in the biennial SAR exercise.[6] The exercise had observers from nine countries, including Australia, Saudi Arabia and South Korea.[7]

Engagement between Navies

Likewise, cooperation between the Indian and Japanese navies has enhanced over the years. A functional integration has been ensured with Japan being included as a permanent participant in the previously bilateral India-US Malabar exercises. Though the Indian navy has been carrying out maritime exercises with other countries such as Singapore (SIMBEX), Sri Lanka (SLINEX), Australia (AUSINDEX), France (VARUNA), South Africa and Brazil (ISAMBAR), the United Kingdom (KONKAN), to name a few, the Malabar exercise has always generated a higher level of interest and attention, more so amongst stake holders in the Indo-Pacific.[8] In 2007, the Malabar exercises were conducted at a multi-lateral level incorporating Japan, Australia and Singapore, in addition to the participation of India and US. China sent demarches to participating countries of Malabar-2007. This indicated the sensitive nature of the exercise and thereafter, it took both India and the US another eight years before it could firmly proclaim the conversion of this bilateral exercise into a trilateral one, with the inclusion of Japan in 2015.

The inclusion of Japan as the third permanent member of the Malabar exercises was noteworthy because it proclaimed India's coming of age to stand up for what it appreciates as its security imperative. The same was heartily welcomed and reciprocated by both Japan and the US. This also brought the navies of India and Japan closer to each other in terms of interoperability and created a better understanding of each other's capabilities.[9] It complemented the special strategic partnership shared by the two countries and underlined the will of the Indian government to create stronger capabilities in conjunction with Japan to deal with maritime challenges in the Indo-Pacific region.[10] Since 2007, the Malabar series of exercises have steadily grown in scope, complexity and participation into a multifaceted exercise with the participation of JMSDF.[11] Malabar 2017 focused on anti-submarine capabilities and the participation of aircraft/helicopter carriers of all three countries made the edition of the Malabar exercise, very significant. As stated by the Indian Navy Eastern Fleet, Flag Officer Commanding, Rear Admiral AK Jain in 2014 "... Malabar Exercises will certainly advance professional interaction and understanding between our sailors and help us to achieve better synergy to tackle common maritime challenges. This will also help us to take naval cooperation between the US, Japan and India to a new level".[12] The growing sophistication of the aspects being undertaken and the naval assets fielded for these exercises is a sign of the growing rapprochement (synergy) between the two countries (refer Table 5.1).

Malabar exercises have enhanced interoperability between participating navies and facilitated dissemination of best practices in the maritime realm.[14] It has also resulted in better training, improved readiness, streamlined SOPs as well as facilitated joint operations and increased the trust quotient among participating sides.[15] The exercises should continue to be conducted to address contemporary security challenges *(SO Strategy: S9O12)*.

Table 5.1: Malabar Exercises 2007–till date

Year, Location and Drills Conducted	Participation	Objectives[13]
Sep 2007 (Off Okinawa Coast) Interception Air combat exercises. Surface and anti-submarine warfare (ASW). Maritime interdiction Visit, board, search and seizure (VBBS) operations. Counter Piracy drills	Ships from five nations (India, US, Japan, Australia and Singapore).	Increase interoperability and develop common understanding and procedures for maritime operations
Oct 2008 (Arabian Sea) Increased inter-operability. Maritime interdiction. Counter-piracy and counter-terrorism operations. VBBS HADR.	US Carrier Strike Group, P3C Orion aircraft. Guided-missile destroyers, replenishment tanker and submarines of both countries.	Focused on functional skills like ASW operations, VBSS techniques, etc.
April 2009 (Off Coast of Japan) VBBS operations. Surface warfare manoeuvres, ASW; Gunnery training, Air defense	Ships from India, Japan and the US	Featured execution of functional skills
April 2010 (Goa) Surface and ASW, Coordinated gunnery exercises Air Defence; VBSS drills.	US Navy's Seventh Fleet. Submarines, surveillance aircraft and special forces detachment of India and US.	Fundamental coordination and communication to more advanced and complex strategic naval operations

Year, Location and Drills Conducted	**Participation**	**Objectives**[13]
April 2011 (Off Okinawa Coast) Professional exchanges and embarks. Communications exercises. Surface action group exercise operations. Formation maneuvering and helicopter cross deck evolutions. Replenishments; HADR; Gunnery exercises; VBBS; ASW.	US, Japan and Indian ships, submarines and surveillance aircraft participated	To enhance military-to-military coordination and help strategize and execute tactical operations in a multinational environment
Apr 2012 (Bay of Bengal) Communications exercises. Surface action group (SAG) operations. Helicopter cross-deck evolutions. Gunnery exercises.	Carrier Strike Group (CSG) 1 of the US Navy along with other maritime assets of US and India.	To advance multinational maritime relationships and mutual security issues
Nov 2013 (Bay of Bengal) Professional exchanges and embarkations; communications exercises; SAG operations; leapfrogs; helicopter cross-deck evolutions; gunnery exercises; VBSS; ASW.	Marine assets of the US and Indian Navies.	To advance multinational maritime relationships and mutual security issue

Year, Location and Drills Conducted	Participation	Objectives[13]
July 2014 (Western Pacific near Japan) CSG operations. Maritime patrol, Anti-piracy and VBSS operations. SAR exercises, helicopter cross-deck landings, Underway replenishment, gunnery ASW	Maritime assets of the US including a carrier group, Japan and India.	To enhance maritime cooperation among the navies of the participating nations
Oct 2015 (Bay of Bengal) Advance multi-national maritime relationships and mutual security. Emphasis on Littoral Operations AD exercise.	Ships from India, US and Japan. Japan became a permanent member of the Exercise.	To enhance naval cooperation among important navies of the Indo-Pacific region which helps in enhancing mutual understanding
Jun 2016 (West Pacific Philippines Sea) CSG Operations Maritime Patrol and reconnaissance operations Surface and ASW VBBS; Focus on Coordination and Joint Capacity to undertake tactical operations; AD exercise; SAR	Ships from India, US and Japan	Increase interoperability amongst the three navies and develop common understanding of procedures.
July 2017 (Bay of Bengal) Shore training - exchanges on CSG operations, maritime patrol and reconnaissance ops; surface- & ASW; VBSS. At-sea training - submarine familiarisation; air-defense and surface-warfare exercises; VBBS drills; ASW.	Aircraft carriers of the US and India and helicopter carrier destroyer of Japan. Other maritime assets including submarines, P-8A Poseidon surveillance and ASW aircraft.	Increase interoperability amongst the three navies as well as develop common understanding and procedures for maritime security operations.

Year, Location and Drills Conducted	Participation	Objectives[13]
June 2018(Guam) Aircraft carrier operations, air defence, ASW; Surface warfare,VBSS, joint manoeuvres and tactical procedures.	India - Three surface warships; a surveillance aircraft and LRMP P8I. US-USS Ronald Reagan with its air wing, four destroyers; Nimitz-class aircraft carrier; an attack submarine and one LRMP Aircraft P8A Japan-Helicopter carrier with integral helicopters; two destroyers; Maritime Patrol Aircraft P1, and a submarine.	To achieve greater inter-operability between the three navies to have a better strategic holding in the Indo-Pacific region. It also seeks to develop working relationships between the countries' maritime forces.

Source: Compiled from various Defence Journals and internet websites.

In addition to the Malabar exercises, both navies are engaged and cooperate on aspects of traditional and non-traditional security. It is imperative to ensure that such exercises are regularly conducted to address issues of interoperability. Maritime operations need to be coördinated for greater effect in order to build upon and advance the working relationship between the US, Japan and India.

Defence Equipment and Technology Cooperation in maritime aspects has been covered in the previous chapter. There will be distinct advantages of having compatible equipment and hardware on both sides of the Malacca Straits.

In September 2017, Indian Defence Minister Arun Jaitely and his Japanese counterpart, Itsunori Onodera, agreed to expand joint anti-submarine warfare training between the Indian navy and JMSDF *(WO Strategy: W3O12)*.[14] Both sides have also agreed to pursue exchanges and training by ASW aviation units such as P-3C.[17]

Security of Sea Lines of Communication (SLOCs)

The major factors that affect SLOC security include the unstable political relationship among regional countries; different interpretations of the freedom of the seas principle; disputes of islands' sovereignty and overlapping maritime jurisdictional claims; the emerging naval build-up of some countries with declared aggressive intent and non-traditional threats such as pollution, piracy, drug-trafficking, etc.[18] Incidentally, SLOCs in the Indo-Pacific are severely affected by several of the factors mentioned above. Security of SLOCs, therefore, become important for countries like Japan which have scarce energy resources and rely for around 95 per cent of their energy needs ex-import and for whom the SLOCs are the lifelines. India is also concerned as 55 per cent of its trade by volume passes through SLOCs in the South China Sea.

Till the starting of the 21st century, US took the lead in ensuring SLOC security in the Indo-Pacific. However, dependence of China on these very SLOCs for its own energy security prompted it to enhance its presence in this region, thereby challenging dominance of the US in the Indo-Pacific and upsetting the status quo. Excessive reliance on the Malacca Strait still poses a potential threat to China's energy security.[19] The phrase "Malacca Dilemma" (*Maliujia kunju*) was first coined by President Hu Jintao, at the closing of a Chinese Communist Party (CCP) economic work conference in November 2003, when he publicly commented on the increasingly complex problem of energy security in the light of China's increasing dependence upon oil imports, especially those from the Middle East.[20] In order to address the Malacca dilemma, the Chinese are seeking land connectivity through different ports to transport oil and cargo, through pipelines and roads. They are exploring different routes like the Lombok and the Sunda Straits; or new openings through the Isthmus of Kra in Thailand. The 'String of Pearls' theory propounded in a report titled *Energy Futures in Asia,* by US defence contractor Booz Allen Hamilton in 2005, suggested, "China is building strategic relationships along the sea lanes from the Middle East to the South China Sea in ways that suggest defensive and offensive positioning at ports of China's choosing to protect its energy interests, as also to serve broad security objectives".[21] According to Mahanian logic, this string of pearls would permit larger-scale military deployments in the future to protect Chinese interests.[22] Port development and related activity in the IOR is currently in progress at Srilanka (Hambantota and Colombo), Myanmar (Kyaukpyu), Pakistan (Gwadar), Djibouti (Obock Harbour), Kenya (Lamu) and Mozambique (Beira and Maputo)[23] (refer Map 5.2).

Map 5.2: Ongoing and Intended Chinese Activity in the IOR

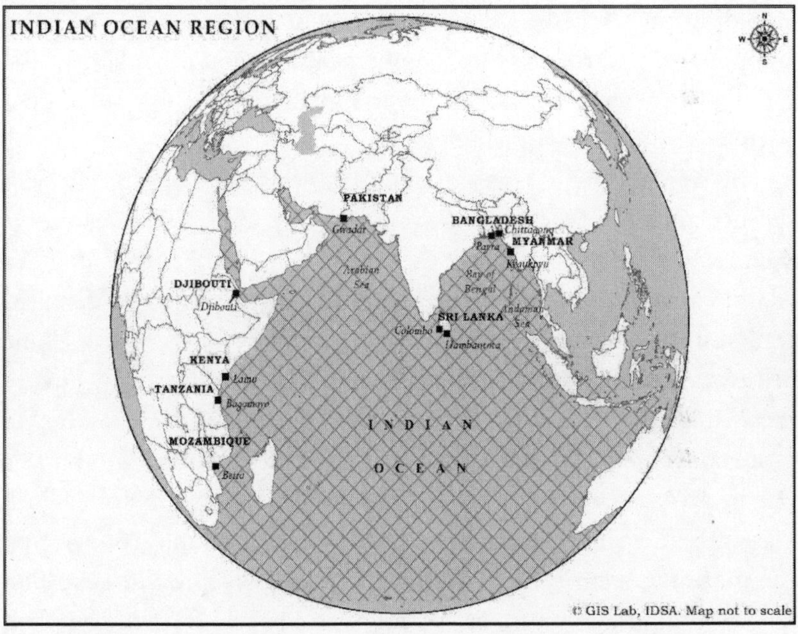

Source: Data compiled from various internet sources. Map prepared by GIS Lab, Manohar Parrikar-IDSA.

Aggressive economic policies, enhanced infrastructure development, establishment of bases and exchanging debt for strategic real estate has resulted in a security environment that is deeply apprehensive and wary of Chinese intentions in the region. The entry of Chinese ships into the Indian Ocean in February 2018, to mark its support for the Maldivian internal upheavals indicates the Chinese intention to play a major role in the region. The reported purchase of the Maldivian atoll by the Chinese for monitoring of the SLOCs has been a major worry for India. The plans for the maritime silk route and the associated lack of transparency are also a cause of consternation. The underwater ocean observation centre in the South China Sea will be serving dual purpose, with civilian and military applications and China's proposal to build such a centre in the Maldives would effectively open a Chinese maritime front against India.[24] The ocean observatory location in Makunudhoo, the westernmost atoll in the north (less than 500 km from India), will allow the Chinese a vantage point of an important Indian Ocean shipping route through which many merchant and other ships pass. It will also be uncomfortably close to Indian waters and test red lines with regard to ties with Maldives.[25]

In West Pacific, China's assertiveness has been on display with the declaration of ADIZ in East China Sea since 2013, extensive land reclamation, positioning of military assets in South China Sea islands and the sending of armed boat patrols near the disputed Senkaku Islands.[26] Japan is especially concerned as the South China Sea is a major conduit for its trade supplies. Consequently, Japan's increasing concern about the protection of its SLOCs has resulted in more convergent stakes with India, in the Indo-Pacific. From Japan's perspective, engaging India in a security cooperation framework was indeed a strategic move as India-Japan maritime cooperation for maritime security in the Malacca Strait will prevent suspicion in the region that continues to retain bitter wartime memories.[27] If Japanese ships start playing an active role in patrolling the SOC the spectre of a 'Greater Asia Co-prosperity Sphere' in another form might lurk in the region, whereas there would be no such reservation about Indian ships and Japan's role will remain limited to extending assistance in the form of equipment, surveillance, capacity-building, etc.[28]

Infrastructure Development: Japan has also focused on infrastructure building in the Indo-Pacific. This is an aspect of convergence between India and Japan, where India with its dominant position and influence can complement Japanese infrastructure and quality standards to provide an alternative to aggressive Chinese activity. The recent agreement to build an LNG hub in Sri Lanka is a sign of such mutual trust and interdependence. Petronet (India) will hold 47.5 per cent stake in the project while Japan's Mitsubishi and Sojitz Corp will take 37.5 per cent stake and the remaining 15 per cent will be held by a Sri Lankan entity.[29] Newspaper reports also point towards a subtle Indian nudge to Bangladesh to ensure that China does not get to build the Sonadia Port for Bangladesh in the Bay of Bengal.[30] In such a dynamic melee, the vision of the AAGC combining the complementary strengths of India and Japan is a refreshing strategic change that points towards a growing and maturing security relationship. A joint India-Japan joint initiative in building Chabahar Port, however, could not make further progress due to political compulsions. Presently, India has gone ahead with the development of the port by itself, for a sum of approximately US$ 150 million.

Certain newspaper reports have hinted at a Japanese funding activity in the Andaman and Nicobar Islands for construction of new Electronic Intelligence (ELINT)/Signals Intelligence (SIGINT) stations and its subsequent link up with the existing US-Japan "Fish Hook" project called Sound Surveillance Systems (SOSUS).[31] The strategic location of the Andaman and Nicobar islands enable monitoring of the naval assets entering and leaving the IOR and collaboration in this regard is a welcome step *(WO Strategy:W1,O10,O12)*.

Maritime security has the potential to be enhanced further with active collaboration of both countries. This cooperation can lay the foundation for a grouping that can be regional or global in nature. However, for any such collaboration to take roots, both countries need to clearly define their red lines in terms of the extent that they are ready to collaborate in facing the challenges of traditional and non-traditional maritime security.

Cooperation in Non-traditional Security

The Action Plan of December 2009 states that exercises, exchanges and training should be conducted on issues such as anti-piracy and transnational crimes and also calls for greater cooperation between the Indian navy and the JMSDF in these areas.[32]

Piracy: Maritime transport is essential to the world's economy as over 90 per cent of the world's trade is carried by sea and it is, by far, the most cost-effective way to move en masse goods and raw materials around the world.[33] Piracy has been a major threat for countries whose supplies move by sea for large distances through various choke points. The Indo-Pacific being one of the busiest shipping lanes has been one of the frequent hunting grounds of the pirates. Increase in pirate attacks in the early 2000s led to formation of various ad hoc security groupings primarily aimed at tackling this menace. Gravely concerned by the threat that acts of piracy and armed robbery pose to the prompt, safe and effective delivery of humanitarian aid to Somalia, the safety of commercial maritime routes, and to international navigation, the UN Security Council adopted at its 5902nd meeting on June 2, 2008, a resolution (Resolution 1816 (2008)) to act under Chapter VII of the Charter of the United Nations.[34] It authorised the states cooperating with the country's transitional government to enter the territorial waters of Somalia and use "all necessary means" to repress acts of piracy and armed robbery at sea, in a manner consistent with relevant provisions of international law.[35]

Currently, there are three main task forces combating piracy in the Gulf of Aden, viz., the Combined Task Force (CTF)-150, CTF-151 and European Union Naval Forces (EU-NAVFOR). The Indian navy has commenced patrolling in the Gulf of Aden since Oct 2008, in order to safeguard Indian ships and Indian citizens who are employed in oceangoing duties. In addition to escorting Indian-flagged ships, ships of other countries are also escorted along the entire length of the (490 nm long and 20 nm wide) Internationally Recommended Transit Corridor (IRTC) that has been promulgated for use by all merchant vessels in the Gulf of Aden.[36] In January 2009, Japan too announced its intention of sending a naval task force to join international efforts to stop piracy off the coast of Somalia.[37] There has been a considerable decrease in piracy incidents post the implementation of anti-piracy measures and coordination between the countries which are part of the anti-piracy groupings. The piracy attacks since 2009 are as shown in Figure 5.1.

Figure 5.1: Pirate Attacks Worldwide

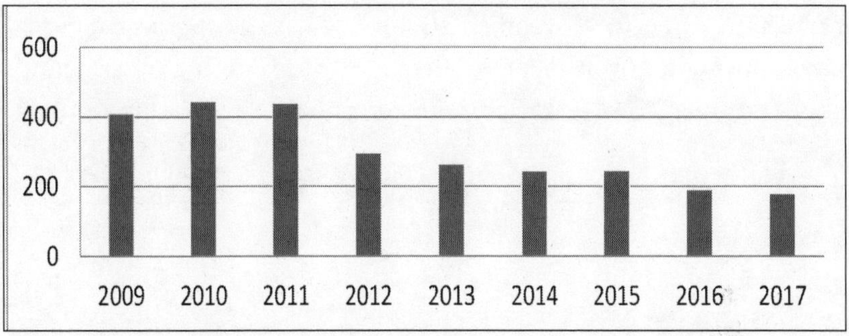

Source: Statista: The Statistics Portal.

The Indian navy has been actively contributing to the anti-piracy effort by continuously deploying one warship in the Gulf of Aden since October 2008. The JMSDF has deployed two destroyers and two P-3C aircrafts off the coast of Djibouti, since 2009, which began patrol missions on June 11, 2009 and have completed more than 1450 mission flights till June 2018.[38] In July 2011, Japan opened a military base in Djibouti, which now assists in combating piracy off the coast of the Horn of Africa.[39] The Japanese patrols, along with those of other countries have been significantly contributing to the overall surveillance of maritime assets by detecting the pirate vessels and giving prompt information to the naval vessels of other countries and nearby merchant ships. The Shared Awareness and Deconfliction (SHADE) initiative commenced in the Gulf of Aden in 2008. This facilitated the coordination and de-confliction of anti-piracy activities between nations and coalitions involved in counter-piracy operations in the Gulf of Aden and the western Indian Ocean. Under the overall framework of SHADE, which comprise of the 33 countries and 14 coalition of forces, India and Japan are cooperating in anti-piracy activities.

Statistics on the piracy incidents region-wise show that the South East Asia region rather than Africa has been the most affected by piracy in the last five years. In order to combat this menace, the Regional Cooperation Agreement on Combating Piracy and Armed Robbery against Ships in Asia (ReCAAP) agreement formally came into force in November 2006. ReCAAP is the first regional government-to-government agreement to promote and enhance cooperation against piracy and armed robbery against ships in Asia.

Figure5.2: Piracy Incidents Region Wise in Last Five Years

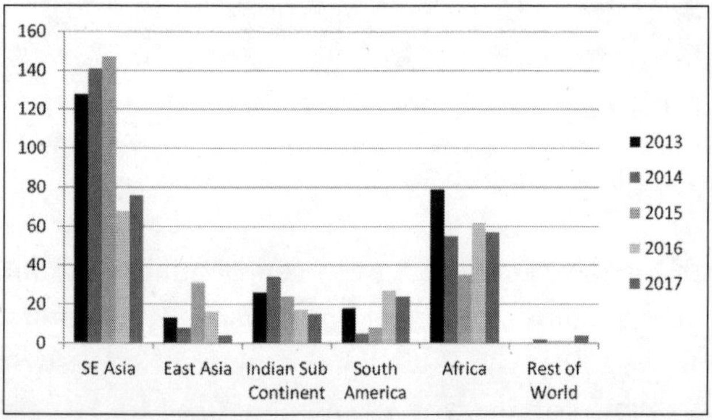

Source: Data compiled from Annual ICC International Maritime Bureau Report 2017.[40]

India and Japan are among the 20 countries that are a part of this agreement. Capacity building, information sharing and instituting cooperative arrangements are the main focus areas of the ReCAAP. Information Sharing Centre which acts as the hub of anti-piracy activity for this grouping. Cooperation between India and Japan in such international groupings, thus, must be maintained and enhanced. This will build up trust, make each side familiar with the functioning of the navies and coast guards and usher in a strong sense of reliability and confidence.

Japan's new partnerships have been consistently backed-up by Abe's rhetoric of preserving the "international order" and ensuring "rule of law" at sea. Through a concerted strategy of maritime diplomacy, Japan is seeking to upgrade the existing regional condition of limited inter-state co-operation over localised issues—such as piracy—to more substantive region-wide maritime co-operation based on shared interests, common threats and larger-scale problems: such as defending East Asia's vital sea lanes; and countering China's growing influence in the maritime arena.[41]

In a bilateral format, the coast guard and navies of India and Japan carry out regular exercises. The coast guards of both nations have decided to further intensify engagement with each other in order to improve their search and rescue skills and carry out joint patrolling, after the Search and Rescue Exercise was held in Jan 2018. As stated by Japan Coast Guard Commandant, Admiral Satoshi Nakajima—"The SAREX-18 was well coordinated and was meaningful ... and indicates how important collaboration between Japan and India is to safeguard maritime boundaries. We will continue to extend our cooperation for peace and prosperity in the Pacific region".[42]

Maritime Terrorism: Japan became the latest victim of the Islamic State's (IS) violence when IS beheaded two of its nationals—a security consultant and a journalist early 2015. Though Japan participated in the US led Iraq war effort through a humanitarian contingent, this violence is a new challenge for Japan.[43] India has been dealing with terrorism for a long time and has acquired greater experience in handling counter terrorism aspects. After the November 2015 terror attack in Paris, Japan declared that a new Japanese Foreign Ministry unit will start collecting information on militant groups such as IS in the countries they are based.[44] With the Mumbai attacks in India in November 2008, maritime terrorism has also come into focus of the security agencies. Japan can thus partner with India in its fight against terrorism through training and related support of this intelligence unit as well as the security forces. The next stage of cooperation can then transcend onto intelligence-sharing on terror-financing.

Internal Security of the Andaman and Nicobar Islands

Andaman and Nicobar islands are strategically located in the IOR.

Their geographic location and spread provides domination of the eastern approaches to the Indian Ocean as it also is a springboard for reaching out to the littorals in the region. However, the security of the islands is a major challenge due to the vast expanse, lack of capability and manpower, inadequate resources and the difficult terrain there. Therefore, poaching of marine and forest resources, illegal migration, use of uninhabited islands for narcotics smuggling and natural disasters are a major challenge.[45] A similar challenge is also faced by Japan, which has more than 6452 islands, most of them uninhabited. There is an opportunity for convergence in this aspect for both the countries. Japan can assist in improving infrastructure in the islands. The Indian coast guards and the marine police lack adequate resources in terms of boats, speed ships, etc. The procurement of US-2 amphibious airplanes will also assist in maintaining security as well as enhancing contact between different islands.

Offensive and defensive operations entail operational infrastructure, which needs to be developed, whereas the existing Indian military facilities are good enough only for routine coastal patrolling, intelligence gathering, and search and rescue.[46] There is a need to position the latest monitoring equipment. In addition, India needs to convert part of the Island chain into a major base that could allow India to create Anti-Access and Area-Denial maritime exclusion zone in the event of a conflict.[47]

Capability Development of Littorals

In response to emerging geopolitical undercurrents, Japan is gradually asserting itself out of the US shadows as an alliance partner and posing as a regional maritime power. It has steadfastly sought to increase its defence outlay and expand its navy as well as coast guard capabilities. Prime Minister Abe has focused on cultivating defence relationships as well as developing closer naval ties with Southeast Asian littorals, seeking to enhance naval capabilities through assistance and agreements. India too has been assuming the role of a regional leader and has been extending assistance to littorals in the IOR. Details of assistance for capability building both by Japan and India in order to enhance regional security and rules based order are given in Chapter 7, where regional security has been discussed in detail. Japan's assistance to the littorals in terms of military assistance are tabulated in Table 5.2.

Table-5.2: Military Assistance by Japan to Littorals

Country	**Assistance By Japan**
Philippines	Two 90-metre patrol ships 10 smaller vessels Five TC-90 reconnaissance planes 600 million yen grant for purchase of high-speed boats and counter-terrorism equipment for the Philippine Coast Guard
Indonesia	Established Japan-Indonesia Maritime Forum to facilitate cooperation. Tokyo will assist with the construction of ports and the development of remote islands, improving Indonesia's capability to defend its maritime sovereignty. Maritime Cooperation labelled 'highest priority'
Vietnam	Agreement for 38 billion yen in Japanese aid to upgrade Vietnamese Coast Guard vessels and improve their patrol capability. Six new patrol vessels in Jan 2017

Source: Defence of Japan 2018.

Ship Building

Ship building Industry is one of the key bases on which the naval power of a nation is based. In addition, the ship building industry also gives a number of secondary and tertiary benefits to the national economy. Indian shipyards contribute just one per cent of the global market share, which is intended to be built up to 5 per cent by 2020 as per the Maritime Agenda 2010–2020.[48] Japan and South Korea have taken great strides in ship building and are amongst the leading ship builders globally. In the defence sector, Japan's leading shipbuilders Mitsubishi Heavy Industries and Kawasaki Heavy

Industries have received request for information (RFI) for the Indian Project 75(I), where the foreign company with its local partner will build six submarines for the Indian navy.[49] Reportedly, the Japanese have not exercised the option of participating in the procurement process. Another RFI for 150 heavyweight torpedoes for submarines at a cost of US$ 300 million have also been floated and Japanese companies are being urged to participate in the global tender.[50]

For India, any endeavour to boost the shipbuilding industry will require drawing up of a national strategy which designates shipbuilding as a priority sector and provides active support in terms of levies, financial subsidies, availability of raw materials, and training of manpower.[51] India has everything it takes to be a warship-building superpower: the springboard of design expertise; cheap and skilled labour; and mounting experience in building successful warships. The only aspect that it lacks is capacity.[52]

Assistance in ship building from countries like Japan and South Korea needs to be taken *(WO Strategy W2,O2,O10)*. With Japan coming in a big way in infrastructure building in India, they should be invited to participate in upgrading ports, constructing new ports, enhancing connecting infrastructure to India's coastal areas, and facilitating hassle-free multi-modal transport. By addressing strategic concerns beyond the realm of security cooperation, the leaders of both nations have found a unique and constructive way to collaborate in the Indian Ocean and beyond.[53]

Conclusion

Maritime security is significant for Japan considering the fact that it is an island nation with scarce natural resources and is dependent on SLOCs for its existence. India with its significant geo-strategic location in the IOR has, thus, become very important to Japan, in order to ensure maritime security. The inclusion of Japan in the Malabar exercises have proved to be beneficial as it facilitates interoperability, establishes common understanding on maritime security operations and helps in tackling both traditional and non-traditional threats. Both countries also need to converge on the issue of assistance to littorals of the Indo-Pacific in order to resist any changes proposed by revisionist countries attempting a change in the status quo. Simultaneously, India needs to develop its own maritime influence in the Indo-Pacific through indigenous ship building assisted by countries like Japan and South Korea.

Notes

1. Admiral Arun Prakash (Retd), Maritime Security Of India: Future Challenges, November 26, 2013, YB Chavan memorial talk, Institute of Defence Studies and Analysis quoting Sardar KM Panikkar.
2. Ibid.
3. https://indiancoastguard.gov.in/content/1732_3_MoU.aspx.
4. Ministry of Foreign Affairs, Japan, Action Plan to advance Security Cooperation based on the Joint Declaration on Security Cooperation between Japan and India, December 29, 2009 at https://www.mofa.go.jp/region/asia-paci/india/pmv0912/action.html, accessed on June 8, 2018.
5. 'Safe Waters', Volume XVII, Issue 2 December 2017 at https://indiancoastguard.gov.in/WriteReadData/ bookpdf/201804201055560111 6741FinalSafeWaters.pdf, accessed on May 28, 2018.
6. *Times of India*, 'India to work with Japan to combat piracy', TNN, January 18, 2018 at https://timesofindia.indiatimes.com/city/chennai/indian-coast-guard-to-expand-collaboration-with-japan-for-search-and-rescue-and-anti-piracy-patrol/articleshow/62546798.cms, accessed on June 7, 2018.
7. Ibid.
8. Adarsha Verma, 'The Malabar Exercises—An Appraisal', Commentary IDSA Website at https://idsa.in/idsacomments/the-malabar-exercises_averma_180717, accessed on July 9, 2018.
9. Ibid.
10. Ibid.
11. Press Release, Exercise Malabar Commences in Bay of Bengal/North Indian Ocean, Press Information Bureau, Government of India, Ministry of Defence, July 10, 2017 at http://pib.nic.in/newsite/PrintRelease.aspx?relid=167276, accessed on May 31, 2018.
12. India, Japan and US navies start Malabar 2014 naval exercise, Naval Technology, July 24, 2014 at https://www.naval-technology.com/news/newsindia-japan-and-us-navies-start-malabar-2014-naval-exercise-4327256/, accessed on May 31, 2018.
13. Jagannath P. Panda, 'India's Call on China in the Quad: A Strategic Arch between Liberal and Alternative Structures', *Rising Powers Quarterly* Volume 3, Issue 2, 2018.

14. Adarsha Verma, note 8.
15. Ibid.
16. Press Information Bureau, Government of India, Joint Press Statement on The India-Japan Annual Defence Ministerial Dialogue, September 6, 2017 at http://pib.nic.in/newsite/pmreleases.aspx?mincode=33, accessed on June 20, 2018.
17. Ibid.
18. Professor Ji Guoxing, 'SLOC Security in the Asia Pacific', Centre Occasional Paper, Asia-Pacific Centre for Security Studies, Honolulu, Hawaii, February 2000 at https://apcss.org/Publications/Ocasional%20Papers/OPSloc.htm, accessed on June 10, 2018.
19. James R. Holmes and Toshi Yoshihara, 'China's Naval Ambitions in the Indian Ocean', *Journal of Strategic Studies,* Vol. 31, Issue 3, 2008, pp. 371 at http:// www.tandfonline.com/doi/full/10.1080/01402390802024700?scroll= top&needAccess=true, accessed on July 28, 2017.
20. Adarsha Verma, 'China's Ambitons in the Indian Ocean', *China Year Book 2017.*
21. Tim Willasey-Wilsey, 'China and the String of Pearls', Gateway House, January 28, 2016 at https://www.gatewayhouse.in/gwadar-and-the-string-of-pearls-2/, accessed on September 28, 2018.
22. Alexandre Sheldon-Duplaix, 'Beyond the China Seas-Will China Become a Global "Sea Power"', China Perspective, No. 2016/3.
23. Adarsha Verma, note 20.
24. Sachin Parashar, 'China's ocean observatory in Maldives sparks fresh security concerns', *The Times of India,* February 26, 2018 at https://timesofindia.indiatimes.com/india/chinas-ocean-observatory-in-maldives-sparks-fresh-security-fear/articleshow/63072040.cms, accessed on September 28, 2018.
25. Ibid.
26. 'Japan's Maritime Diplomacy Mission in Southeast Asia', Michael Hart, *The Diplomat* August 28, 2017 at https://thediplomat.com/2017/08/japans-maritime-diplomacy-mission-in-southeast-asia/, accessed on March 25, 2018.
27. Raja Ram Panda, 'Changing Dynamics of India-Japan Relations: Future Trends' at http://src-h.slav.hokudai.ac.jp/rp/publications/no06/01_Panda.pdf, accessed on September 30, 2018.
28. Ibid.
29. Petronet, 'Japanese company to set up $300 million LNG terminal in Sri Lanka', *The Economic Times,* February 11, 2018 at https://economictimes.indiatimes.com/industry/energy/oil-gas/petronet-japanese-company-to-set-up-300-million-lng-terminal-in-sri-lanka/articleshow/62871145.cms, accessed on September 28, 2018.

30. Sudha Ramachandran, 'China's Sinking Port Plans in Bangladesh', China Brief Volume 16 Issue 10 at https://jamestown.org/program/chinas-sinking-port-plans-in-bangladesh/, accessed on June 20, 2018.
31. Prakash Panneerselvam, 'Indo-Japan Maritime Security Cooperation in a Changing Environment', East Asia Research programme, August 19, 2016 at http://earp.in/en/indo-japan-maritime-security-cooperation-in-a-changing-environment/, accessed on June 7, 2018.
32. Ministry of Foreign Affairs, Japan, 'Action Plan to advance Security Cooperation based on the Joint Declaration on Security Cooperation between Japan and India', December 29, 2009 at https://www.mofa.go.jp/region/asia-paci/india/pmv0912/action.html, accessed on June 7, 2018.
33. International Maritime Organisation, Overview of IMO Profile at https://business.un.org/en/entities/13, accessed on June 8, 2018.
34. United Nations Press Release, Security Council condemns acts of piracy, armed robbery off Somalia's coast, authorizes for six months 'all necessary means' to repress such acts, June 2, 2008 at https://www.un.org/press/en/2008/sc9344.doc.htm, accessed on June 8, 2018.
35. Ibid.
36. The Year That Was, Indian Navy in 2011 at https://www.indiannavy.nic.in/sites/default/themes/indiannavy/images/pdf/year-gone-by-2011.pdf, accessed on September 28, 2018.
37. Ministry of Foreign Affairs, Japan, Japan's Actions against Piracy off the Coast of Somalia at https://www.mofa.go.jp/policy/piracy/ja_somalia.html, accessed on September 28, 2018.
38. Ministry of Foreign Affairs website, Japan's Actions against Piracy off the Coast of Somalia at https://www.mofa.go.jp/policy/piracy/ja_somalia_1210.html, accessed on June 8, 2018.
39. Ibid.
40. The report is available at https://www.hellenicshippingnews.com/wp-content/uploads/2018/01/2017-Annual-IMB-Piracy-Report-Abridged.pdf.
41. Michael Hart, 'Japan's Maritime Diplomacy Mission in Southeast Asia', *The Diplomat,* August 28, 2017 at https://thediplomat.com/2017/08/japans-maritime-diplomacy-mission-in-southeast-asia/, accessed on July 10, 2018.
42. *Times of India*, 'India to work with Japan to combat piracy', TNN, January 18, 2018 at https://timesofindia.indiatimes.com/city/chennai/indian-coast-guard-to-expand-collaboration-with-japan-for-search-and-rescue-and-anti-piracy-patrol/articleshow/62546798.cms, accessed on June 7, 2018.
43. Sameer Patil, 'India balances Asian security with Japan', Gateway House, December 17, 2015 at https://www.gatewayhouse.in/india-japan-bullet-train-nuclear-deal/, accessed on September 28, 2018.

44. Kiyoshi Takenaka, 'Japan to launch new intelligence unit focused on Islamic militants', Reuters, December 4, 2017 at https://in.reuters.com/article/france-shooting-japan/japan-to-launch-new-intelligence-unit-focused-on-islamic-militants-idINKBN0TN0IG20151204, accessed on July 11, 2018.

45. Air Marshall Dhiraj Kukreja, 'Andaman and nicobar Islands—A Security Challenge for India', *Indian Defence Review*, 28.1 Jan–Mar 2013, September 16, 2013 at www.Indiandefencereview.com, accessed on September 28, 2018.

46. Ibid.

47. Ibid.

48. Government of India, Ministry of Shipping, Press Information Bureau, January 11, 2011 at http://pib.nic.in/newsite/PrintRelease.aspx?relid=69044.

49. Handing over P75(I) submarine project to Mazagon will sound death-knell for private players, *The Financial Express,* April 30, 2018 at https://www.financialexpress.com/defence/handing-over-p75i-submarine-project-to-mazagon-will-sound-death-knell-for-private-players/1150991/, accessed on September 28, 2018.

50. Ibid.

51. Admiral Arun Prakash (Retd), 'Maritime Security Of India: Future Challenges', November 26, 2013, YB Chavan memorial talk, Institute for Defence Studies and Analyses.

52. Ajai Shukla, 'India: Global hub for warship-building', December 15, 2009 at http://www.rediff.com/money/column/guest-india-global-hub-for-warship-building/20091215.htm, accessed on June 2018.

53. Darshana Baruah, Japan-India's unique maritime partner, November 17, 2016 at https://carnegieindia.org/2016/11/17/japan-india-s-unique-maritime-partner-pub-66192, accessed on June 7, 2018.

6

Cooperation in UN Peacekeeping Operations

Abstract

Cooperation in UN Peacekeeping activities is one of the areas where India-Japan Security Cooperation has a lot of potential. Japan's participation in UN peacekeeping operations is fairly nascent as compared to the huge experience that India has, through participation in various peacekeeping missions. Whereas Japan has always been amongst the top three financial contributors to the UN budget, India has always been amongst the top five contributors of uniformed personnel for UN peacekeeping missions. Both countries can cooperate with each other, tapping on their respective strengths in order to enhance global peace and security.

Introduction

Peacekeeping operations have played an important role in maintaining international peace and security, more so in the current post-Cold War period. These missions also play a significant role in bringing uniformed forces of different countries together for a cause which is just, noble and has a universal appeal—peacekeeping. It is easier to transcend legal, physical and nationalistic boundaries in the name of peacekeeping. Forces train with each other and bond together during long periods of operations in peacekeeping missions, in a way which is more intensive than the inter-operability achieved during routine bilateral or multilateral short duration exercises and training. UN peacekeeping operations are counted amongst the important engagements between nations that strive for cooperation in security matters and find mention in all security cooperation declarations. In the same spirit, in the Declaration of Security Cooperation signed in October 2008, UN peacekeeping operations were considered an important element of cooperation between India and Japan.

The significance of the UN peacekeeping operations can be recognised from the fact that presently there are 14 missions around the world and more than 100,000 personnel deployed in peace keeping activities. Details of UN Missions around the globe and the numbers deployed in peacekeeping activities are tabulated in Table 6.1.

Table 6.1: UN Missions Around the Globe

UN Mission		**Deployed Personnel**
MINUJUSTH	UN Mission for Justice Support in Haiti	1600
MINURSO	UN Mission for Referendum in Western Sahara	467
MINUSCA	UN MULTI Dimensional Integration Stabilisation Mission in the Central African Republic	14588
MINUSMA	United Nations Multidimensional Integrated Stabilisation Mission In Mali	15514
MONUSCO	United Nations Organisation Stabilisation Mission in the Democratic Republic of Congo	19074
UNAMID	African Union - United Nations Hybrid Operation in Darfur	13980
UNDOF	United Nations Disengagement Observer Force	1100
UNFICYP	United Nations Peacekeeping Force in Cyprus	1061
UNIFIL	United Nations Interim Force in Lebanon	11282
UNISFA	United Nations Interim Security Force for Abyei	4817

UN Mission		Deployed Personnel
UNMIK	United Nations Interim Administration Mission in Kosovo	349
UNMISS	United Nations Mission inRepublic of South Sudan	18983
UNMOGIP	United Nations Military Observer Group in India and Pakistan	115
UNTSO	United Nations Truce Supervision Organization	373
	Total	103303

Source: Data taken from UN Peace keeping website.

Both India and Japan have always aspired to be positive contributors to global peace and stability. However, there have been considerable differences in the approach of both countries towards peacekeeping. These differences stem from varied cultural lineages, historical baggage and domestic compulsions. Both countries have, however, realised that international peacekeeping activities need to be supported both with troops on ground and with budgetary support.

The Declaration of Security Cooperation signed in October 2008, between India and Japan, has identified peacekeeping and peace building activities as one of the areas in which both countries can extensively cooperate, given the rich Indian experience in peacekeeping and Japan's drive for "Proactive Contribution to Peace" in the world. SWOT Analyses at Appendix A also mentions Cooperation in UN Peace Keeping as a strategy for enhanced India-Japan Security Cooperation *(SO Strategy: S3Oj5)*.

Japan and Peacekeeping

The Japanese participation in UN Peace keeping operations has its genesis in Article 9 of the Japanese Constitution which states:

- *'Aspiring sincerely to an international peace based on justice and order, the Japanese people forever renounce war as a sovereign right of the nation and the threat or use of force as means of settling international disputes.'*

- *'In order to accomplish the aim of the preceding paragraph, land, sea, and air forces, as well as other war potential, will never be maintained. The right of belligerency of the state will not be recognized'.*

This constitutional prohibition of not maintaining forces and other war potential questions the legality of despatching SDF for peacekeeping operations. In 1954, when the SDF was established, its despatch abroad for any operations was prohibited. The first request for Japanese participation by the UN Secretary General Hammarskjold was rejected citing incompatibility with domestic laws but a national debate ensued on the possibilities of contribution towards world peace and international peace. In 1980, the then LDP government interpreted that Article 9 did not restrain the participation of SDF in peace keeping operations. The government presented before the Diet its official position wherein it mentioned that participation of SDF in UN Ceasefire Observation groups and similar employment (which did not entail the use of force) was possible.[1] However, there was no deployment of SDF for any UN peacekeeping mission.

During the Gulf War in 1991, Japan refused to provide manpower and resources for the coalition effort citing legal and constitutional issues. However, it provided US$ 13 billion as aid for the war effort.[2] This large financial contribution was not appreciated by the international community and Japan had to bear the brunt of criticism especially from its ally, the US, due to lack of commitment of resources and boots on ground. Post the Gulf War, it was debated and appreciated amongst political leaders in Japan that contribution in terms of resources and peacekeepers in consonance with its national strength was also mandatory to be considered as a responsible country in the international community. The Japanese government thereafter formulated the UN Peace Cooperation Bill, which was enacted as the peacekeeping cooperation law in June 1992.[3] With this development,

Japan cautiously stepped into the uncharted realm of peacekeeping by tasking SDF troops with cease-fire monitoring.[4] Thereafter, in 2007, international peace cooperation activities, which used to be regarded as one of the supplementary activities of the SDF of Japan, were upgraded to become part of the primary missions of the SDF, alongside the defence of Japan and the maintenance of public order.[5] Japan has also committed its engineering units and staff officers as being available to deployment for the UN peacekeeping missions as part of the UN launched Peacekeeping Capability Readiness System (PCRS).

Japan's UN Peace keeping contribution is based on the following five principles in accordance with the International Peace Cooperation Act and Article 9 of the Japanese Constitution:[6]

- Agreement on a cease-fire shall have been reached among the parties to armed conflicts.
- Consent for the undertaking of UN Peacekeeping Operations as well as Japan's participation in such operations shall have been obtained from the host countries as well as the parties to the armed conflicts.
- The operations shall strictly maintain impartiality, not favouring any of the parties to the armed conflicts.
- Should any of the requirements in the above-mentioned principles cease to be satisfied, the Government of Japan may withdraw SDF contingent.
- The use of weapons shall be limited to the minimum necessary to protect the lives of personnel, etc.

Japan's Participation in UN Peace Keeping Operations (UNPKO)

In 1989, 27 electoral observers from Japan were sent to Namibia as part of the United Nations Transition Assistance Group (UNTAG). This marked Japan's entry into the realm of UN peacekeeping. Thereafter, with the passage of the International Peace Cooperation Law in 1992, Japan was empowered to despatch both uniformed personnel as well as civil personnel for UN peace keeping tasks. Thereon, Japan undertook peacekeeping operations in various parts of the globe including Cambodia, Mozambique, Angola, El Salvador and Timor-Leste. Japan also cooperated in international election monitoring activities in Bosnia and Herzegovina (in 1998 and 2000), Kosovo (in 2001) and in Timor-Leste (in 2001 and 2002).[7]

A chronology of Japan's participation in UNPKO and in international humanitarian assistance activities is tabulated in Table 6.2.

Table 6.2: Chronology of Japan's Participation in UNPKO

Year	Event
1990-1991	The Gulf Crisis
August 1992	International Peace Cooperation Law was enacted.
Sep-Oct 1992	United Nations Angola Verification Mission (UNAVEM II)
Sep 1992 to Sep-1993	United Nations Transitional Authority in Cambodia (UNTAC)
May 1993- Jan 1995	United Nations Operation in Mozambique (ONUMOZ)
Mar-Apr1994	United Nations Observer Mission in El Salvador (ONUSAL)
Sep-Dec1994	Self-Defence Forces dispatched to Zaire to conduct humanitarian assistance activities for the Rwandan refugees
Jan1996	United Nations Disengagement Observer Force (UNDOF)
Feb 2002-Jun 2004	United Nations Mission in Timor Leste (UNMIT)
Mar 2007-Jan 2011	United Nations Mission in Nepal (UNMIN)
Oct 2008	United Nations Mission in Sudan (UNMIS)
2011-2017	United Nations Mission in South Sudan (UNMISS)

Source: Data taken from the website of Ministry of Foreign Affairs, Japan.

Over a period of time, Japan has upgraded its rapid deployment capability for the UN peacekeeping missions. In 2007, the Ministry of Defence, Japan created a Central Readiness Force (CRF) of around 4,000 soldiers for rapid response to any situation on either Japanese or foreign soil, including peacekeeping operations and unconventional warfare.[8]

The number of Japanese uniformed personnel in UNPKO over the years is shown in the chart below. Further deployment of the engineering unit in UNMISS were halted and troops pulled out in May 2017. Presently Japan has no troops (except staff officers) in UN peace keeping efforts.

Figure 6.1: Japanese Uniformed Personnel in UNPKO

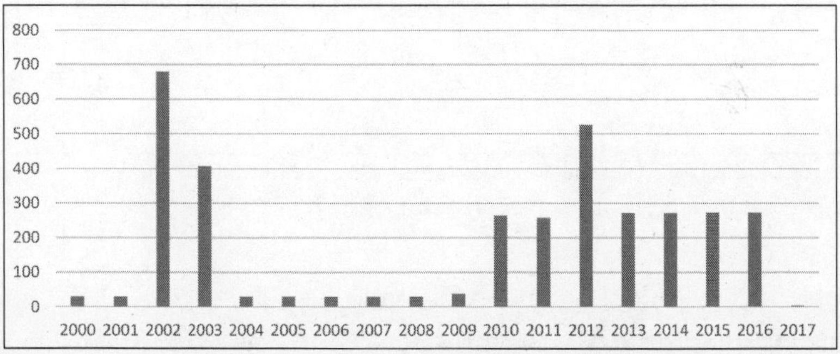

Source: Data compiled from IPI PeaceKeeping Database, Providing for Peacekeeping at http://www.providingforpeacekeeping.org/2014/04/03/contributor-profile-japan/.

An analysis of the contributions by countries over the last 10 years reveals that Japan has been the second-largest contributor to the peacekeeping budget at the international body after the United States and presently provides 9.7 per cent of its annual funding.[9]

Peacekeeping in Cambodia, Timor-Leste and South Sudan

Japan contributed a total of 1,300 personnel, including SDF personnel, civilian police officers and election monitors to the United Nations Transitional Authority in Cambodia (UNTAC), which was established by the Paris Peace Agreements.[10] It was the first full-scale PKO deployment for Japan under the International Peace Cooperation Law enacted in June 1992. The Special Representative of the Secretary General (SRSG) in UNTAC was Yasushi Akashi, who was also the first Japanese national to hold the post of SRSG.[11] Thereafter, in 2002, Japan sent around 680 SDF personnel (as part of engineer units) and another 10 Peace Keeping Force (PKF)

Figure 6.2: Top Contributors to UN Budget

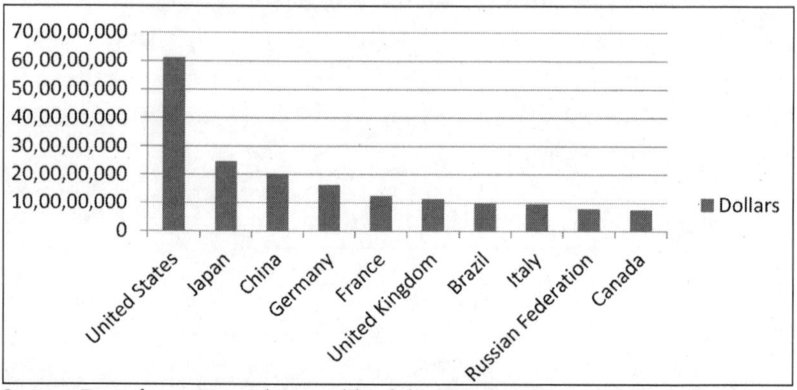

Source: Data from General Assemblyof the UN Committee on Contributions at https://www.un.org/en/ga/contributions/budget.shtml.

personnel to United Nations Mission in East Timor (UNAMET). In this mission, the SDF was entrusted with the task of reconstruction in terms of maintenance and repair of roads and bridges, for carrying out logistic support tasks and also acting as electoral observers to the presidential elections.

The deployment of Japanese SDF in South Sudan needs special mention as it leads to an intricate understanding of the public opinion to conflict and peacekeeping. This also will facilitate analysis of the ways and means through which India can cooperate with Japan in peacekeeping activities.

An engineering company of the SDF was deployed in the UNMISS in 2011. The major achievements of the SDF Company in South Sudan include a total of approximately 260 km of road repairs and a total of approximately 500,000 square metres of engineering works and infrastructure development. When fighting broke out among the opposing groups in Juba, South Sudan (where the SDF Company was based), it spilled over to areas within the UN Camp. With fighting continuing in and around the UN Camp, the SDF based on their country's legal restrictions could use weapons only in self-defence but not to protect other UN personnel and civilians. The inability of a uniformed force to protect others from physical harm did not auger well for the reputation of the SDF. Additionally, as per the five principles of UN Peacekeeping deployment in Japan, the SDF is permitted to be deployed only in locations where the conditions of the five principles of Peacekeeping have been met, which includes that ceasefire between opposing groups exists and the troops are not exposed to combat-like situations. The public questioned the deployment of the SDF against these principles, and though then Defence Minister Tomomi Inada, tried to scale down the reports of fighting in Juba as mere armed clashes, the war diaries of the SDF unit mentioned the conditions as otherwise. The row eventually led to the resignation of Defence Minister Inada and the subsequent withdrawal of SDF from UNMISS in May 2017.[12] In the interim, the LDP government passed the "kaketsuke-keigo" legislation that allows the JSDF to use their weapons to assist civilians and fellow peacekeepers in need, under conflict conditions, in UNPKO.

Overall, the withdrawal of the SDF has dampened the spirit of Proactive Contribution to Peace by the Japanese government. Japan wanted to increase its global footprint and image with greater UN peacekeeping contribution through boots on ground. It is already doing enough to ensure that adequate funds flow in. Even when vacating the SDF location at South Sudan, it handed over most of its engineering equipment including heavy engineering equipment worth US$ 24 million to the UNMISS as a token of remembrance.[13] However, soon after the withdrawal of the UNMISS SDF company, Chief Cabinet Secretary Suga responding in a press conference stated, "... under the banner of proactive contribution to peace, Japan remains committed to making further active contributions in the field of international peace cooperation, including enhancing capacity building assistance, and dispatching units and personnel, by leveraging Japan's strengths based on its past achievements concerning PKO activities".[14] Future participation in peacekeeping activities will definitely bear the ghost of this UN mission for a long time.

Japan Peace Keeping Training and Research Centre: The Japan Peacekeeping Training and Research Center (JPTRC) of the Joint Staff College offers basic and specialised courses on international peace keeping activities for the SDF. In a bid to enhance international cooperation, international students are also called for these courses. So far, Indian students/officers have not been sent to the JPTRC because the nature of courses offered to India are not commensurate with the duties envisaged by Indian peacekeepers. Moreover, unlike the JPTRC, which is a nascent centre, the Centre for UN Peacekeeping (CUNPK) in India is well established with rich experience on UN matters. However, the numbers of Japanese peacekeepers coming to India are few and on an average two to four Japanese students visit the CUNPK in India every year for getting trained.[15] More cooperation including visits from both sides needs to be pursued to chalk out future courses for student exchange among the two peacekeeping centres.

As part of future efforts at peace building, Japan aims at achieving the same through a three-pronged effort as under:[16]

- "Human resource development for peace building, wherein the number of Japanese capable of contributing to peace building efforts will be increased. The experience gained in peace building in Asia will be used for missions across the world.
- By strengthening intellectual contributions by contributing to the development of discussion on peace building as well as launching related initiatives in the UN.
- Strengthening engagements on ground by bolstering ODA for peace building as well as promoting international cooperation for peace by legal frameworks and increasing contribution of peace keepers".

India and Peacekeeping

India is a land where many faiths have found expression. Birthplace of many religions of the world—Buddhism, Jainism, Hinduism and Sikhism, India has taught tolerance throughout ages. Tolerance and reconciliation were the reasons for the conquerors and the defeated merging into the same culture in years; reconciliation has led to practitioners of different faiths merging to evolve new beliefs and practices. "Vasudhaiva Kutumbakam", enshrined as part of the Maha Upanishads has been our guiding principle from the 12th century. The same now adorns the entrance hall of the Parliament of India where all policy decisions are taken.

With its rich cultural background, participation of India in the UN peace keeping activities was thus a natural transition after Independence. Historically, India has provided almost 200,000 troops in nearly 50 of the 71 peacekeeping missions mandated over the past six decades, including 13 of the current 14 missions. Indian contribution to Peace Keeping Operations worldwide is tabulated in Table 6.3.

Table 6.3: Indian Contribution to UNPKO

Year	**Country/Location**	**Troops (Including Awards and other remarks)**
1950-54	Korea	60 Indian Para Field Ambulance Unit was deployed. (Awarded citations by Chiefs of US 8th Army and the ROK Army. Special mention in House of Lords, London. Commendations by commanders of various formations. Individual honours included four US Bronze Stars, two Mahavir Chakras, six Vir Chakras and 25 Mention-in-Despatches. Unit was also awarded the President's Trophy on 10 March 1955 by then President of India, Dr. Rajendra Prasad, the only unit to be awarded, till date.)
1954–70	Indo-China (comprising three states of Vietnam, Cambodia and Laos)	Infantry Battalion and supporting troops.

Year	Country/Location	Troops (Including Awards and other remarks)
1956-1967	Middle East (UNEF)	Infantry Battalion and supporting troops.
1960-1964	Congo (ONUC)	Two Infantry Brigades. One Flight of six Canberra bombers. (39 personnel of the Indian contingent laid down their lives. Capt GS Salaria was awarded posthumously the Param Vir Chakra for action in Katanga, Southern Congo.)
1992-1993	Cambodia (UNTAC)	One battalion group.
1992-1994	Mozambique (ONUMOZ)	Two Engineer companies, HQ company, logistics company, staff officers and military observers
1993-1994	Somalia (UNITAF and UNOSOM II)	Infantry Brigade Group Indian Navy also deployed four warships
1994-1996	Rwanda (UNAMIR)	Infantry Battalion Group, Staff Officers, Military Observers (One of the three Force Commanders was an Indian)
1989-1999	Angola (UNAVEM)	Infantry Battalion Group, Engineer Company. (One Indian Deputy Force Commander)
1999-2001	Sierra Leone (UNAMSIL)	Two Infantry Battalion Groups Two Engineer Companies. Staff Officers. (Attack Helicopter Unit, Medical Unit and Logistics Unit also participated.)
2006-2008	Ethiopia-Eritrea (UNMEE)	Infantry Battalion Group, Engineer Company. Force reserve company and staff officers
Since Dec 1998	Lebanon (UNIFIL)	Infantry Battalion Group, Level II hospital, Staff Officers.

Year	Country/Location	Troops (Including Awards and other remarks)
Since Jan 2005	Congo (MONUSCO)	Infantry Brigade Group, Military Observers, Staff Officers, Two Formed Police Units, Army Aviation Contingent with Utility helicopters. (One Force Commander)
Since April 2005	UNMIS/UNMISS	Two Infantry Battalion Groups, Sector HQ, Engineer Company, Signal Unit, Level II hospital, Military Observers, Staff Officers. (Two Indian Peacekeepers lost their lives while ensuring Protection of Civilians.) One Deputy Force Commander, One Deputy Police Commissioner.
Since Feb 2006	Golan Heights (UNDOF)	Logistics Battalion (One Force Commander)
Since Apr 2004	Ivory Coast (UNOCI)	Staff Officers and Military Observers
Since Dec 1997	Haiti (MINUSTAH)	Three Formed Police Unit Staff Officers
Since April 2007	Liberia (UNIMIL)	Formed Police Unit, One Rapid Action Force One Acting Police Commissioner

Source: Data collected from various websites.

India currently deploys more than 6,700 military and police personnel to UN peace operations in Afghanistan, the Democratic Republic of the Congo, Haiti, Lebanon, Liberia, the Middle East, South Sudan, Sudan and the Western Sahara and has been among the top five largest troop contributor countries [TCC].[17]

Table 6.4: Top Five Contributor Nations to UNPKO
(as in May 2018)

Country	Uniformed Personnel (Police, Military Experts, Staff Officers, Troops)
Ethiopia	8417
Bangladesh	7099
Rwanda	6945
India	6712
Pakistan	5996

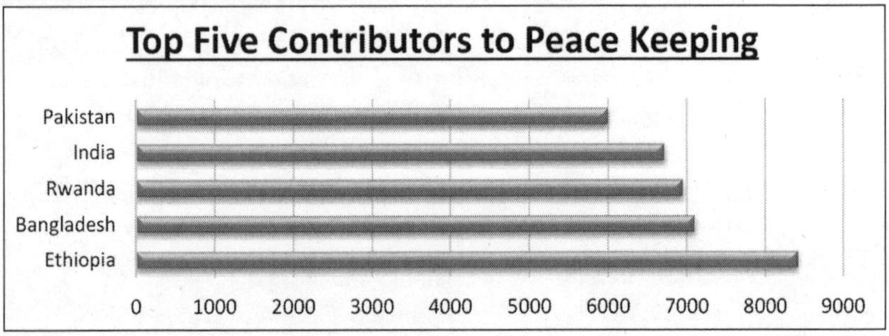

Source: Data taken from UN Peacekeeping Troop and Police Contributors at https://peacekeeping.un.org/sites/default/files/2_country_ranking_report.pdf.

This amazing contribution has shown India's strong commitment to peace building and peacekeeping. One hundred and sixty-three Indian peacekeepers have given the ultimate sacrifice by laying down their lives for global peace under the UN Flag. India has consistently been among the top five contributors of peacekeepers in UN Peacekeeping activities.

Of particular importance is the first mission of independent India in Korea, when India rushed a Paramedical unit, which was deployed in the thick of battle and sometimes behind enemy lines to tend to casualties. India also provided a custodial force under Maj Gen SPP Thorat comprising approx. 6,200 personnel. Over the past seven decades and more, even though India faces security challenges of its own region, no country has contributed more to UN peacekeeping than India. Presently, India has a huge troop contribution in Congo and South Sudan. In both countries,

Indian peacekeepers have shown their mettle by employing holistic and wide-ranging methods. These methods include provision of humanitarian aid, creating suitable environment for sustaining peace and enhancing reconciliation between warring groups. This is done by visiting hospitals, attending church services, providing medical and veterinary support ensuring vulnerable population is protected with the ultimate aim of rebuilding institutions and focusing on sustainable peace, justice and reconciliation.

Training for UNPKO: Training for UNPKO for Indian troops is carried out in the CUNPK, which is one of the leading institutions in the world imparting high quality training to peacekeepers. The CUNPK also conducts courses for international students and is abreast of the latest developments in the field of peacekeeping.

The high standards of performance maintained consistently by the Indian peace personnel under challenging circumstances have won them high regard worldwide. India's unique combination of being the largest democracy in the world with a strong tradition of respect for rule of law and the successful experience in nation building makes it particularly relevant in the context of 21st century peace-building. India is a member of the Organisational Committee of the Peace Building Commission (PBC) and is strongly supportive of nationally-led plans for peace consolidation.

Enhancing India-Japan Cooperation

There exists a huge potential for cooperation in peacekeeping activities between both countries. The doctrinal convergence of India and Japan, in that both desire peace and stability and believe in non-interference in domestic issues, can be built upon to create the necessary space for coordinated activity. Some of the aspects that can be developed for enhanced cooperation in UN peacekeeping activity have been analysed in the succeeding paragraphs.

Composite Peacekeeping Task Forces: Indian peacekeepers actively participate in the UNPKO around the world, under the mandate of the UN Security Council. Indian peacekeepers have participated as battalion groups enforcing peace, as engineering companies involved in reconstruction activity, as signal and communication units providing support to the mission, as aviation units, medical units, police and so on, performing a variety of tasks. They are deployed in Chapter VI and VII missions without any restrictions on their employment, and guided by the mandate of the mission. The SDF, on the other hand, when participating in such missions is governed not only by the UN Security Council Mandate by also by their national laws, which lays restrictions on the employment of SDF and the use of weapons. Resultantly, Japanese peacekeepers are involved only in non-combat activities like engineering and re-construction efforts. For a start, a combined/composite grouping of Japanese engineering company with Indian peacekeepers can form an effective mission group that would be responsible for both, capacity building/reconstruction as well as ensuring/enforcing peace in a sector. This composite task force can thus operate independently in the given sector. Such task forces would be self-contained, led by the battalion group commander and would not require additional intervention from the Force Headquarters for each separate engineering task that needs to be done (which is now the case when SDF companies operate independently). This will pave the way for future cooperation in many other combinations for peacekeeping missions around the world between Indian and Japanese forces such as composite Japanese medical and Indian infantry units, composite communication units coupled with Indian infantry units and so on. Composite units are not new in the Indian context as a similar training is conducted wherein troops from India and Kazakhstan have trained to participate together in a peace keeping mission.

Exchange of Peacekeepers: Since August 2012, two Liaison Officers (LO) from Australian Defence Force (ADF) had been a part of the SDF engineer unit in UNMISS. Their duties included supporting the unit in coordinating engineering tasks not only with the UNMISS components, but also with the government of South Sudan. Additionally, they had been contributing to enhance the Japan-Australian cooperation in the African continent. During this time, support was provided based on the Japan-Australia Acquisition and Cross Servicing Agreement (ACSA) to implement various procedures smoothly.[18] In an interview, one of the Australian officers who was part of the SDF unit in Juba, South Sudan, said, "... one of the reason behind my position being established is to form stronger bonds between Japan and Australia at the operational level, so that the two countries can work together in the future should there be a need to support humanitarian crises closer to the Australasian region".[19] In a similar arrangement, Indian officers can be part of the SDF and assist them in a variety of tasks including liaison and communications. Indian peacekeepers have earned a very good reputation for themselves in the UN fraternity and are sought after as staff officers for liaison and policy making. Such arrangements will also enhance the bonds at the lower levels and assist better understanding of each other's security perspectives.

Logistics in UN Peacekeeping Missions: When any Indian military regiment is earmarked for participation in any UN peacekeeping mission, it carries all its equipment along with it. Some of these stores are unit equipment (peculiar to the unit proceeding for the UN mission) and some stores are left behind in the mission area for subsequent units to utilise. However, the logistic challenge of procurement, transportation from India and maintenance of equipment in the UN mission area involves effort and is cost intensive. The logistics process of procurement and packaging into relevant groups in India commences almost six months prior to the move of the unit abroad and a battery of clerks and a few officers continuously need to monitor the overall logistic build up, packaging and transportation. At times, if the equipment being used is not as per the specified configuration or as per UN standards, India gets back only a partial reimbursement from the UN. This challenge can be mitigated to a very large extent by utilising the logistics infrastructure of other countries that is already available near the mission area. Japan, being one of the largest contributors of equipment and vehicles to the UNPKO, has a vibrant infrastructure and a well-established supply chain at many locations around the world. India can utilise the available supply chain infrastructure to equip own forces in UN missions. This will definitely be economical though the calculations for the same have not been carried out in detail. A case in point is the recent initiative by Nissan Motor Co. Ltd, which plans to start assembling vehicles in Kenya, bolstering government plans to develop a regional auto-manufacturing hub in East Africa's biggest economy.[20] Once established, the Kenyan facility will feed the East African market and will be in addition to the Nissan Motor Co. plant in South Africa as well as an assembly line in Nigeria.[21]

Another option to this arrangement could be that India establishes its manufacturing base closer to the mission area and utilises the established Japanese supply chain architecture for its own logistics needs. India needs to collaborate with Japan in setting up joint manufacturing bases, which can provide the much needed UN equipment and vehicles to UN missions in Africa. In addition to collaborating in locations where Japan already has bases, India can think of new bases like Adis Ababa in Ethiopia, which is also the Headquarters of the African Union.[22] Such manufacturing units will not only enhance employment, and give fillip to the Indian economy, but also assist in propagating Indian influence abroad. Avoiding transportation of equipment required in UN peacekeeping missions, as well as catering for its life cycle maintenance through maintenance hubs set up in proximity will save money for the government. Being especially tailor-made for the peacekeeping missions, the equipment and vehicles will be fully reimbursed by the UN, thereby ensuring that there is no loss to the government exchequer, as is presently the case when particular equipment does not perform as per laid down specifications leading to partial reimbursements only. It will also ensure that our contingents are better equipped, well stocked and present a better image of the nation. Government to government understanding on this aspect and detailed executive level planning is a must for such logistics integration to exist.

Training of Peacekeepers: When Japan decided to contribute troops for peace keeping in 1992, India should have taken the opportunity to build up a stronger relationship by offering to train the SDF. However, opportunity for training still exists with the current enhancement in the security relationship. In India, the CUNPK trains peacekeepers, both Indian and international, for peacekeeping duties. However, only two to four Japanese peacekeepers subscribe to the courses run by the CUNPK every year.[23] No Indian peacekeeper has undertaken a course in Japan at the Japanese Peace Keeping Institute, as yet. There is a need to identify the strengths of both the institutes and impart peacekeeping training accordingly. As the Indian CUNPK is well advanced in its training curriculum, there may be no need for a cross-training presently, but should the two militaries agree to operate in UN peace keeping missions jointly, cross-training in each other's institutes will be beneficial. Joint training for peacekeepers can also transcend classroom teaching and move onto joint exercises and drills. Both countries may even think of holding annual peacekeeping exercises on the lines of the planned Counter-Terrorism exercise planned between the two countries. These can be held along with the annual HADR exercises held in Japan or India.[24] As a future step, India and Japan can think of a regional peacekeeping exercise involving other countries of the region.

Soft Power and Post Conflict Economy: Peacekeeping offers one of the finest spaces for propagating soft power. Both the countries should, therefore, look beyond short term gains towards the propagation of soft power, which is one of the spinoffs of peacekeeping operations.[25] Along with this, Japan and India should also be looking at post-conflict engagement in economic reconstruction in such countries. With the basic intent of Japan and India, of acting for the common good of locals, their actions for social development would not be considered invasive or exploitative of local resources.

UNSC Reforms: The United Nations was initially established by 51 countries, about 70 years ago. Presently, the UN has 193 member states that discuss and decide on global issues that are very different from the situation as was obtained in 1945, when the UN was founded.[26] Despite a threefold increase in world population, the massive increase in the number of member countries and a change in power dynamics shifting focus from the West to the East, UN structures and procedures remain as archaic as the early founding years. The UNSC has undergone reforms only once, in 1965, when it expanded the number of non-permanent seats from 11 to 15, when the number of UN member states increased from the original 51 to 118.[27] The membership now stands at 193, a significant increase again since 1965. This has sparked calls for further reforms of the UNSC.[28] The G4 nations are the four countries of India, Brazil, Germany and Japan that have asked for an increase in the number of permanent members of the UNSC and stake claims to be a part of it. These countries also support the candidature of one another as permanent members of UNSC with veto power. The economic and political influence of each of these countries has grown significantly and some are comparable to those of the existing permanent members. India and Japan along with the other G4 countries need to come together to press ahead for an early reform of the UN so that it conforms to geo-political realities. During a meeting of foreign ministers of the G4 countries in September 2017, the ministers reiterated their commitment as aspiring new permanent members of a reformed council, as well as their support for each other's candidatures.[29] There are countries which do not support this cause for geo-political reasons. Pakistan does not want India to gain a permanent seat in the UNSC, neither do China, South Korea and North Korea want Japan to become a permanent member of the UNSC. Some of the regional rivals have formed a group amongst themselves informally known as the Coffee Club and later as the "Uniting for Consensus" (UfC) Group, thereby trying to derail the G-4 proposal and putting forward a proposal favouring an increase of only the non-permanent seats.[30] In fact, out of the G4, the candidature of Japan is the least likely, given the opposition to it by China, which also holds the veto power and is unlikely to relent. China views the prospects of its Asian peers, Japan and India joining the council's permanent membership as a strategic nightmare.[31] India and Japan need to cooperate further with like-minded countries to ensure that a whelming majority support their case for permanent member status in the UNSC. Cooperation between G4 is imperative in order to ensure that the UNSC reform process is taken up in due earnest and is not scuttled by hardball diplomacy of the P5 countries as was the case in 2005.

A section of experts think that with the growing clout of the G4 nations, they should strongly represent against the inertia of the UN to reform itself by being non-cooperative as they are amongst the top contributors of peacekeepers and funds to the UN. Whatever be the strategy, India and Japan along with Brazil and Germany will need to cooperate to ensure that the reforms are not stalled. Another section of experts on the subject propagate that India is diminishing its chances of being considered for permanent membership in the UNSC by clubbing along with countries such as Japan and Germany, which have regional competitors and strong historical baggage.

China Factor: Currently China provides a substantial contribution to the UN budget, being the second largest contributor to the peacekeeping budget and the third largest contributor to the UN budget. It is also the largest contributor in terms of troops to UN peacekeeping force, amongst the permanent members of the UN Security Council. This translates into an increased influence of China, in matters of UN peacekeeping. The CSIS report of September 2017 states that China has used its veto only 12 times, but two were cast where its economic interests were involved, like in Myanmar and Zimbabwe despite these being low on human rights records.[32] Another two vetoes were cast for influencing opinion against Taiwan when China was against sending UN peacekeepers to Guatemala and Macedonia because they had established diplomatic ties with Taiwan. When this act of casting vetos "over concerns over territorial integrity pertaining to Taiwan" is linked with Beijing's other recent coercive actions such as those against Mongolia due to a Dalai Lama visit, and against Japan when it is said to have halted exports of rare earth metals following the arrest of a Chinese trawler captain, the increasing front-lining of China in international affairs via the UN has an ominous ring.[33] Therefore, India and Japan need to seek closer integration with respect to each other in this regard.

In the Action Plan chalked out to advance India Japan Security Cooperation, which is based on the Joint Declaration on Security Cooperation dated December 29, 2009, both countries have agreed to institute under mentioned measures (refer Appendix D):

- 'Regular dialogue and cooperation on UN reform including early realisation of permanent membership of the UNSC of Japan and India, at the level of Deputy Vice-Minister, MoFA / Additional Secretary, MEA.[34]
- Mutual dispatch of lecturers/participants to UN peacekeeping operation-related seminars to be hosted by each side and exchange of experiences/information related to staff training.[35]
- Regular Dialogue and cooperation on UNPKO, including exchanges between Japanese Central Readiness Force/ International Peace Cooperation Activities Training Unit and CUNPK/Units experienced in peacekeeping operations from India, training of Japanese officers at the CUNPK, and sharing experience in and information on UNPKO and peace building.[36]

Divergences

There is a deep division amongst the countries that provide maximum funds for peacekeeping operations (large donors) like US, UK, Japan and Germany and the largest troop contributing countries (TCC) like India, Bangladesh, Pakistan, which send troops on ground. This is called the "gold versus blood debate", in which the TCCs are demanding a greater say in making the mandates for UN missions and more funding as current mandates have got tougher without a commensurate increase in funding or equipment.[37] India, as a leading troop contributor, has always lent its support for increasing the emoluments and reimbursements for the soldiers on ground and seeks simpler missions with greater freedom to the troops on ground. India and Japan are, therefore, at the opposite ends of the table in this debate. Were India and Japan able to cooperate within the UN on peacekeeping and, perhaps, evolve ways to bridge the contentious gold versus blood debate, they would not only make peacekeeping more effective but might also win kudos from African nations where most of the peace operations occur.[38]

Conclusion

UNPKO are significant avenues for countries to facilitate integrated operations of their uniformed personnel, thereby enhancing security cooperation. Being politically less sensitive and more acceptable to the international community, UNPKO can be an important plank where India and Japan can come together for greater cooperation amongst their armed forces. Moving towards a peacekeeping exercise between the two countries or having regional peacekeeping exercises will facilitate greater interoperability and integration amongst the militaries, and also be more acceptable to the peace-loving Japanese public. Divergences should be resolved through considerate understanding of each other's positions towards the greater good of humankind.

Notes

1. Akiho Shibata, 'Japanese Peacekeeping Legislation and Recent Developments in U.N. Operations', 19:2, *Yale Journal of International Law* at http://digitalcommons.law.yale.edu/cgi/viewcontent.cgi?article=1648&context=yjil, accessed on July 2, 2018.
2. https://www.reuters.com/article/us-japan-military-history-insight/gulf-war-trauma-began-japans-retreat-from-pacifism-idUSKBN0U300D20151220.
3. Ministry of Foreign Affairs, Japan, Japan's Response to the Gulf Crisis at http://www.mofa.go.jp/policy/other/bluebook/1991/1991-2-2.htm.
4. SDF still seeking UN opportunities 25 years after peacekeeping law's passage, JIJI, *The Japan Times*, June 17, 2017 at https://www.japantimes.co.jp/news/2017/06/17/national/politics-diplomacy/sdf-still-seeking-u-n-opportunities-25-years-peacekeeping-laws-passage/#.Wq9SAdR97Gg, accessed on March 18, 2018.
5. Defence of Japan, 2017 (Activities prescribed in Article 8 of the SDF Law (miscellaneous provision) or supplementary provisions 2 Missions defined in Article 3 of the SDF Law. The primary mission is to defend Japan. The secondary missions are the preservation of public order, activities in response to situations in areas surrounding Japan (in 2007) and international peace cooperation activities. In accordance with the entry into force of the Legislation for Peace and Security in 2016, "situations

in areas surrounding Japan" was revised to "situations that will have an important influence on Japan's peace and security".

6. Japan's Contribution to UN Peacekeeping Operations (PKO), Ministry of Foreign Affairs of Japan at http://www.mofa.go.jp/fp/ipc/page22e_000683.html.
7. Ministry of Foreign Affairs, Japan, Japan's Contribution to UN Peacekeeping Operations at https://www.mofa.go.jp/policy/un/pko/pamph2005.html, accessed on July 8, 2018.
8. Prof. Katsumi Ishizuka, Peacekeeping Contributor Profile: Japan at http://www.providingforpeacekeeping.org/2014/04/03/contributor-profile-japan/
9. Seana K. Magee, 'UN sizes up Japan as peacekeeper', *The Japan Times,* August 21, 2014 at https://www.japantimes.co.jp/news/2014/08/21/national/politics-diplomacy/u-n-sizes-up-japan-as-peacekeeper/#.WwmcpO6FPIU, accessed on July 24, 2018.
10. 'Japan's Efforts on Peace building—Towards Consolidation of Peace and Nation Building', Ministry of Foreign Affairs, Japan at https://www.mofa.go.jp/policy/un/pko/effort0704.pdf, accessed on September 27, 2018.
11. Saifuddin Ahmed and Md. Harun or-Rashid, 'Japan's Contribution to UN Peacekeeping Operations: Domestic and International Legal Perspective', *Law Journal Bangladesh*, January 4, 2017 at http://www.lawjournalbd.com/2017/01/japans-contribution-to-un-peacekeeping-operations-domestic-and-international-legal-perspective/, accessed on July 8, 2018.
12. The official version, however, is that the SDF Engineering Company had fulfilled its task in South Sudan and was no longer required there. As the author was personally deployed in South Sudan around this time, the perception as was prevalent in the environment has been mentioned.
13. UNMISS, 'Japanese Government Hands over its Peacekeepers' Equipment to UNMISS', May 23, 2017 at https://www.ss.emb-japan.go.jp/files/000259295.pdf, accessed on October 13, 2018.
14. Press Conference by the Chief Cabinet Secretary, June 13, 2017 at https://japan.kantei.go.jp/tyoukanpress/201706/13_p.html.
15. Data based on interaction with the Centre for UN Peace Keeping, New Delhi.
16. Ministry of Foreign Affairs, note 10.
17. Contributors to UN PKO by country and post, May 2018 at https://peacekeeping.un.org/sites/default/files/msr_may_2018.pdf, accessed on July 24, 2018.
18. *Defence of Japan, 2017*, Part III, Section 3 Efforts to Support International Peace Cooperation Activities, 3) Cooperation between Japan and Australia in UNMISS at http://www.mod.go.jp/e/publ/w_paper/pdf/2017/DOJ2017_3-2-3_web.pdf.

19. Complete transcript of the interview available at Ministry of Defence, Japan at http://www.mod.go.jp/e/jdf/sp/no63/sp_specialfeature.html, accessed on March 25, 2018.
20. 'Nissan eyes bigger share of East Africa market with vehicle plant in Kenya', *The Japan Times*, April 6, 2018 at https://www.japantimes.co.jp/news/2018/04/06/business/corporate-business/nissan-eyes-bigger-share-east-africa-market-vehicle-plant-kenya/#.WwrWsu6FPIV, accessed on May 2, 2018.
21. Ibid.
22. Inputs acquired during an interview with Dr Chandrasekhar, Professor, School of International Studies, Jawaharlal University, New Delhi.
23. Data acquired after an interaction with Director, CUNPK, India.
24. For the HADR exercises being held by Japan, Indian army personnel have been invited to participate as observers. This was stated in the Joint Press Statement on the India-Japan Annual Defence Ministerial Dialogue when the Defence Minister of India Arun Jaitley was on a bilateral visit to Japan from September 5–6, 2017. The Joint Press Statement is available at http://www.mod.go.jp/j/press/youjin/2017/09/05_jpr_e.html.
25. Author's Interview of Prof. CSR Murthy, Professor, School of International Studies, July 2, 2018.
26. Jakkie Cilliers, 'Does the UN Security Council need reform?', *World Economic Forum,* April 9, 2015 at https://www.weforum.org/agenda/2015/04/does-the-un-security-council-need-reform/, accessed on July 7, 2018.
27. Jakkie Cilliers, 'Does the UN Security Council need reform?', *World Economic Forum* at https://www.weforum.org/agenda/2015/04/does-the-un-security-council-need-reform/, accessed on July 7, 2018.
28. Ibid.
29. Ministry of Foreign Affairs, Brazil, Joint Press Statement—New York, Meeting of the Foreign Ministers of the G4 countries—Brazil, Germany, India and Japan—on United Nations Security Council Reform, September 21, 2017 at http://www.itamaraty.gov.br/en/press-releases/17475-meeting-of-the-foreign-ministers-of-the-g4-countries-brazil-germany-india-and-japan-on-united-nations-security-council-reform-joint-press-statement-new-york-september-20-2017, accessed on July 7, 2018.
30. Yeshi Choedon, 'A Setback for the Prospect of UN Security Council Reform!', Institute for Defence Studies and Analyses Comment, August 17, 2015 at https://idsa.in/idsacomments/ASetbackfortheProspectofUNSecurityCouncilReform_YeshiChoedon_170815, accessed on September 26, 2018.
31. Brahma Chellaney, *Asian Juggernaut—The Rise of China, India and Japan*, HarperCollins, New York, 2010, p. 270.

32. Manmohan Bahadur, 'The Power Play in Peacekeeping', *The Hindu,* December 12, 2017 at http://www.thehindu.com/opinion/op-ed/the-power-play-in-peacekeeping/ article21420388.ece, accessed on May 28, 2018.
33. Ibid.
34. Ministry of Foreign Affairs, Japan, 'Action Plan to advance Security Cooperation based on the Joint Declaration on Security Cooperation between Japan and India', December 29, 2009 at https://www.mofa.go.jp/region/asia-paci/india/pmv0912/action.html, accessed on June 7, 2018.
35. Ibid.
36. Ibid.
37. W.P.S. Sidhu, 'Keeping peace among peacekeepers', *The Mint,* June 22, 2015 at https://www.brookings.edu/opinions/keeping-peace-among-peacekeepers/, accessed on October 13, 2018.
38. WPSSidhu,'EnhancingtheIndia-Japanpartnership',Livemint,March1,2018 at http://www.livemint.com/Opinion/l91NGJCoDUJ0XvHTe1ZoGO/Enhancing-the-IndiaJapan-partnership.html, accessed on May 28, 2018.

PART III
Strategic Affinity

7

Consolidating the Strategic Partnership in a Regional Context

Our past has desired us to stand together. Our present is encouraging us to work together.

—PM Narendra Modi at CII Keidanren Luncheon[1]

Abstract

India Japan strategic partnership commenced in the early years of the 21st century initiated by a number of visits of senior leaders from both sides. The rise of China, though very significant, is not the only driver of this strategic partnership. Domestic factors have also played an important role in getting the two countries together. Along with these drivers, the concept of the Indo-Pacific has also ensured that both countries accept a sense of inclusiveness. These factors have led to a strategic affinity between the two countries. The prospects of convergence in the Indo-Pacific are bright but the relationship is also beset with challenges and divergences. Both countries need to take conscious initiatives to ensure that the strategic partnership delivers tangible results.

Background

The converging strategic interests of the two largest democracies of Asia owes a lot to the rise of China in the region and the consequent concerns of having to cope with a new regional order built on Chinese terms and conditions. The signing of the US-

India Nuclear deal in 2006 and subsequent prodding of Japan by the US to further open up to India was one of the triggers to break the logjam created by the conduct of the nuclear tests by India in 1998.

The Alondra Rainbow incident of October 1999 in which Indian navy and the Indian coast guards were instrumental in retrieving the hijacked Japanese ship, dramatically changed the way Japan looked at India. Then Foreign Minister of India, Jaswant Singh was invited to Japan in November 1999 and the Defence Minister George Fernandez paid a visit to Japan in Jan 2000. In the same year, post the visit of US President Clinton to India in March 2000, PM of Japan, Yoshiro Mori paid a visit to India, which recast the ties and paved the way for an India-Japan Global Partnership in the New Asian era. This broke the impasse that had developed due to imposition of sanctions by Japan post the Indian nuclear tests.[2] Other than economic factors, Japan recognised that India was emerging as a 'regional and global power' aided by robust economic growth. In Japan's quest for 'new friends' India with its new found policy of 'Look East', opening up of the economy and significant geo-strategic position in the IOR stood out as a very important country. This basis led to the signing of the India Japan Joint Security Declaration, in October 2008, asserting that the strategic partnership between the two countries would become 'an essential pillar for the future architecture of the region'.[3] This was followed by various initiatives from leaders of both sides and the relationship was upgraded to a Special Strategic and Global Partnership in 2014. Currently exchanges are held at various levels with the Annual Defence Ministerial Dialogue, the National Security Advisers' dialogue, the "2+2" Dialogue, the Defence Policy Dialogue and the Service-to-Service staff talks. The chronology of events of India-Japan Security relations has been shown at Table 7.1.

Table 7.1: Recasting India Japan ties in the 21st Century

Year	Event
2000	Visit of Indian Defence Minister George Fernandez to Japan.
2000	Visit of PM Yoshiro Mori to India. "Global Partnership between Japan and India" established between the two countries.
2005	Visit of PM Koizumi to India. An Eight-fold Initiative for Strengthening Japan-India Global Partnership in New Asian Era worked out.
2006	Dr Manmohan Singh visits Japan. Japan-India relationship elevated to "Global and Strategic Partnership".
2007	PM Shinzo Abe visits India. Delivers the 'Confluence of Two Seas' speech in the Indian Parliament. Road map drawn to realise this partnership.
2008	Dr Manmohan Singh visits Japan. India-Japan Joint Security Declaration signed.
2009	PM Hatoyama visits India. Action Plan laid down to advance the Joint Security Declaration.
2010	Vision Statement Of Strategic Partnership given out.
2011	PM Noda visits India. Enhancement To Vision Statement agreed to.
2012-2014	Yearly Summit Meetings Of PMs, Joint Naval Training Agreement signed. The Emperor and Empress of Japan visit India.
2014	Japan-India relationship upgraded to Special Strategic and Global Partnership.
2015	PM Shinzo Abe visits India. Japan-India Vision 2025 announced. Agreement on the "Transfer of the Defence Equipment and Technology" and Agreement concerning "Security Measures for the Protection of Classified Military Information" signed.
2016	Signing of "India Japan Civil Nuclear Deal". Both PMs agree to coordinate the "Free and Open India and Pacific Strategy" and the "Act East" policy.
2017	"Year of Japan India Friendly Exchanges" observed.

Source: Compiled from Various Sources.

Elements Driving the Strategic Partnership

The rising power of China is seen as a common geo-political challenge by both India and Japan, bringing them closer in a hedging strategy. However, it would be incorrect to say that this challenge is the sole factor governing the relations between the two countries. Drivers of this strategic partnership have been identified through an Impact-Uncertainty graph (refer Appendix E for details). The drivers of this strategic partnership and efforts by India and Japan to enhance the same have been discussed in the subsequent paragraphs.

The China Factor and Efforts to Counter Chinese Influence

The aggressive rise of China and its claims over the South China Sea and islands based on the nine-dash line is a cause for concern to both India and Japan as major SLOCs pass through it. SLOCs are the life-line of Japan with over 90 per cent of its requirement of natural resources passing through it. India also has huge stakes in the South China Sea with 55 per cent of its trade moving through it. Though Japan considers the Japan-US alliance as the cornerstone of Japan's diplomatic and security policies, it has realised that the waning influence of the US and the disinterest of the present Trump regime obligates it to seek new friends and partners, in order to affect prevalence of a rules based order.[4] Japan finds in India a comfortable partner enshrined with similar democratic values, a follower of international norms and rule of law and an emerging global power. PM Modi's policy of hedging by diversifying partners and its growing interests in the Indo-Pacific, coupled with an emphasis on short-term deliverables, made New Delhi amenable to closer ties.[5]

Sri Lanka: Japan-Sri Lanka relations, which have grown since 1960 has seen a boost with Japan competing to expand economic and military engagements due to the strategic location of Sri Lanka which lies merely 12 nautical miles north of the busiest East West shipping lane in the IOR. India and Sri Lanka, on the other hand have historical and cultural relations which span back to around 2500 years. India is Sri Lanka's closest neighbour and both sides have built upon a legacy of intellectual, cultural, religious and linguistic intercourse."[6] China with its focus on becoming a major player in the IOR has aggressively courted Sri Lanka, given its strategic location and has come up with a number of investments and infrastructure building projects through its economic might and well developed construction capabilities.

Resultantly, both India and Japan share similar geopolitical concerns over the ever increasing presence of China in the IOR, which is being gauged through its push to maintain bases and ports. In Sri Lanka, China has struck a 'Concession Agreement' and has commenced full scale operations through the Hambantota International Port Group (HIPG) and Hambantota International Port Services (HIPS), two new companies set up by the China Merchants Port Holdings Company and the Sri Lanka Ports Authority in December 2017.[7] This will be a 99-year lease of the Hambantota Port as a result of conversion of Colombo's US$ 6 billion debt into equity. Beijing, having "invested" around US$ 1.6 billion in building the port, reaped the benefits when Colombo was unable to make repayments on the "loan" and was thus, forced to sell a 70 per cent stake to the China Merchants Ports Holdings.[8] Hambantota is strategically located about 10 nautical miles from the important SLOCs in the Indian Ocean, which permit passage of two-thirds of the world's oil and half of all container shipments with more than 60,000 ships navigating the vital SLOCs.

In an effort to counter the growing Chinese influence in Sri Lanka, India and Japan have agreed to set up a US$ 250 million LNG import terminal in Sri Lanka at Kerawalapitiya on western Sri Lankan coast, where Sri Lanka plans to build a 300 MW gas-fired power plant adjoining an existing power plant.[9] The existing plant, which uses oil to generate power would also be converted to LNG once the terminal is set up and gas imports start.[10] The Indian company Petronet and a Japanese company have agreed to set up the LNG terminal as a 50:50 joint venture.[11] On its part, India also looks towards quarantining Chinese influence at Hambantota, by gaining control of the Mattala Rajapaksa International Airport, some 25 miles (40 km) away from the Hambantota port, dubbed the world's emptiest airport, in order to monitor Beijing's growing presence in the country.[12] In terms of defence cooperation and procurements too, there exists a sharp competition to nullify the Chinese and Pakistani influence. Sri Lankan efforts to procure 12 JF-17 fighter aircrafts built in Pakistan in collaboration with China, was met by an Indian offer of Tejas, still in its trial period, as an alternative.[13] When China offered an US$ 11 million loan to buy an offshore patrol vessel in 2016 (a purchase yet to be completed), Japan, in return, has offered to provide two patrol vessels.[14] This competition can also be seen in Sri Lanka's recent joint training mission with India, as well as an ongoing joint hydro graphic survey to update maritime navigation charts of the increasingly busy nearby shipping lanes.[15] Incidentally, 65 Japanese MSDF ships have visited the Port of Colombo from 2008 to 2017, which is second only to Indian warships visiting Sri Lanka.[16] Japan has provided patrol boats to the Sri Lankan coast guard based on an agreement signed by the Sri Lanka Government and the Japan International Cooperation Agency (JICA) in June 2016 and is also planning to offer used P-3C patrol planes to Sri Lanka in addition to sending its coast guard ships to Sri Lanka to train the Sri Lankan navy in coastal security duties.[17] In order to further enhance its economic integration with Sri Lanka, Japan has offered a US$ 1.85 billion equivalent loan to build a light rail transit system in Colombo with easy payment terms (an annual interest of 0.1 per cent, a 12-year grace period and a payback over 40 years).[18]

Bangladesh: India and Bangladesh relations are anchored in history, culture, language and shared values of secularism, democracy and countless other commonalities between the two countries.[19] Bangladesh shares around 4156 km of international border with India, which is among the top five longest land borders in the world. On the other hand, Bangladesh-Japan relations, established in February 1972, have also seen a boost with Japan emerging as a trusted development partner providing loans and aid to Bangladesh. The bilateral relations between the two countries have gradually enhanced in areas of trade and investments.

In recent times, the Chinese influence in Bangladesh has been evident with Beijing having supplied Dhaka with five maritime patrol vessels, two corvettes, 44 tanks, and 16 fighter jets, as well as surface-to-air and anti-ship missiles since 2010.[20] In addition, Dhaka has also ordered new Ming-class submarines from China.[21] China is engaged in upgrading Chittagong port, has won a US$ 705 million contract for a two-lane tunnel under the Karnaphuli River connecting Chittagong port and Karnaphuli River Valley and many other infrastructure projects such as the US$ 4.47 billion Padma Bridge rail link project, power distribution projects, and improvement of transmission lines in Bangladesh.[22] Chinese investors are also keen to shift labour-intensive industries such as garment manufacturing to Bangladesh in order to exploit its cheap labour.[23] In 2005, China overtook India as Bangladesh's major source of imports most notably in defence trade and Bangladesh is now the second largest importer of Chinese arms in the world after Pakistan. Out of the three promised Belt and Road Initiative (BRI) mega projects in Bangladesh, the Payra Coal power project is under construction and the other two, viz. the Dhaka-Jessore rail line and the Karnaphuli underwater tunnel are in the planning stage.[24]

Increasing Chinese influence, therefore, presents a threat within the immediate neighbourhood of India, For India, Bangladesh is a very important part of its Act East policy as well as provides a direct land access from India to Myanmar and South East Asia. In order to enhance Indian influence in Bangladesh, Indian PM Narendra Modi visited Dhaka in June 2018 and signed agreements with the Hasina government, including a Land Boundary Agreement, which ended a four-decade old border dispute, and demarcated borders and river water sharing between the two countries. A commitment of US$ 2 billion line of credit was made and a previously committed US$ 800 million was also assured to be released shortly. A total of 22 agreements were signed, including those on maritime security and the establishment of special economic zones in Bangladesh.[25] Indian businessmen visiting Dhaka also promised to invest over US$ 11 billion in a number of infrastructure projects, which included an LNG plant and a gas pipeline from Odisha to Bangladesh. According to media reports, India's state-owned Bharat Heavy Electricals Limited (BHEL) is soon to sign a US$ 1.6 billion power station construction contract with Bangladesh after undercutting China's Harbin Electric International Company.[26] This thermal power project with an installed capacity of 1,320 MW is planned to be located in the Khulna district of South Bangladesh and would be the largest project abroad by any Indian power company. The Sonadia sea port development was previously agreed to have been assigned to China, however, when Prime Minister Hasina visited Beijing in 2014, she did not sign the agreement, reportedly due to pressure from some countries.[27] Japan, on the other hand, would build a new port in Matabari, a few kilometres away from Sonadia.[28] Beijing said it wanted to develop another port at Payra.[29] However, the Payra Port Authority under the shipping ministry of Bangladesh and Belgium-based company Jan De Nul signed an agreement in December 2017 to jointly conduct dredging on the main channel of the country's third seaport Payra in Patuakhali. Petronet has also signed preliminary agreement to build a 7.5 MT LNG terminal in Bangladesh.

Bangladesh seems to be walking the balancing rope between the three major powers India, Japan and China, in Asia and is attempting to garner for itself, maximum benefits for investment and infrastructure.

Tussle Over Maldives: The Maldives, comprising of nearly 1200 islands is located alongside key SLOCs in the IOR, and hence, strategically important. Traditionally under the Indian sphere of influence, China stepped up its engagement in Maldives as it realised that this island country was key to its "Belt and Road Initiative". Under President Abdulla Yameen, Maldives drew closer to China and utilised Chinese investments to build infrastructure in the country. They include a US$ 830 million investment to upgrade the Maldives airport, build a 2 km (1.3-mile) bridge to link the airport island with the capital Male and construction of a 25-storey apartment complex and hospital.[30] China and Maldives also proposed developing a Joint

Ocean Observation Station in Makunudhoo, the westernmost atoll in Maldives. This development had the capability to pose as another pearl in the 'String of Pearls theory' for India. Meanwhile, some 306,000 Chinese tourists visited the Maldives in 2017—accounting for 21 per cent of the country's total number of visitors. Docking of ships in Male in 2017 further aggravated India's concerns.

Meanwhile, the India—Maldives relations deteriorated under President Yameen. Maldives declined to participate in the biennial maritime exercise 'Milan' in 2018 conducted by India. It also initiated a process to return helicopters, personnel and other assets given by India. Renewal visa applications for Indians were cancelled without valid reasons and pro-Indian Maldivian leaders arrested. Scales tipped in favour of India only when in the elections held in September 2018, President Yameen was ousted and opposition leader Ibrahim Mohamed Solih, who is considered pro-Indian was democratically elected. It was, however, reported that the Chinese investments were mounting a debt burden on the Maldives and the estimated US$ 1.3 billion debt to China was more than a quarter of its GDP and was about 80 per cent of the overall foreign debt owed by Maldives.[31]

Chinese Bases in the Indo-Pacific: In addition to wielding influence through infrastructure and port building activities, Chinese strategic interests in the IOR have taken concrete shape with the establishment of bases at Djibouti and Gwadar. The Djibouti base became operational in August 2017. It is located astride Bab-el-Mandeb—the key chokepoint connecting Asia and Europe and greatly improves the ability of the Chinese navy to protect China's overseas interests. Purportedly, China has deployed this base for support to anti-piracy, to assist UN peacekeeping activities as well as to assist the huge Chinese diaspora in the Middle East and Africa, when required. The evacuations of more than 35,000 Chinese nationals in February-March 2011 and of more than 900 Chinese from Libya in August 2014 were well appreciated by the international community and are examples of the emergence of a new diplomatic imperative: overseas citizen protection. The second base being constructed at Gwadar will be the culmination of the China Pakistan Economic Corridor (CPEC) through Pakistan. Gwadar is strategically located astride the SLOCs emanating from the Gulf of Aden and dominates the SLOCs towards the West Coast of India. Before Chinese intentions in Djibouti were clear, a 2014 article by experts from the PLAN-affiliated Chinese Naval Research Institute listed the following locations as possible sites for a Chinese military outpost in the IOR: the Bay of Bengal; Sittwe (Myanmar); Gwadar (Pakistan); Djibouti (Djibouti); Seychelles; Hambantota (Sri Lanka); and Dar es Salaam (Tanzania). These places were explicitly mentioned because of their strategic or economic importance, but most likely both.[32]

More so, Chinese activities of island building in the South China Sea, deploying military assets on these islands and infrastructure building activity have raised concerns amongst the littorals in the Western Pacific and has highlighted the vulnerability of littoral nations who find it increasingly difficult to safeguard national interests in the wake of the Chinese economic heft and military muscle. In order to ensure status quo and security, both India and Japan have realised the imperative to assist littoral countries to possess strong maritime capability as a deterrent to forcible changes. Assistance in terms of military equipment and capability building, being provided by Japan to littoral countries in the West Pacific has already been mentioned in Chapter 5.

Certain additional capacity building measures undertaken by Japan are tabulated in Table 7.2.

Table 7.2: Capacity Building of East Asia Littorals by Japan

Country	**Areas of Capacity Building Activities**
Timor Leste	HADR; Civil Engineering
Cambodia	Civil Engineering
Vietnam	Underwater Medicine, PKO, Aviation Safety, HADR, Aviation Medicine, International Aviation Law
Indonesia	Oceanography; International Aviation Law; International Maritime Law

Country	Areas of Capacity Building Activities
Mongolia	Military Medicine
Myanmar	Civil Engineering; Underwater Medicine; HADR, Aviation Meteorology
Papua New Guinea	HADR; Military Music
Philippines	HADR International Aviation Law; Diesel Engine Maintenance
Malaysia	International Aviation Law; HADR
Laos	HADR
Thailand	International Aviation Law; Aviation Safety
ASEAN Countries	HADR

Source: Defence of Japan 2017.

India too has been proactively engaging littorals in the IOR to extend material, training and infrastructure support in order to facilitate the build-up of a strong indigenous maritime capability. Efforts by India in this regard are tabulated in Table 7.3.

Table 7.3: India's Engagement with Littorals of the IOR and the Pacific

Seychelles	• Very close ties. Prevented couple of coups in the 1980s. • Maritime advisor of Seychelles is an Indian navy officer. • Has provided financial support (US$ 100 million in 2018) to augment defence capabilities and equipment including Dornier Do 228 aircraft and Chetak helicopters. • Renovation of airfield and construction of deep sea port in Assumption Island by India. • Gifted patrolling ships and interceptor boats. • Eight Coastal Surveillance Radar Systems (CSRS) established in 2015.
Mauritius	• Provided US$ 500 million credit for security. • Agreements on opening up of blue economy. • Transport Infrastructure (sea and air links) for Agalega Islands.
Indonesia	• Joint Drills in CI Training.
Cambodia	• Training of Cambodian Air Force pilots.

Malaysia	• Training of Malaysian Air Force pilots of Su-MKM.
Singapore	• Joint Exercises. • Provide basing facilities to armed forces assets and personnel from Singapore.
Myanmar	• Cooperation in flushing out militants. • Cooperation in technology crucial for maintaining Internal Security and coastal maritime patrolling capability.
Vietnam	• Deepening security cooperation. • Training of Air Force fighters and Submariners. • Provision of spares of combat equipment.

Source: Data compiled by the Author from various sites and research.

Indian armed forces also conduct various joint exercises with other militaries to enhance interoperability, standardises procedures and address common issues of interest and concern. As part of the Indian government's vision of SAGAR (Security and Growth for All in the Region), the Indian navy has also been involved in assisting countries in the IOR with EEZ surveillance, Search and Rescue, HADR and other capacity-building and capability-enhancement activities.[33] India's joint exercises with South East Asian Countries are as under:[34]

Table 7.4: Joint Exercises of India with South East Asian Countries

Country	**Exercise**
Myanmar	IMBAX (Army Exercise) India-Myanmar Coordinated Patrol (IMCOR) (Navy Exercise)
Thailand	Maitree (Army Exercise) India-Thailand Coordinated Patrol (Indo-Thai CORPAT)
Indonesia	Garuda Shakti (Army Exercise) CORPAT and Bilateral Maritime Exercise
Singapore	Bold Kurukshetra SIMBEX Annual Exercise (Navy Exercise) SINDEX (AF Exercise) Agni Warrior
ASEAN	Exercise Force 18 (Army Exercise)
Sri Lanka	Slinex Mitra Shakti

Country	Exercise
Bangladesh	Sampriti
Mongolia	Khan Quest Nomadic Elephant
Nepal	Surya Kiran
Seychelles	Lamitye
Oman	Naseem Al Bahr, Al Nagah
Maldives	Ekuverin
Vietnam	Vinbax
Malaysia	Harimau Shakti
Multi National Naval Exercise in the Indian Ocean	Milan

Source: Data compiled by the author from various sources.

Domestic Factors as Drivers

The China threat theory might have triggered substantial political and security cooperation between India and Japan, but over-emphasizing the 'China threat' has not helped deepen bilateral cooperation because of different diplomatic and security situations.[35] Other domestic factors that have played an important role in paving the way to a meaningful relationship between the two countries are enumerated in succeeding paragraphs.

Economic Growth: In addition to the China factor as a driver, domestic factors in both India and Japan have also contributed towards the converging strategic partnership between India and Japan. Japan, with an economy, which is projected to reach 1.25 per cent growth in 2018 and 2019 is reaching outwards to enhance its economic growth momentum. Traditionally, consumer spending, which has a major role in overall economic growth, has been restricted in Japan. On the other hand, India with its population of 1.3 billion presents a huge market to Japanese manufactured products. With a median age of only 27.6 years in India, the long term benefits of entering such a market for Japan are obvious.

Infrastructure: Japanese Prime Minister Shinzo Abe's Enhanced Partnership for Quality Infrastructure in Asia (EPQI) aims to consolidate Japan's regional clout among the emerging Asian economies.[36] EPQI, which is often viewed as a competing formulation vis-à-vis the Chinese mega infrastructure designs, is critical to achieving the goals of Japan's national growth strategy. The Japan Business Federation has identified Asia and countries like Indonesia, Vietnam, India and Myanmar, where it aggressively intends pursuing an EPQI strategy. The 2010 Research Report entitled "The Comprehensive Asia Development Plan", which was commissioned by the Japanese government, Japan's Economic Research Institute for ASEAN and East Asia lays down that Japan's vision for infrastructure connectivity in Asia is composed of three initiatives: the well-known East-West Economic Corridor (running from the port of Danang in central Vietnam through Laos and Thailand to the port of Mawlamyine in Southeast Myanmar); the Mekong India Economic Corridor (connecting Ho Chi Minh City, Phnom Penn, Bangkok and potentially extending to the port of Dawei in southern Myanmar and beyond); and the third initiative being the Maritime ASEAN Economic Corridor that would consolidate port development, marine economic development and information, communications, and technological networks connecting Brunei, Indonesia, Malaysia, the Philippines and Singapore.[37]

A comparison of the infrastructure projects of Japan and China in South East Asia gives an indication of the intense competition that is prevailing between China and Japan in the region.

Table 7.5: Comparison of Infrastructure Projects of China and Japan

Country	China Based Projects	Japan Based Projects
Cambodia	20	2
Indonesia	46	47
Laos	31	6
Malaysia	30	16
Myanmar	6	8

Country	China Based Projects	Japan Based Projects
Philippines	7	28
Singapore	12	23
Thailand	5	22
Timor-Leste	4	1
Vietnam	30	84
Total	191	237

Source: *BMIResearch*[38]

In addition to the finished goods, Japan also intends to export infrastructure in sectors such as railways, airports, ports, harbours, telecommunication and power plants to an infrastructure-hungry and infrastructure-deficit India. Connectivity and infrastructure development are important aspects of economic collaboration between India and Japan. Several such projects have been implemented in India with Japanese collaboration. Some projects currently under implementation include the Mumbai Ahmedabad High Speed Rail, Metro rail projects in various cities of India, the Delhi-Mumbai Industrial Corridor and the Western Dedicated Freight Corridor.[39]

Strategically, infrastructural development in the North East region, which serves as a gateway for India's Act East policy has been the focus of Japan in a regional context. India is working on a number of road and bridge projects to improve connectivity with its neighbours in the East. The Cabinet Committee on Economic Affairs chaired by Prime Minister Modi has approved the upgradation and widening of 65 km of the Imphal-Moreh Section of NH-39 in Manipur at a cost of Rs 1630.29 crore.[40] The project is being developed with ADB's loan assistance under the South Asian Sub-Regional Economic Cooperation (SASEC) Road Connectivity Investment Programme, which aims at upgradation of road infrastructure in Bangladesh, Bhutan, Nepal and India (BBIN), thereby improving regional connectivity.[41] This corridor forms part of the India-Myanmar-Thailand Trilateral (IMT) highway or the Asian Highway No. 01 (AH01). This highway can be considered as India's Gateway to the East and will connect Moreh in Manipur to Mae Sot in Thailand via Myanmar. Thus, trade, commerce and tourism in the region will get a boost.[42]

Map 7.1: The India Myanmar Thailand Highway

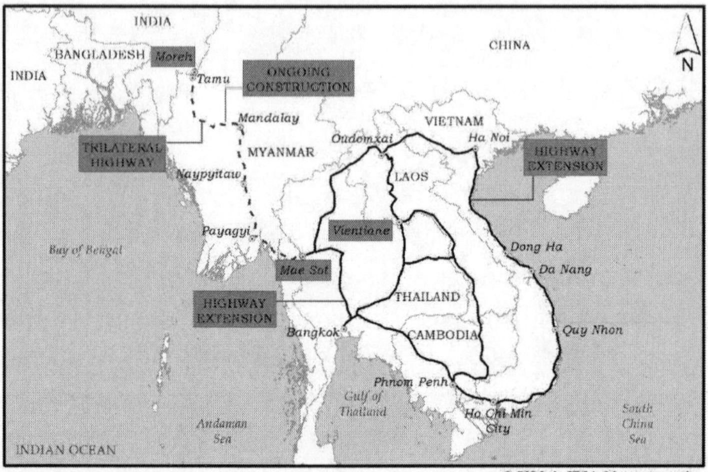

© GIS Lab, IDSA, Map not to scale.

Source: Ministry of External Affairs, India.

The security implications of these developments, however, cannot be ignored. A good network of infrastructure facilitates prompt mobilisation of own forces, whenever necessary. A weak infrastructural support is a logistical nightmare for military planners in terms of supplies, movement, transport of heavy armament and subsequent support during a conflict situation. Aspects such as evacuation of casualties, movement of reinforcements and provision of medical aid are very important and such issues are automatically catered for through an enhancement in connectivity and infrastructure. Given Japan's historic connection to North East India, it has offered to provide loan and aid for social and highway development, which will complement the connectivity initiatives pursued by India in Bangladesh, Myanmar and beyond, besides BBIN (Bangladesh, Bhutan, India, Nepal). Japan's contribution through its Expanded Partnership for Quality Infrastructure (EPQI) will assist in speeding up connectivity amongst nations in the region.

Make in India: In addition, India looks towards Japan for introducing technology in the manufacturing sector through its Make in India programme. In security terms, dual use technology and defence equipment technology will facilitate capability development and indigenisation. Various institutes have opened up in India to impart necessary skills that will assist interactions and understanding of Japanese methods and business practices. The total number of Japanese companies registered in India as of October 2017 was 1,369 (an increase of 64 [5 per cent growth] from 1,305, as of October 2016) and the total number of Japanese business establishments was 4,838 (an increase by 248 [6 per cent growth] as compared to 4,590 as of October 2015).[43]

Therefore, domestic agendas of both governments are also playing an important role as drivers for this strategic relationship. The strategic relations have been induced with an additional element of inclusivity with the acceptance of Indo-Pacific as a concept instead of the Asia-Pacific.

The Concept of the Indo Pacific

The term Indo-Pacific has gained relevance over the past few years, and has come to replace the earlier used 'Asia-Pacific' in strategic discourse in this part of the world. From an Indian geopolitical perspective, it represents the inclusion of the Western Pacific within the range of India's security interests, thus stretching beyond the traditional focus on the Indian Ocean theatre.[44] The concept of 'Indo-Pacific' gained prominence during the visit of President Trump to Asia in November 2017, where-in the US administration repeatedly emphasized the term in lieu of the earlier used term 'Asia Pacific'. This basically denotes that the swath of the region being referred to earlier as the Asia Pacific has been enlarged. The Indian Ocean, by its geographical expanse brings India into the context of any event being referred to. Way back in 2007, PM Shinzo Abe while delivering his famous 'Confluence of Two Seas' speech in the Indian Parliament in October 2007 also referred to the same idea of a geographical expanse touching the Eastern coast of Africa and encompassing the entire Western Pacific and its littorals.

For India, this concept may seem appealing as it represents an opportunity to project that India's security interests are also the shared concerns of the US and that they are not alone in protecting their own turf from increased Chinese aggressiveness. It meshes in very well with India's Act East policy, giving it a sort of inclusiveness in the East Asian matters. For Japan, this has become one of the key concepts in contemporary foreign policy and the promotion of this concept has been one of the six priorities of the Japanese FM Taro Kono.[45] Trump's willingness to carry the strategy first propagated by Abe in 2007 as the regional policy of the US underlines that the US has not given up on its responsibilities of ensuring a rules-based regional order. Not only Japan, but it has also reassured other nations in this region of continued US stakes albeit shared stakes in the region. For Japan, at the core of this Free and Open Indo-Pacific Strategy lies the opportunity to promote free trade, infrastructure investment and development to countries in the vast expanse of Asia, Middle East and Africa. Japan aims at presenting "Free and Open Indo-Pacific" as a system in which international maritime areas remain a global common, which are governed by the rule of law and not might-makes-right, and that will allow small and large trading states to flourish alike.[46] This concept also provides a fillip to the prevalent cooperation in aspects of non- traditional maritime threat such as piracy, maritime terrorism, illegal fishing, and smuggling.

The concept of a seamless connectivity between the two oceans has reinforced the idea of having close cooperation between the two countries by way of supporting each other logistically in this vast expanse. India and Japan can cooperate by signing the Acquisition and Cross Servicing Agreement (ACSA) wherein both can provide access to each other's military assets in their respective bases and ensure easy provision of supplies, repairs and maintenance. The issue of seamless Maritime Domain Awareness, which has been mentioned earlier in the previous chapters, also gets facilitated.

India in the meantime, is seeking a wider footprint in the IOR. The signing of an agreement with Indonesia to develop a port in the city of Sabang has been a strategic move related to maritime security in the western entrance to the Strait of Malacca. A pact with Singapore on logistical support for ships, submarines and military aircraft during visits, also ensures a greater acceptability in the region. Again, for the first time, India has carried out naval exercises with the Vietnamese navy in the South China Sea. The signing of an agreement with Oman for unrestricted access to the port of Duqm in Oman will ensure logistics support to Indian naval ships for sustained operations in the western IOR. Signing of a logistics agreement with France also opens up French military bases in the IOR.

The Chinese response to the development of a change in the perception of the region from Asia-Pacific to Indo-Pacific has been met with concern and scepticism. Liu Zongyi, a Chinese scholar believes that "Indo-Pacific" and "Asia-Pacific" are just different terms; the key point will be their substance.[47] China's growing economic influence, potentially rewriting the existing economic rules and norms, is a key factor behind the four nations- US, India, Australia and Japan, coming closer. If [the Indo-Pacific] the concept were developed as a counterbalancing mechanism against China's "Belt and Road Initiative with a different set of economic rules—based on freedom, openness, transparency and fairness, China would feel uncomfortable, resulting in harsher competition over regional economic hegemony.[48] China has said that regional cooperation should neither be politicised nor exclusionary, responding to US President Donald Trump's use of the term "Indo-Pacific" during his trip to Asia.[49] Asked about China's view of the Indo-Pacific concept, Chinese Foreign Ministry spokesman Geng Shuang said that peaceful development and win-win cooperation were the trends of the times.[50] As per him, "All sides can come up with their own plans and positions on how to promote regional cooperation, but we hope that plans and positions can accord with and conform to this trend, can suit the general trend of events in the world, and that the relevant plans and positions are open and inclusive, benefiting the promotion of win-win cooperation by all sides, and avoid politicised or exclusionary arrangements".[51]

Partnership Prospects in the Indo-Pacific

Japan desires a "free and open Indo-Pacific", a theme Sonoura expounded on at the Raisina Dialogue held at New Delhi in 2018. There he stated that it was a coming together of Japan's Indo-Pacific policy and India's Act East policy.[52] "We need to share the importance of rule of law and freedom of navigation among related countries; the next step is infrastructure development based on global standards, so that connectivity among countries is increased; the third step would be maritime law enforcement and disaster management that would ensure the stability and prosperity in the Indo-Pacific region.[53] Therefore, we would like to connect and combine our Indo-Pacific strategy and India's Act East policy as one big picture. That's the synergy we seek",[54] This is the kind of grand strategy that incorporates a stronger bilateral relationship as well as a multilateral one, between Japan-India-US, Japan-US-Australia and the Quadrilateral, Japan-US-India-Australia, seeking to tilt the strategic balance away from China.[55] Japan has been invited to invest in various areas in this region and the India-Japan Act East Forum was set up to focus on strategic projects such as connectivity and road network development, electricity, and disaster management.[56] A similar cooperation for infrastructural upgradation in the Andaman and Nicobar Islands is also emerging with Japan constructing a 15-megawatt diesel power plant on South Andaman Island and a Japanese firm having been awarded the contract to lay an OFC connection between Chennai and Port Blair. Incidentally, no other country has been allowed to invest in the strategic regions of the North East and Andamans before. This displays the levels of trust and confidence that have been built over the years between the two countries. Both countries are also collaborating in regional outreach from Asia to Africa.

The term Indo-Pacific has yet to crystallise in the form of a coherent policy or a definition. Ironically, the concept of Indo-Pacific reinforces the reality that the US may no longer be able to maintain the strategic status quo in the Pacific and Indian Oceans.[57] Both India and Japan are acutely concerned about the possibility of a US-China 'G2' to manage Asian affairs based on respective national interests. For Japan, a US-China condominium and the 'abandonment' of Japan is the worst of all strategic scenarios.[58] Therefore, by forging a strong partnership with each other, India and Japan are also signalling to the US and China that no regional order in Asia will be viable without their active participation.[59] Some experts believe that although Japan must secure the peace and stability of the Indo-Pacific region, the concept may not be sufficient to guarantee Japan's survival. The silver lining is, however, that countries like India are willing to exercise collective responsibility to supplement US efforts in the region. Whether it remains a mere rhetoric or realistically defines the dynamics of the Asia and Pacific regions with an underlying India Japan collaborative theme, needs to be seen. Nevertheless, as an indication of growing rapprochement, both countries have agreed to collaborate together in Africa for enhanced connectivity between Asia and Africa through the AAGC.

Asia Africa Growth Corridor (AAGC): As an indication of converging economic and security interests in the Indo-Pacific, India and Japan developed the idea of the AAGC, which was highlighted in the joint declaration issued by Prime Ministers Narendra Modi and Shinzo Abe in November 2016.[60] The AAGC will envisage people-centric sustainable growth strategy, details of which would be evolved through a process of detailed consultations across Asia and Africa, engaging various stakeholders.[61] India has had historical ties with Africa. India's bilateral trade with Africa has risen five-fold in the last decade, from US$ 11.9 billion in 2005–2006 to US$ 56.7 billion in 2015–2016 and is expected to reach US$ 100 billion by 2018.[62] Calling the synergy at the third India Africa Forum, the power of 55 (India and 54 African countries), Prime Minister Modi said, "Today, the dreams of one-third of humanity have come together under one roof." The declaration at the forum placed development cooperation at the heart of India-Africa partnership, with India unveiling US$ 10 billion in Lines of Credit for a host of development projects over the next five years and pledging a grant assistance of US$ 600 million.[63] The AAGC is proposed to be raised on the four pillars of Development and Cooperation Projects, Quality Infrastructure and Institutional Connectivity, Enhancing Capacities and Skills, and People-to-People partnership.[64] The centrality of people to people partnership would be the unique feature of this initiative and the strengths of AAGC will be aligned with the development priorities of different countries and sub-regions of Africa, taking advantage of simultaneous homogeneity and heterogeneity among them.[65]

Japan promotes collaborative development in Africa through the multilateral platform of Tokyo International Conference on African Development (TICAD), set up in 1993.[66] This forum meets every five years in partnership with the United Nations Office of Special Adviser on Africa, the United Nation Development Programme, the World Bank and the African Union Commission.[67] Apart from the TICAD initiative, Japan after the end of Cold War has emerged as the top contributor to ODA programme benefitting several African nations.[68] At the last TICAD summit, Prime Minister Shinzo Abe pledged US$ 30 billion in the form of public and private sector investments in Africa.[69] As India's engagement with the continent is consultative and to a large extent, driven by the demands of the African countries, India postulates that its partnership is an amalgam of African development priorities in keeping with the African Union's long term plan and the Africa Agenda 2063, as well as India's development objectives.[70] Therefore, both India and Japan have been intensely engaging African nations in the recent years. A Research Support Unit (RSU) comprising of the Research and Information System for Developing Countries (RIS), New Delhi, the Economic Research Institute for the ASEAN and East Asia (ERIA), Jakarta, and the Institute of Developing Economies (IDE-JETRO), Tokyo, have developed a Vision Document for AAGC based on consultations with Asian and African think-tanks. The RSU will conduct the preparation of the Asia Africa Growth Corridor Study in 2017–2018, and present it to the Governments of India and Japan, and other Leaders and policy makers of Asia and Africa in 2018.[71] Overall, the AAGC aims at sustainable growth and development, cooperation between important stakeholders of Asia and Africa, development of institutional and industrial corridors between Asia and Africa as well as contribution to a holistic integration of Asia and Africa.[72] It is also a test bed for the convergence of complementary strengths of India, in Human Resource Development and of Japan, in quality capacity building.

Strategic Economic Partnership: Other than the AAGC, both countries are also cooperating in the aspect of REM—a strategic resource, 90 per cent of which was, hitherto, controlled solely by China. India also has a fair amount of reserves of REM, which has now been tapped by Japan for extraction and its imports. Rare earths are a series of chemical elements found in the Earth's crust that are vital to many modern technologies.[73] Their unique magnetic, luminescent, and electrochemical properties are the reason why these elements help make many technologies perform with reduced weight, reduced emissions, and energy consumption; or give them greater efficiency, performance, miniaturisation, speed, durability, and thermal stability.[74] There are 17 elements that are considered to be rare earth elements—15 elements in the lanthanide series (in the Periodic Table) and two additional elements that share similar chemical properties.[75] Rare earth metals are used in iPads, plasma TVs, lasers, and catalytic converters for car engines.[76] For example, Dysprosium, a rare earth metal, is crucial because it is the strongest magnet in the world and remains stable at very high temperatures; Neodymium is used in hybrid cars; and Terbium cuts power use for low-energy light bulbs by 40 per cent.[77] The rare earth metals are also used in precision-guided weapons, missiles such as the Hellfire, military avionics, satellites, and night-vision equipment such as the US M1A2 Abrams tank and the Aegis Spy-1 radar, both of which rely on Samarium.[78]

In a recent discovery, scientists of Japan's Agency for Marine-Earth Science and the University of Tokyo have found deposits that are just two to four metres from the seabed surface at higher concentrations than found anywhere on the globe.[79] This is the second such discovery after an announcement of a break-through in extracting gas from methane hydrates under the ocean floor done previously. It points towards a technology that is likely to prove costly but could meet Japan's gas needs for a century.[80] Heavier rare earth metals like dysprosium, terbium, europium, and ytterbium are most difficult to find but are also the most important amongst the 17 rare earth elements. China has a near total monopoly on the heavier end of the spectrum, though it is also the dominant supplier of rare earth metals after driving rivals out of business in the 1990s.[81] Presently, China accounts for 97 per cent of the total global supply of rare earth metals. Beijing has been following unfair trade practices by restricting exports, thereby pushing foreign companies to re-locate to China, from where their technology could be absorbed by Chinese domestic markets. The rare earth metals that have been discovered by Japan are thought to be 1000 times that of all land-based deposits, some of it in French waters around Tahiti. Incidentally, Japan is the largest importer of REM. in the world and utilises about half the total rare earth metals of the world in its electronics, cars and environmental industries. In 2010, tensions between Japan and China flared up when a Chinese trawler collided with a Japanese Coast Guard vessel near the waters of the Senkaku Islands. It was widely reported that as a consequence to the arrest of the Chinese captain by Japanese coast guard, exports of REM from China to Japan were restricted as a pressure tool. Though the use of coercion tactics was denied by China, Japan has thereafter been searching for alternate sources under its "Strategy for Ensuring Stable Supplies of Rare Metals". A joint venture in Vietnam that once looked promising has so far yielded only lighter rare earths.[82]

India is known to have significant reserves of REMs.[83] Rare earths minerals found in India include ilmenite, sillimanite, garnet, zircon, monazite and rutile, collectively called Beach Sand Minerals (BSM) and India has almost 35 per cent of the world's total beach sand mineral deposits.[84] On November 2016, a trade pact allowing the import of 4100 tonnes of Rare Earth Elements (REE) material (amounting to roughly 10 to 15 per cent of Japan's peak annual demand) from India was signed by the two countries.[85] Signing of this pact can be seen as a step forward for the strategic cooperation between the two countries. Japan has already commenced investments in rare earth industry in India. Toyotsu Rare Earths India Pvt. Ltd., which is a subsidiary of Toyota Tsusho and is based at Vishakhapatnam, Andhra Pradesh is engaged in production of certain rare earth elements. In addition to the supply of REM by India to Japan, both nations have also proposed to engage with other countries like Afghanistan and Kazakhsthan where REMs are available for excavation. The rare-earth resources in Afghanistan (Helmand province) are estimated to be one million tonnes; and, particularly for India, engagement in Afghanistan has considerable strategic significance too.[86] With regard to Kazakhstan too, India and Japan aim to undertake joint development of rare-earth assets.[87] Japan has also planned to invest in the coastal stretch of around 2,500 hectares at Bramhagiri (Puri district), Odisha where huge reserves of Rare Earth Elements (REE) have been discovered. A US$ 1.5 billion corpus for developing alternative sources of rare earths has been earmarked by Japan and in this regard, India can be of great help. Most REMs are not that rare but they are hard to find in viable concentrations, and the metallurgy is complex.[88] Brazil, Malaysia, Vietnam and the Democratic Republic of the Congo also have reserves of REM without processing power, while the US, Japan and Western Europe have had processing capacity without reserves, until now.[89]

Deep Sea Mining: The International Seabed Authority (ISA) regulates and manages deep sea bed mining. As an intergovernmental organisation, established by treaty, the decision making in the ISA are as far as possible, by consensus.[90] The organisation has established a regime of Pioneer Investors (of which both India and Japan are a part) and developed a legal framework for the development of the deep sea bed resources. Incidentally, Japan is the largest financial contributor to the ISA.[91]

The Ministry of Earth Sciences of the Government of India has focused on the development of deep sea mining to extract polymetallic nodules from the ocean bed. The polymetallic nodules containing copper, cobalt, nickel and manganese are viewed as potential resources to meet the increasing demand for these strategic metals worldwide.[92] The ISA has allotted a site to India, in the Central Indian Ocean Basin (CIOB), for exploration and technology development for polymetallic nodule mining.[93] As per the National Institute of Ocean Technology (NIOT), these nodules are strewn across 10–18 million sq km of ocean floor in the Indian Ocean, and about 380 million tonnes of nodules are present in the licensed exploration area of 150,000 sq km.[94] Deep-sea Technologies and Ocean Mining Group of NIOT of India, has been actively involved in development of technology for polymetallic nodules mining from 6000 m water depth.[95] India aims to increase its self-sufficiency by harnessing the deep sea resources as also to meet its growing mineral requirements.

Japan, like India is also a pioneer investor in this field and is perhaps the only country till date, to experiment mining the deep sea hydrothermal vents.[96] Hydrothermal vents form when the hot magma from the earth's crust come in contact with the near-freezing waters of the sea bed. The minerals which are contained in the magma solidify as fine-grained sulfides of minerals forming chimney-like structures. They are generally formed at convergent plate boundaries and are a sort of hot springs. Deep Ocean Resources Development Co. Ltd., (DORD) of Japan is actively involved in deep sea mining. In 2017, Japan became the first nation to successfully mine zinc and other minerals from deep-sea vents, confirming the possibility of exploiting this untapped source.[97] Certain areas around Japan have also been allotted by the ISA for deep-sea mining. The Okinawa Trough, northwest of Okinawa Islands, and the Bayonnaise submarine caldera, believed to contain among the world's richest seabed deposits of gold, silver and rare earth elements are areas where Japan is focusing its deep sea bed mining efforts.[98]

Deep sea mining is expensive and effort intensive. It thus makes for an attractive option for both countries to collaborate, pool in resources and mitigate threats of monopoly on minerals and rare earth metals.

Regional Frameworks: Besides the bilateral relations, both India and Japan are part of a number of multi-lateral frameworks in Asia some of them being, the ADMM Plus, East Asia Summit and ReCAAP. An analysis of the partnership in some of these regional forums reveals that both nations can optimise realisation of their national interests by collaborating and synchronising their responses to regional and global issues.

The ADMM-Plus is a platform for the ASEAN and its eight dialogue partners to strengthen security and defence cooperation for peace, stability and development in the region.[99] The inaugural ADMM-Plus convened in Ha Noi, Vietnam in October 2010, agreed on five areas of practical cooperation namely maritime security, counter-terrorism, HADR, peacekeeping operations and military medicine. The areas of cooperation were increased to humanitarian mine action in 2013 and cyber security in 2016. ADMM Plus has conducted a total of 12 exercises in the seven designated areas of cooperation: counter-terrorism, cyber security, HADR, humanitarian mine action, maritime security, military medicine and peacekeeping. ADMM Plus provides the ideal platform for India and Japan to contribute towards enhancement of regional capacity building and to provide better poise to the ASEAN to face complex security challenges. Both countries can play a major role on issues like the formulation of the SCS Code of Conduct (CoC), exploring creative approaches to combating terrorism and encouraging stronger intelligence sharing on terror-financing, after due coordination. The strengths of both countries in the chosen fields of cooperation along with resources can be pooled to create a regional capacity to deal with such challenges.

Similarly, in the East Asia Summit (EAS) where Japan facilitated the entry of India, both countries can coordinate approaches to complex issues like energy security, climate change and management of financial institutions. Tokyo's support of the Indian membership of the EAS was in itself indicative of its positive outlook towards New Delhi, in addition to the need for balancing the presence of China in the grouping. The EAS has, in fact, become a common regional institutional platform where both India and Japan have come together with common aims and objectives.[100] Whereas Japan looks at EAS through the lens of a 'broader Asia', India perceives the EAS as an opportunity to 'put in place a regional architecture for greater cooperation and economic integration amongst countries of East Asia'.[101]

Likewise, in order to combat non-traditional maritime threats, Asian nations formed a new legal framework, the Regional Cooperation Agreement on Combating Piracy and Armed Robbery against Ships in Asia (ReCAAP) with an Information Sharing Centre (ISC) at Singapore in 2006. India and Japan, as part of ReCAAP, can share maritime experiences within member countries and assist in the overall capacity building by providing patrol vessels under bilateral agreements and despatching experts. As maritime law enforcement capabilities of those countries rise, activities performed by ReCAAP and its ISC will likewise increase in effectiveness.[102] With their powerful coast guards and navies, both India and Japan can coordinate to provide a more secure and peaceful environment in the Indo-Pacific.

The Civil Nuclear Agreement

The signing of the Agreement for Cooperation in Peaceful Uses of Nuclear Energy with Japan in November 2015 displays the strategic importance accorded by both countries, to each other. This Agreement will pave the way for enhanced cooperation in energy security and clean energy.[103] The Agreement seeks to promote full cooperation between the two countries in the development and use of nuclear energy for peaceful purposes on a stable, reliable and predictable basis.[104]

As Japan is the only nation to have undergone the agony of being a victim of nuclear bombings, the Japanese public turned away from any kind of nuclear proliferation. Their society at large abhors the use of force as a means of settling international disputes and is pushing for a world without nuclear weapons. Therefore, when India conducted the 1998 nuclear tests, Japan's reaction was swift and harsh. Japan halted its aid programme in order to chasten India so that it signs the Non Proliferation Treaty (NPT), and along with Costa Rica, Slovenia and Sweden brought in a motion in the UNSC against India for conduct of the nuclear tests.[105]

However, post the signing of the India-US civil nuclear deal, Japan came around to negotiate a civil nuclear deal with India, after exhaustive domestic deliberations considering its security and economic interests. The signing of the Agreement for Cooperation in Peaceful Uses of Nuclear Energy on November 11, 2016 was an important milestone. The signing of the Agreement displays a mature understanding of the Indian position by Japan with regards to nuclear energy, in contrast to the stand it had taken after the 1998 nuclear tests.[106] India is the only non-NPT signatory with whom Japan has signed the civil nuclear deal and this speaks volumes of the initiative taken by the Abe government.[107] Currently, India has civil nuclear agreements with eleven countries; Australia, Argentina, Kazakhstan, Canada, France, Mongolia, South Korea, Namibia, Russia, United Kingdom and the United States. However, today, the largest and best-known supplier of heavy forgings (required for components of nuclear plants) is Japan Steel Works (JSW), which claims 80 per cent share of the world market.[108] Hence, a nuclear agreement with Japan was imperative in order to establish nuclear projects in India. This agreement also gives a new lease of life to the nuclear business houses, especially after the Fukushima disaster and to energy-starved India to open new nuclear power plants. It has been reported that Japan is willing to undertake joint manufacture of nuclear power plants under the 'Make in India' scheme.

Operationalisation of India Japan civil nuclear agreement is also in consonance with India's goal of enhancing the share of nuclear power generation and its drive towards clean energy in India. India currently has 5.7 gigawatts (GW) of nuclear power generation capacity, which accounts for 2 per cent of the total power capacity.[109] This is expected to change with a sharp increase in power generation from atomic plants over the next 16 years as Asia's third largest economy moves away from fossil fuels for its energy needs.[110] India's Department of Atomic Energy's target is to have 63 GW of nuclear power capacity by 2032.[111]

In addition to the bilateral civil nuclear deals with other countries, India has also been making efforts at being part of the four important multi-lateral export control regimes, viz. the Missile Technology Control Regime (MTCR), the Wassenaar Arrangement, the Australia Group and the Nuclear Suppliers Group (NSG). In the Japan-India Joint Statement 'Toward a Free, Open and Prosperous Indo-Pacific' signed in September 201, the Prime Minister of Japan Shinzo Abe, welcomed India's accession to the MTCR and the Hague Code of Conduct against Ballistic Missile Proliferation (HCOC) and its intensified engagement with the export control regimes.[112] The two prime ministers reaffirmed their commitment to work together for India to become a full member in the remaining three international export control regimes: NSG, Wassenaar Arrangement and Australia Group, with the aim to strengthen the international non-proliferation efforts.[113] Currently, India is a member of three of the four export control regimes. This change has been possible because of a change in the attitude of the non-proliferation order towards India too, from seeing India as a country of proliferation concern to a partner in non-proliferation.[114] A brief analysis of the control regimes reveals that membership of India has been in the interests of both because of India's growing profile in the technology exports and the overall changing political equations between India and the major powers.[115]

MTCR: The MTCR is an informal, voluntary group of 37 countries that prevents the proliferation of missiles and drones that can carry a payload of over 500 kg for more than 300 km.[116] India had voluntarily committed to follow MTCR export control guidelines in 2008, and in June 2015, formally applied for membership of the regime.[117] The move was, however, blocked by Italy which wanted to secure the release of its marine and his return to Italy. Once the matter was resolved, Italy relented and based on the process of silent approval, India was admitted to this control regime in June 2015. Presently, India continues with the development of its indigenous ballistic missile programme. Admission to the MTCR has opened the doors to India for the procurement of high-end missiles and unmanned vehicle technology. Unmanned aerial vehicles from the US and collaboration in unmanned ground vehicles with Japan have been facilitated due to India being a member of the MTCR.

Wassenaar Arrangement: The Wassenaar Arrangement on Export Controls for Conventional Arms and Dual-Use Goods and Technologies is an export control regime established in September 1996 with the aim of promoting transparency and great responsibility in transfers of conventional arms and related dual-use goods and technologies, thus preventing destabilising accumulations.[118] Participating states are required to implement export controls based on control lists and procedures agreed by the Wassenaar Arrangement.[119] At the 23rd Plenary Meeting of the Wassenaar Arrangement held on December 6 and 7, 2017 in Vienna, India's application to become a participating state was unanimously approved. India became the Wassenaar Arrangement's 42nd participating state. After the Wassenaar Arrangement decision to admit India into its folds, the Ministry of Foreign Affairs statement said, 'India would like to thank each of the forty-one Wassenaar Arrangement Participating States for their support for India's membership. We would also like to thank Ambassador Jean Louis Falconi of France, 2017 Plenary Chair of the Wassenaar Arrangement for his role in facilitating India's accession to the Arrangement.[120] India also notes the valuable contribution of Japan and France as co-rapporteurs, and Ambassador Philip Griffiths, Head of WA Secretariat, for their guidance during the preparatory process'.[121] Thus Japan played an important role as a co-rapporteur along with France facilitating India's entry, as outlined in the joint statement between the prime ministers in September 2017. In its Ministry of Foreign affairs, Japan has stated, 'Japan welcomes India's participation in the Wassenaar Arrangement, which will contribute to strengthening export controls on conventional arms and related dual-use goods and technologies in the Asian region'.

Australia Group: Australia Group is a cooperative and voluntary group of countries working to counter the spread of materials, equipment and technologies that could contribute to the development or acquisition of chemical and biological weapons by states or terrorist groups.[122] On January 19, 2018, India formally became the 43rd member of the Australia Group (AG), the cooperative and voluntary group of countries working to counter the spread of materials, equipment and technologies that could contribute to the development or acquisition of chemical and biological weapons (CBW) by states or terrorist groups.'

NSG: Interestingly, the NSG was formed in 1975 with the aim of restraining transfer of nuclear wares from would be proliferators.[123] India has repeatedly attempted to gain entry into this elite club but has been blocked as it is not a signatory to the Non-Proliferation Treaty (NPT). While India, which is backed by the US and a number of western countries has garnered the support of a majority of the group's members, China has stuck to its stand that new members should sign the Nuclear Non-Proliferation Treaty (NPT), making India's entry difficult as the group is guided by the consensus principle.[124] In September 2008, after the U.S. applied diplomatic pressure to a number of states that had raised reservations or objections to making an exception for India, the NSG by consensus granted the exception; as a consequence India today may import NSG-listed items from participating governments.[125] It is, however, reported that the support for the India-specific exemptions in the guidelines of the NSG came quite late from Japan.[126] And the general understanding is that the US had to intervene in order to get these through.[127] Since 2011, the NSG has considered including India as a member without reaching a necessary consensus agreement.[128] Since 2016, China has departed from its previous expressions of ambiguous reluctance to support India's membership in the NSG in favour of a position that appears to categorically exclude India.[129]

However, changed geo-politics has resulted in the Western powers including Japan being supportive of the inclusion of India in the NSG. Presently, US-based nuclear reactor maker Westinghouse, a unit of Japan's Toshiba Corp, has made substantial progress towards an agreement to build six nuclear reactors in the state of Andhra Pradesh. Such a deal on completion will be the first to have resulted from the India-US deal signed a decade ago. The fact that Japan has strategically partnered with India in nuclear issues, despite India not being a signatory to the NPT depicts the pragmatism in the

Japanese political dispensation despite extreme public opinion and opposition pressures in the domestic front. Though, the economic benefits that will accrue to Japan and other countries have been the prime motivator, the civil nuclear deal with India can definitely be counted as one of the important bilateral deals made by Japan.

Challenges

Trade Volumes: A reality check on the relations of India and Japan reveal that both have considerable stakes in their economic dealings with China. India-China and India-Japan trade statistics are shown below. India Japan bilateral trade in 2016–2017 is US$ 13.48 billion and is a matter of concern in view of the fact that there is high potential for faster progress on goods and services trade.[130] The India-China trade volume of the same year was US$ 84.4 billion about six times that of the India-Japan trade volume.[131] Similarly, the Japan-China trade volume of US$ 297.28 billion is again twenty times the Japan-India trade figures. The economies of trade, thus, do not seem to be in congruence with the strategic relations. China is the largest trading partner for both countries. Will India and Japan partner each other on security issues to the point of antagonising China, is a moot question.

Figure 7.1: Trade Statistics (India)

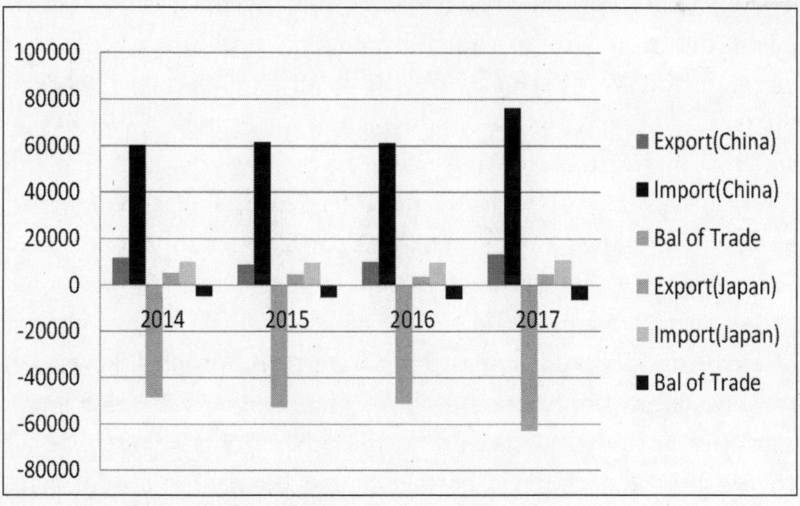

Source: Ministry of Commerce, India.

Figure 7.2: Trade Statistics (Japan)

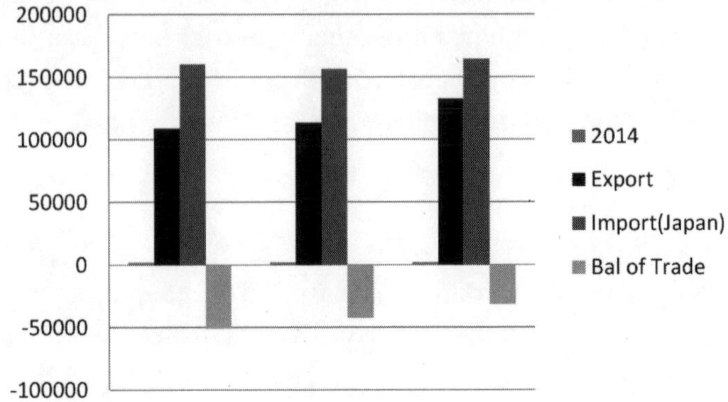

Source: Ministry of Commerce, India and World Integrated Trade Solution.

Reciprocation to Each Others' Security Challenges: The second issue is of political and military reciprocation to each other's security issues. The testing of intercontinental missiles over Japanese territory is definitely a matter of severe security concern for Japan. Japan looks towards India for support for mitigation or resolution of the North Korean threat. However, till date, India has only been able to empathise with Japan in joint statements and joined in condemnation of this blatant disregard for international norms by North Korea. There has been no tangible action by India in this regard. This is partly due to a lack of capability and political will to influence events in the West Pacific as well as a spirit of non-interference in bilateral issues of countries in the region. Incidentally, India has an embassy in North Korea and is one of the few countries that can leverage its relations with North Korea. In a similar vein, Japan has also not shown any particular empathy to security concerns of India vis-à-vis Pakistan. Japan maintains cordial relations including provision of substantial aid to Pakistan, which is a known abettor of terrorism, despite being a victim of terrorism itself. Likewise, in the case of any confrontation with China, neither India nor Japan can offer unequivocal support to the other. For a robust security cooperation and strategic partnership to flourish, it is important that both countries fully comprehend the security dynamics and take visible actions assisting each other to mitigate security risks posed by neighbouring countries.

Lack of Pro-activity to Enhance Relationship: Over the years it has been observed that in the realm of security relations, US has been more experimental and spontaneous in its dealings with India. Japan has been in a followers camp and conservative. India too has not been very pro-active to enhance the relations with Japan, either. A brief chronology of security related events between the three countries points towards a possible nudge from Washington before India and Japan came together for strategic commitments.

Table 7.6: Corresponding Events—US and Japan

Mar 2000	Visit of US President to India (First in 20 years)	→	Aug 2000	Visit of PM Mori. (India-Japan Global Partnership)
Jan 2004	India-US Strategic Partnership			
July 2005	India-US Civil Nuclear Agreement Next Steps in Strategic Partnership (NSSP)	→	Dec 2006	India-Japan Global and Strategic Partnership
			2007	Participation in Malabar Exercise
			Oct 2008	Joint Declaration of Security Cooperation
Jan 2015	US-India Joint Strategic Vision for Indo-Pacific region	→	Dec 2015	India-Japan Vision 2025 Permanent Member Malabar Ex
June 2016	US-India Enduring Global Partnership	→	Nov 2016	India-Japan Civil Nuclear Agreement

Source: *South Asia Journal.*[132]

Though the veracity of this claim cannot be indisputably established, it points towards a need for both India and Japan to come forward and take initiative.

The security narrative in Asia is dynamic with a conspicuous four way power struggle between China, the United States, India and

Japan. The power struggle is happening in the context of a perceived decline of the United States, the rise of China, the effort by Japan to recover its role in the region, and India as a rising power.[133] The East Asian region is also being shaped by international events like the North Korean crisis, the South China Sea imbroglio and the US push towards a nationalist policy in trade and security. Status quo powers need to build strategic cooperation but the future depends on how evolving challenges are addressed by both countries. Developing multiple overlapping triangular dialogues will give much-needed depth to the India-Japan partnership.[134] There is, thus, a need to form multi-lateral alignments and groupings with countries of the region like Vietnam, Singapore and Indonesia. Developing multiple overlapping triangular dialogues will give much-needed depth to the India Japan Partnership.[135]

This year (2018), the Asian Department of the Japanese Ministry of Foreign Affairs set up a new 'South Asia Department' specifically responsible for the affairs of India, Pakistan and Southeast Asia, showing Japan's attitude toward India. The Department of Industrial Policy & Promotion (DIPP), India, on its part, has set up a Japan Plus in October 2014—a special management team to facilitate and fast track investment proposals from Japan.[136] This team comprises of representatives from Government of India and Ministry of Economy, Trade and Industry, (METI) Government of Japan. The mandate of the "Japan Plus" team runs through the entire spectrum of investment promotion—research, outreach, promotion, facilitation and after-care. The team will support the Government of India in initiating, attracting, facilitating, fast tracking and hand-holding Japanese investments across sectors.[137] Notwithstanding the efforts taken by both sides, there appears to be very slow progress in security and strategic matters. On the other hand, in its relations with China, India has been vacillating between appeasements, hedging and confronting in its policies, thereby sending out mixed signals. As an emerging regional power with global aspirations, it is India that needs to take the initiative of furthering the partnership more than Japan does.

Conclusion

India and Japan can effectively partner each other in the Indo-Pacific. Converging interests have resulted in partnership in the AAGC and in strategic economic issues. Complementarities exist on a large number of issues which needs to be exploited for mutual gains. Partnership in regional and global forums reveals that both nations can optimise realisation of their national interests by collaborating and synchronising their responses to regional and global issues. Challenges to the optimal realisation of the potential of this strategic partnership need to be surmounted with deeper understanding, empathy and initiative. Though the security cooperation and strategic partnership is progressing rapidly, the trajectory of the current engagement needs to be accurately assessed and corrected, if need be, to achieve greater heights. The same has been carried out with limited quantitative data in the next chapter.

Notes

1. The Japan visit: An Eastward Sojourn, e-book, Ministry of External Affairs, Government of India e-book, December 8, 2016 at http://www.mea.gov.in/japan/index.html#, accessed on April 5, 2018.
2. Satish Kumar (ed.), *India's National Security: Annual Review 2015-16*, Foundation for National Security Research, Routledge, London and New York, 2017, p. 274.
3. David Brewster, 'The India-Japan Security Relationship: An Enduring Security Partnership?', *Asian Security Journal,* 6:2, 2010, pp. 95–120 at https://doi.org/10.1080/14799851003756550.
4. Alliance with US key to Japan's foreign policy: Abe, *The Straits Times,* January 21, 2017 at https://www.straitstimes.com/asia/east-asia/alliance-with-us-key-to-japans-foreign-policy-abe, accessed on July 23, 2018.
5. W.P.S. Sidhu, 'Enhancing the India-Japan partnership', The Livemint, September 25, 2017 at https://www.livemint.com/Opinion/l91NGJCoDUJ0XvHTe1ZoGO/Enhancing-the-IndiaJapan-partnership.html, accessed on July 23, 2018.
6. Ministry of External Affairs, India-Sri Lanka Relations at www.mea.gov.in, accessed on February 12, 2019.
7. Ankit Panda, 'Sri Lanka Formally Hands Over Hambantota Port to Chinese Firms on 99-Year Lease', *The Diplomat,* December 11, 2017 at https://thediplomat.com/2017/12/sri-lanka-formally-hands-over-hambantota-port-to-chinese-firms-on-99-year-lease/, accessed on September 2, 2018.

8. Ibid.
9. India, Japan JV to set up LNG import terminal in Sri Lanka http://www.thehindubusinessline.com/economy/policy/india-japan-jv-to-set-up-lng-import-terminal-in-sri-lanka/article9711648.ece.
10. Ibid.
11. Ibid.
12. Tara Francis Chandec, India is buying world's emptiest airport in its battle for territorial dominance with China, Business Insider, December 13, 2017 at https://www.businessinsider.in/India-is-buying-worlds-emptiest-airport-in-its-battle-for-territorial-dominance-with-China/articleshow/62046916.cms, accessed on May 18, 2018.
13. Franz-Stefan Gady, 'Sri Lanka to Buy 8 Sino-Pak JF-17 Fighter Jets', *The Diplomat,* January 7, 2016 at https://thediplomat.com/2016/01/sri-lanka-to-buy-eight-sino-pak-jf-17-fighter-jets/, accessed on September 2, 2018.
14. China, India, and Japan Are Very Interested in Sri Lanka—Here's Why, Global Risks Insights, April 17, 2017 at https://www.financialsense.com/global-risk-insights/china-india-japan-interested-sri-lanka, accessed on May 18, 2018.
15. Ibid.
16. Admiral Dr. Jayanath Colombage, Director Centre for Indo-Lanka Initiatives, Pathfinder Foundation, 'Rising sun for Japan-Sri Lanka maritime relations' Daily News, April 18, 2017 at http://www.dailynews.lk/2017/04/18/business/113341/%E2%80%98rising-sun-japan-sri-lanka-maritime-relations%E2%80%99, accessed on June 30, 2018.
17. Ibid.
18. Economy Next, January 4, 2019 at https://economyeast.com/Japan soft loan for Sri Lanka LRT at low interest, 40 year payback-3-13054.html, accessed on February 12, 2019.
19. Ministry of External Affairs, India-Bangladesh Relations at www.mea.gov.in, accessed on February 12, 2019.
20. Shannon Tiezzi, 'China, Bangladesh Pledge Deeper Military Cooperation', *The Diplomat,* December 4, 2015 at https://thediplomat.com/2015/12/china-bangladesh-pledge-deeper-military-cooperation/, accessed on May 18, 2018.
21. Increasing Geopolitical Rivalry: China, India and Japan Focus on Bangladesh, Indian Defence Update, June 20, 2016 at https://defenceupdate.in/increasing-geopolitical-rivalry-china-india-japan-focus-bangladesh/, accessed on September 27, 2018.
22. Ibid.
23. Ibid.
24. Ishrat Hossain, 'Bangladesh balances between big brothers China and India, East Asia Forum', June 6, 2018 at http://www.

eastasiaforum.org/2018/06/06/bangladesh-balances-between-big-brothers-china-and-india/?utm_source=subscribe2&utm_medium=email&utm_campaign=post notify&utm_id=129898&utm_title=Bangladesh+balances+between+big+brothers+China+and+India, accessed on June 7, 2018.

25. Sarath Kumara, 'Indian power deal with Bangladesh highlights geo-political rivalry', World Socialist Web Site, March 5, 2016 at https://www.wsws.org/en/articles/2016/03/05/bang-m05.html, accessed on September 27, 2018.
26. Ibid.
27. Economy Next, note 18.
28. Ibid.
29. Sarath Kumara, 'Chinese defence minister seeks to boost ties with Bangladesh', World Socialist Web Site, June 16, 2016 at https://www.wsws.org/en/articles/2016/03/05/bang-m05.html, accessed on September 27, 2018.
30. Bertil Lintner, 'India wins, China loses in Maldives elections', *Asia Times*, September 25, 2018 at http://www.atimes.com/article/india-wins-china-loses-in-maldives-election/, accessed on October 9, 2018.
31. Ibid.
32. Monica Wang, 'China's Strategy in Djibouti: Mixing Commercial and Military Interests', Council on Foreign Relations, April 13, 2018 at https://www.cfr.org/blog/chinas-strategy-djibouti-mixing-commercial-and-military-interests, accessed on July 23, 2018.
33. Press Information Bureau, Government of India, Ministry of Defence, India–Indonesia Coordinated Patrol (IND-INDO CORPAT), June 6, 2018 at http://pib.nic.in/newsite/PrintRelease.aspx?relid=179826, accessed on October 22, 2018.
34. Vignesh Ram, 'India's Defence Diplomacy with South East Asia: An impetus to Act East', *Journal of Defence Studies*, April-September 2018, p. 64.
35. Toru Ito, 'China Threat Theory in Indo-Japan Relations', Chapter 5 in Takenori Horimoto and Lalima Varma (eds), *India–Japan Relations in Emerging Asia*, Manohar Publishers, New Delhi, 2013, p. 125.
36. Titili Basu, 'Mapping India in Japan's infrastructure agenda', Institute for Defence Studies and Analyses Commentary , April 29, 2016 at https://idsa.in/idsanews/mapping-india-in-japans-infrastructure-agenda, accessed on October 9, 2018.
37. Hong Zhao, 'Chinese and Japanese infrastructure investment in Southeast Asia: from rivalry to cooperation?', Institute of Developing Economies, Japan External Trade Organization (IDE-JETRO) at http://www.ide.go.jp journal or publication title IDE Discussion Paper volume 689 year 2018-02 (http://hdl.handle.net/2344/00050160), accessed on October 9, 2018.

38. Siegfrid Alegado, 'Japan Still Beating China in Southeast Asia Infrastructure Race', Bloomberg Economics, February 9, 2018 available at https://www.bloomberg.com/news/articles/2018-02-08/japan-still-beating-china-in-southeast-asia-infrastructure-race, accessed on October 9, 2018.
39. Rajya Sabha Starred Question No. 223 Collaboration With Japan For Regional Connectivity March 15, 2018.
40. Press Release, Cabinet Committee on Economic Affairs (CCEA), Press Information Bureau, Government of India, Cabinet approves SASEC Road Connectivity Investment Program—Tranche 2, July 12, 2017 at http://pib.nic.in/newsite/PrintRelease.aspx?relid=167351, accessed on May 20, 2018.
41. Ibid.
42. Ibid.
43. Press Release, The Embassy of Japan and JETRO, Japanese Business Establishments in India—2017 (Summary of Updated List of Japanese Business Establishments in India, as of October 2017, with the cooperation of Japanese Chamber of Commerce and Industries in India) at http://www.in.emb-japan.go.jp/PDF/2017_co_list_en_pr.pdf, accessed on September 15, 2018.
44. Shyam Saran, 'Mapping the Indo-Pacific', *The Indian Express*, October 29, 2011 at http://archive.indianexpress.com/news/mapping-the-indopacific/867004/, accessed on July 26, 2018.
45. James D.J. Brown, 'Japan's Values-Free and Token Indo-Pacific Strategy', *The Diplomat*, April 3, 2018 at https://thediplomat.com/2018/03/japans-values-free-and-token-indo-pacific-strategy/, accessed on July 26, 2018.
46. https://www.japantimes.co.jp/opinion/2018/04/03/commentary/japan-commentary/japans-indo-pacific-strategy-falls-short/#.WsWp5tR97Gg.
47. Liu Zongyi, senior fellow at the Institute for International Strategic Studies at the Shanghai Institutes for International Studies, Shanghai, China, 'Indo-Pacific': containment ploy or new label for region beyond China's backyard? at http://www.scmp.com/news/china/diplomacy-defence/article/2119412/indo-pacific-containment-ploy-or-new-label-region, accessed on October 17, 2018.
48. Takashi Terada, international relations professor at Doshisha University, Kyoto, Japan; visiting fellow at the National University of Singapore at http://www.scmp.com/news/china/diplomacy-defence/article/2119412/indo-pacific-containment-ploy-or-new-label-region, accessed on July 26, 2018.
49. https://www.ndtv.com/world-news/as-trump-sticks-to-indo-pacific-not-asia-pacific-china-reacts-1774888.
50. Ben Blanchard, 'China says regional cooperation should not be politicized', Reuters, November 13, 2017 at https://www.reuters.com/article/us-trump-

asia-china-diplomacy/china-says-regional-cooperation-should-not-be-politicized-idUSKBN1DD0WA?il=0, accessed on September 28, 2018.

51. Ibid.
52. India, Japan to introduce AI, robotics in defence sector, *Times of India,* January 22, 2018 at https://timesofindia.indiatimes.com/india/india-japan-to-introduce-ai-robotics-in-defence-sector/articleshow/62597018.cms, accessed on September 28, 2018.
53. Ibid.
54. Ibid.
55. Ibid.
56. Utpal Bhaskar, 'India, Japan join hands for big infrastructure push in Northeast', *The Livemint,* August 3, 2017 at https://www.livemint.com/Politics/8T9Q9wBg1s4JKRwFgChMDO/India-Japan-join-hands-for-big-infra-push-in-Northeast-Indi.html, accessed on September 28, 2018.
57. Kuni Miyake, 'The Indo-Pacific is Nothing New', *The Japan Times*, June 4, 2018 at https://www.japantimes.co.jp/opinion/2018/06/04/commentary/world-commentary/indo-pacific-nothing-new/#.W7tN5WgzbIU, accessed on October 8, 2018.
58. 'Evolution of India-Japan Ties: Prospects and Limitations', in Rajesh Basrur and S.N. Kutty (eds), *India and Japan: Assessing the Strategic Partnership*, Palgrave Macmillan, Singapore, 2018, p. 37.
59. Ibid.
60. Executive Summary, A Vision Document, AAGC at http://www.eria.org/Asia-Africa-Growth-Corridor-Document.pdf, accessed on May 20, 2018.
61. Ibid.
62. Akinwumi Adesina, 'President of the African Development Bank Africa and India—sharing the development journey' available at African Development Bank Website, May 25, 2017 at https://www.afdb.org/en/news-and-events/africa-and-india-sharing-the-development-journey-17038/, accessed on February 3, 2018.
63. India Africa Forum Summit, Ministry of External Affairs, Magic book at http://mea.gov.in/india-africa-forum-summit-2015/index.html, accessed on September 28, 2018.
64. AAGC Vision Document at http://www.eria.org/Asia-Africa-Growth-Corridor-Document.pdf.
65. Ibid.
66. Government of Japan, "Uniqueness of TICAD" at http://www.mofa.go.jp/af/af1/page22e_000767.html.
67. Ruchita Beri, 'India's New Initiative in Africa: The Asia–Africa Growth Corridor', Institute for Defence Studies and Analyses, June 13, 2017 at https://idsa.in/idsacomments/indias-new-initiative-in-africa-asia-africa-growth-corridor_rberi_130617, accessed on September 28, 2018.

68. Africa—Opportunities for Trade, Investment and Triangular Cooperation (India-Africa-Japan), ASSOCHAM Study, December 20, 2017 at http://publication.assocham.tv/data/product-file/20171204_Africa%20Study%202017_final.pdf, accessed on May 20, 2018.
69. 'As conference wraps up, Japan, African leaders vow to fight terrorism, stress rules-based maritime order', *Japan Times,* August 29, 2016 at http://www.japantimes.co.jp/news/2016/08/29/national/politics-diplomacy/...
70. ASSOCHAM Study, note 68.
71. AAGC Vision Document at http://www.eria.org/Asia-Africa-Growth-Corridor-Document.pdf, accessed on September 28, 2018.
72. Ibid.
73. What Are Rare Earths?, *Rare Earth Technology Alliance* at http://www.rareearthtechalliance.com/What-are-Rare-Earths, accessed on July 10, 2018.
74. Ibid.
75. Ibid.
76. Ibid.
77. Ibid.
78. Ibid.
79. Ambrose Evans-Pritchard, 'Japan breaks China's stranglehold on rare metals with sea-mud bonanza', *The Telegraph,* March 24, 2013 at https://www.telegraph.co.uk/finance/comment/ambroseevans_pritchard/9951299/Japan-breaks-Chinas-stranglehold-on-rare-metals-with-sea-mud-bonanza.html, accessed on September 28, 2018.
80. Ibid.
81. Ibid.
82. Ibid.
83. Ajay Lele, 'India-Japan Join Hands to Challenge China's Rare Earth Monopoly', November 20, 2012 at https://idsa.in/idsacomments/IndiaJapanJoinHandstoChallengeChinasREE_AjeyLele_201112.
84. KVL Akshay, 'India not realising potential of rare earth industry', *Economics Times Bureau,* October 19, 2018 at https://economictimes.indiatimes.com/industry/indl-goods/svs/metals-mining/india-not-realising-potential-of-rare-earth-industry/articleshow/54940321.cms, accessed on July 10, 2018.
85. Ajay Lele, note 83.
86. Ibid.
87. Ajay Lele, note 83.
88. Kuni Miyake, note 57.
89. Emailed on April 13, 2018 by the hustle, Underwater Japan discovers enough rare metal to supply the world for 400+ years at https://thehustle.

co/japan-finds-rare-earth-metals-underwater/, accessed on July 10, 2018.

90. International Seabed Authority, ISA—Japan Cooperation at http://www.isa.org.jm/news/isa-japan-cooperation, accessed on September 27, 2018.
91. Press Release, Ministry of Foreign Affairs, Courtesy call on State Minister for Foreign Affairs Nobuo Kishi by Mr. Michael LODGE, Secretary-General of International Seabed Authority (ISA) at https://www.mofa.go.jp/press/release/press4e_001512.html, accessed on September 27, 2018.
92. Ministry of Earth Sciences, Development of Deep Sea Mining Machine, available at http://www.moes.gov.in/programmes/development-deep-sea-mining-machine-continuing, accessed on September 27, 2018.
93. Ibid.
94. Mining at Deep Sea, Richard Mahapatra, Anupam Chakravartty, *Down to Earth,* July 8, 2015 at Richard Mahapatra, Anupam Chakravartty, accessed on September 27, 2018.
95. Deep Sea Technologies, Website of National Institute of Ocean Technology, Ministry of earth Sciences, retrieved on September 27, 2018.
96. Philip Budgen, 'Hydrothermal vent mining, Japan experiments the new frontier threatening our oceans', *Lifegate,* November 23, 2017at https://www.lifegate.com/people/news/hydrothermal-vent-mining-japan, accessed on September 27, 2018.
97. Ibid.
98. Monika Chansoria, 'How deep sea mining can enrich India's energy future', *Daily O,* November 16, 2015 at https://www.dailyo.in/politics/modi-government-india-japan-ties-indian-ocean-region-dae-deep-sea-mining/story/1/7351.html, accessed on September 27, 2018.
99. ADMM Plus, About the ADMM Plus, available at https://admm.asean.org/index.php/about-admm/about-admm-plus.html.
100. Arpita Mathur 'Japan's Approach to Regionalism: Outlook towards the EAS and EAC', *Strategic Analysis*, 33:5 (2009), pp. 675–685, DOI: 10.1080/09700160903064505 at https://doi.org/10.1080/09700160903064505.
101. Ibid.
102. JapanGov, Government of Japan, 'ReCAAP Ensures the Safety of Asian Waters', Autumn/Winter 2017 at https://www.japan.go.jp/tomodachi/2017/autumn-winter2017/reaccp_ensures_the_safety.html, accessed on August 14, 2018.
103. Press Release Ministry of External Affairs, Government of India, The entry into force of India-Japan Agreement for Cooperation in the Peaceful Uses of Nuclear Energy, July 20, 2017 at https://mea.gov.in/press-releases.htm?dtl/28678/The_entry_into_force_of_IndiaJapanAgreement_for_Cooperation_in_the_Peaceful_Uses_of_Nuclear_Energy, accessed on September 26, 2018.

104. Ibid.

105. Security Council Condemns Nuclear Tests By India And Pakistan, Resolution 1172 (1998) at https://www.un.org/press/en/1998/sc6528.doc.htm, accessed on October 15, 2018.

106. Adarsha Verma, 'Prime Minister Modi's Visit to Japan', IDSA Commentary, November 18, 2016 at https://idsa.in/idsacomments/prime-minister-modi%E2%80%99s-visit-to-japan_averma_181116, accessed on September 25, 2018.

107. Ibid.

108. Ibid.

109. Elizabeth Roche, 'India, Japan sign landmark civilian nuclear deal', The Livemeint, November 12, 2016 at https://www.livemint.com/Politics/alJ9XsoWmUkcyPYO0HDDOK/India-Japan-sign-civil-nuclear-deal.html, accessed on September 26, 2018.

110. Ibid.

111. Ibid.

112. Japan-India Joint Statement 'Toward a Free, Open and Prosperous Indo-Pacific' at https://www.mofa.go.jp/files/000289999.pdf, accessed on September 26, 2018.

113. Ibid.

114. Rajeswari Pillai Rajagopalan, 'What Does India's New Australia Group Admission Mean for its Old NSG Bid?', *The Diplomat,* February 1, 2018 at https://thediplomat.com/2018/02/what-does-indias-new-australia-group-admission-mean-for-its-old-nsg-bid/, accessed on September 26, 2018.

115. Ibid.

116. 'India becomes member of Missile Technology Control Regime', *India Today* New Delhi, June 27, 2016 at https://www.indiatoday.in/education-today/gk-current-affairs/story/india-becomes-a-member-of-missile-technology-control-regime-16525-2016-06-27, accessed on September 26, 2018.

117. Kelsey Davenport, 'The Missile Technology Control Regime at a Glance', Arms Control Association, July 2017 at https://www.armscontrol.org/factsheets/mtcr, accessed on September 26, 2018.

118. Press Release, Ministry of Foreign Affairs, 'Japan, India's Participation in the Wassenaar Arrangement', December 8, 201 at https://www.mofa.go.jp/press/release/press4e_001835.html, accessed on September 26, 2018.

119. Ibid.

120. Dipanjan Roy Chaudhury, 'Significance of Wassenaar Arrangement for India', *Economic Times*, July 12, 2018 at https://economictimes.indiatimes.com/news/defence/siginfiance-of-wassenaar-arrangement-for-india/articleshow/61993284.cms, accessed on September 26, 2018.

121. Ibid.

122. Boost for NSG membership, India joins Australia Group, *The Economic Times,* January 19, 2018 at https://economictimes.indiatimes.com/news/defence/boost-for-nsg-membership-india-joins-australia-group/articleshow/62568821.cms, accessed on September 26, 2018.

123. Mark Hibbs, 'A More Geo-Politicised Nuclear Suppliers Group', Carnegie Endowment for International Peace, December 14, 2017 at https://carnegieendowment.org/2017/12/14/more-geopoliticized-nuclear-suppliers-group-pub-75027, accessed on September 26, 2018.

124. World Press Trust of India, US advocates for India's membership in Nuclear Suppliers Group, says New Delhi meets all qualifications, September 13, 2018.

125. Ibid.

126. Rajiv Nayan, 'India-Japan Strategic Partnership', IDSA Comment, June 11, 2013 at https://idsa.in/idsacomments/IndiaJapanStrategicPartnership_rnayan_110613, accessed on September 26, 2018.

127. Ibid.

128. Akinwumi Adesina, note 62.

129. Ibid.

130. Embassy of India, Tokyo, Japan, 'India Japan Economic Relations' at https://www.indembassy-tokyo.gov.in/india_japan_economic_relations.html accessed on August 6, 2018.

131. China-India trade volume reaches new high, *The Global Times,* April 26, 2018.

132. Dr. Thomas F. Lynch III, 'The Phases of Growth: India-Japan Strategic Partnership in the 21st Century', *South Asia Journal,* September 16, 2017 at http://southasiajournal.net/the-phases-of-growth-india-japan-strategic-partnership-in-the-21st-century/, accessed on August 7, 2018.

133. This interview was conducted by Yomiuri Shimbun New Delhi Correspondent Shigeki Tao. Kanwal Sibal Former Foreign Secretary of India at http://the-japan-news.com/news/article/0004192605.

134. C Raja Mohan and Rishika Chauhan, 'India-Japan Strategic Partnership', in Rohan Mukherjee and Anthony Yazaki (eds), *Poised For Partnership: Deepening India-Japan Relations in the Asian Century*, Oxford University Press, New Delhi, 2016, p. 200.

135. Ibid.

136. Japan Plus, Department of Industrial Policy and Promotion, Ministry of Commerce and Industry.

137. Press Release, Ministry of Commerce & Industry, "Japan Plus" constituted to fast track Japanese investments Press Information Bureau, Government of India, October 9, 2014 at http://pib.nic.in/newsite/PrintRelease.aspx?relid=110398, accessed on July 24, 2018.

PART IV
Quantitative Analyses and Recommendations

8

Quantitative Assessment: Criteria for India-Japan Security Cooperation

Abstract

A quantitative assessment of the India Japan Security Cooperation reinforces the qualitative research work done on the subject. In order to arrive at a quantitative assessment of the levels of security cooperation, a model has been worked upon, keeping the realities of the security environment in Asia, external dynamics of international relations, domestic politics and the bilateral relations between India and Japan. A questionnaire survey has been used to arrive at the inter-se degree of importance of each criterion of the model and its effect on the overall levels of cooperation in figurative terms. The quantitative results arrived at the end of the analyses can then be compared by the reader with the qualitative analyses of security cooperation carried out earlier.

Introduction

In order to gain an insight into the dynamics of India-Japan relationship a limited quantitative assessment of the security cooperation between India and Japan has been carried out in this chapter. The aim is to verify whether the qualitative perspective given in the previous chapters match up to the perception in the environment regarding India-Japan Security Cooperation.

In order to validate this relationship through quantitative means, a model for security cooperation has been evolved based on the internal and external security dynamics of both countries. Other than the research on security aspects, this model has been inspired by two reports—first, the report of the Clingendael Institute (Netherlands Institute of International Relations) on *Defence Cooperation Models* by Dick Zandee, Margriet Drent and Rob Hendriks and second, the RAND Corporation Testimony presented before the House Armed Services Committee in October 2015 where seminal work has been recorded on the criteria for defence and security cooperation amongst nations.[12]

This model involves defining certain criteria for robust security cooperation between two nations. Though the criteria defined may not be considered as water-tight factors, they do cover the middle ground of parameters required for any security cooperation. The criterion has been arrived at considering the contribution of following aspects in influencing security relations between countries, with specific reference to India and Japan:

- External Dynamics
- Domestic Aspects
- Bilateral aspects between countries

External Dynamics: The criteria in the model related to external dynamics pertain to Japan's relations with the US, the security alliance between the two countries as also the geo-strategic significance of India to Japan.

Domestic Aspects: Criteria in the model pertaining to domestic aspects cover issues related to the Japanese society, and its legal and security framework. Specifically, it covers the public opinion of pacifism, restraints due to domestic laws and principles, the economy, role and capabilities of Japanese SDF and involvement of political leaders in decision making in order to enhance the security cooperation.

Bilateral Aspects Between Countries: Criteria related to bilateral aspects pertain to issues that are bilateral in nature and covers historical and cultural linkages, whether a convergence can be attained in the objectives of the security cooperation, trust that can be developed between the countries, willingness to share technology and intelligence, engagement between the militaries and equipment interoperability between the two militaries.

Table 8.1: Criteria for Quantitative Assessment Model of India Japan Security Cooperation and its Explanation

Ser No	Criteria	Explanation of the Criteria
1.	Historical Linkages	This criterion examines the influence of historical linkages based on culture and religion on security cooperation between India and Japan.
2.	Geo-strategic Significance	Examines whether geographical location and consequently the geo-strategic importance of a country assists furtherance of national interests through cooperation with the partner.
3.	US-Japan Security Alliance	Assesses whether levels of security cooperation is affected due to either of the partners being part of an already established alliance with a third country.
4.	Restraints (Constitutional/ Cultural/Political)	Examines how constitutional bindings or foreign policy orientations of the partner countries hinder security cooperation. Specifically, it focuses on the pacifist constitution of Japan and the Indian stance of strategic autonomy.
5.	Alignment of Objectives	Examines whether there is congruence in terms of the objectives of this cooperation and the desired end state of security cooperation between the two countries.
6.	Economy	This criterion assesses whether such security cooperation will lead to mutual economic benefit for both partners.

Ser No	Criteria	Explanation of the Criteria
7.	Trust	Examines whether India and Japan can build up mutual trust that diplomatic or military support will be made available, when needed.
8.	Partner Willingness	Assesses the willingness of either partner to share high end technology and critical intelligence inputs.
9.	Military Engagements, Training and Exercises	Assesses whether military experts, especially at the operational and tactical levels, are engaged in understanding each other's security imperatives, military thought, application of force, and equipment capability. Also looks into the periodicity and levels of exercises and training held between the armed forces of the partner nations.
10.	Involvement of Parliaments	Assesses whether law-making bodies of both partner nations are involved in enhancement of the security relationship.
11.	Interoperability of Equipment	This criterion assesses whether equipment of both countries are interoperable and whether they can operate in conjunction with each other, when the need arises.
12.	Expeditionary Capability	Examines whether both nations have the will and capability to influence situations at any point of choosing based on security challenges of the partner nation.

Source: Prepared by the author based on Model proposed.

Each of these factors have been analysed through a questionnaire sent to respondents with five options for responding. Each option selected for a particular criterion was simplified for a universal understanding but kept strictly within the purview of the meaning of the criteria and the aspect it wanted to measure. Details of the questionnaire, responses received and statistical inferences are part of Appendix D. Each option has been quantified on a Likert's

Scale of 5,4,3,2 and 1. The direction of options to the questions on various criteria has been varied to avoid a mechanical response. Any aspect, which the respondent is not sure of, or unaware of, can be marked with a 'Cannot Say' option, which has been given a central value of 3.

From the total responses received to the questionnaire survey, a 'mean' (average) has been worked out for each question (criteria). This 'mean' (or *xi*) denotes the 'stand-alone' value of the criteria in the overall ambit of security cooperation. Therefore, if each criterion equally affects the overall robustness of the security cooperation, the contribution of each criteria will be given by the respective 'mean'. However, each criterion does not affect the overall security cooperation equally as certain criteria are more important than others. In order to overcome this challenge, the questionnaire contains a requirement in which the respondents rank the criteria against one another. When an average of the rankings of all responses is taken, a final ranking is obtained which is actually the weightage (*wi*) of that particular factor. A multiplication of the weightage of a particular criteria with that of its standalone mean $((xi)X(wi))$, gives the weighted mean, which is a representation of the contribution of the factor to the overall security cooperation posture. Finally, when the weighted means are added and divided by the total weightage, the overall posture of the security cooperation is obtained (worked out at a base of 100).The broad analysis of each criterion and its response has been briefly discussed in subsequent paragraphs.

Historical Linkages: Deep historical linkages serve as a platform from which security cooperation between partner nations can take off. The questionnaire has tried to investigate the extent to which historical linkages affect India-Japan security cooperation. It is also said that when two countries have nothing other than historical linkages to fall back upon, their relationship is not moving forward. However, as discussed in Part I of this book, India and Japan have had a rich cultural bonding through Buddhism, Hindu Gods and the Sanskrit language. Based on the question asked, 60 per cent respondents agreed that the criteria of historical and cultural linkages between India and Japan has an overall positive effect on the security relationship. This indicates that strengthening the historical linkages will be a boost to the security cooperation between the countries.

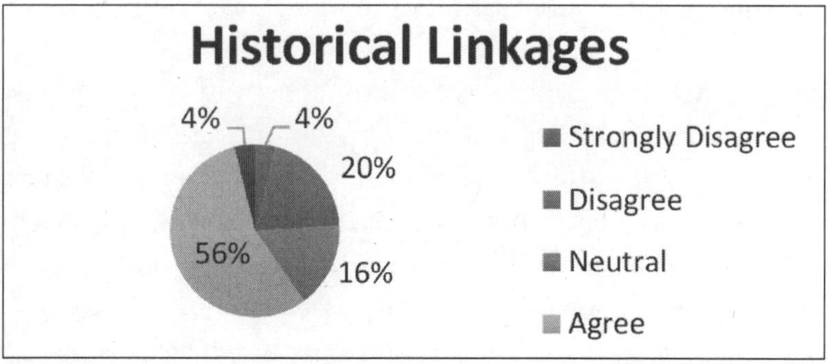

Source: Prepared by the author based on response to Questionnaire.

Geo-Strategic Significance: Geo-strategy describes where a state concentrates its efforts by projecting military power and directing diplomatic activity. Located at a dominating position in the IOR, India is strategically located to influence events in a region which is very important to Japan and where its reach being limited, it has traditionally been reliant on US support. Ninety-six per cent respondents have agreed that India's prominent location in the IOR and consequent geo-strategic significance was one of the important factors, which led to Japan establishing a security relationship. This has also been qualitatively analysed in Part I of this book.

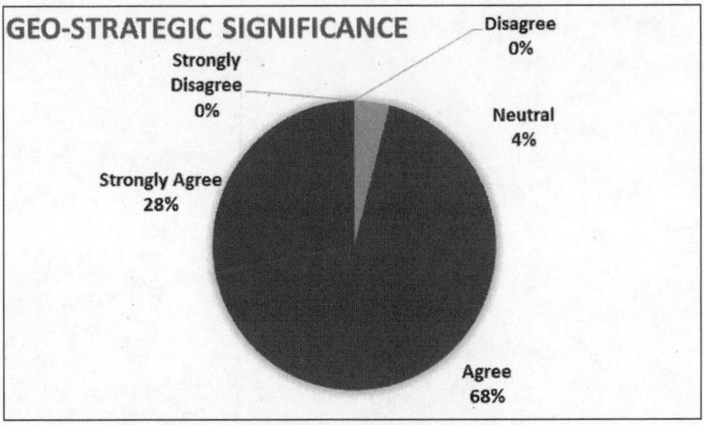

Source: Prepared by the author based on response to Questionnaire.

US-Japan Security Alliance: More the number of partners in security cooperation, greater are the number of problems of integration and cooperation. This increases the risk of diverging interests and national sensitivities endangering the overall aim of a security relationship. This criterion measures the effect that the US-Japan alliance will have on a security relationship of Japan with India. In the case of Japan, the US has always been very welcoming of India-Japan ties and has urged both nations to further engage each other. Sixty-eight per cent respondents agree that US-Japan Security alliance has had a positive effect in enhancing the security cooperation between India and Japan. The nudge given by US to both countries to form closer ties has also been analysed in Chapter 7 (Strategic Affinity). However, for any bilateral relations between Japan and India, the complementarities need to be strong and the security relations between Japan and India cannot be solely dependent on external stimuli, like the *rise of China* or the *security relationship with the US*.

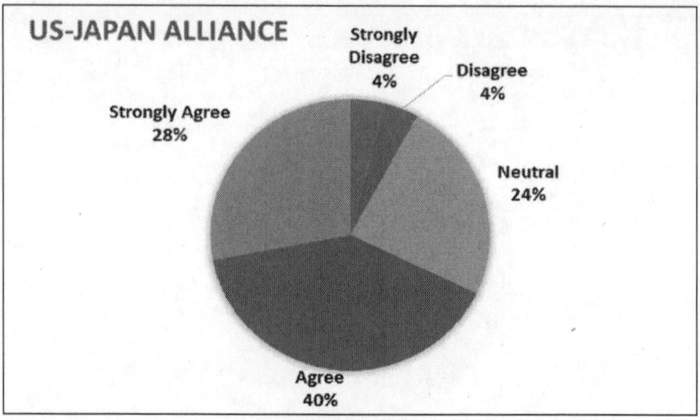

Source: Prepared by the author based on response to Questionnaire.

Constitutional/Political Restrictions: Article 9 of the Constitution of Japan renounces war as a sovereign right of the nation and the threat or use of force as means of settling international disputes. Despite the pacifist character of Japan's Constitution, the LDP government has successfully interpreted the constitution to cater to the basic security imperatives facing the country. The security legislations of 2015 have strengthened the hand of the SDF and the government to deal with various security challenges, which were otherwise hindered by the old legal provisions. The question related to this criterion intended measuring the perception whether the pacifist Constitution hindered successful security cooperation between the two countries. Forty-seven per cent respondents have agreed that constitutional restrictions will be a hindrance to successful India-Japan Security Cooperation. Similarly, the Indian policy of strategic autonomy can be seen as a hindrance to successful India-Japan security cooperation. Since these restraints are governed by various compulsions and opinions, both nations need to work around them to progress towards meaningful security relations.

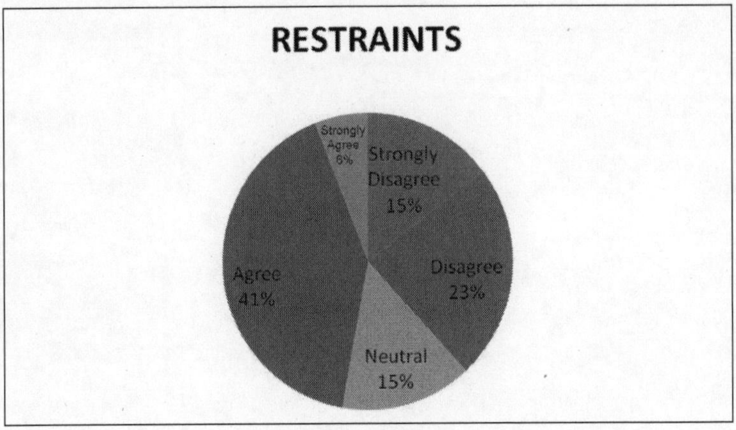

Source: Prepared by the author based on response to Questionnaire.

Objectives: A similarity of objectives facilitates two partner nations coming closer in a security relationship. Countries should have the same intentions, be open and clear about the goals of cooperating together and define realistic objectives.[3] Realism assists in maintaining relations at an optimum level with no false sense of expectations from each other. However, it should be noted that nations have multiple objectives some of which are ambiguous and some even change with time. In the case of India and Japan, presently there seems to be a degree of convergence in the objectives of security cooperation. Whereas Japan desires an order based on rules and maintenance of status quo in the region, India, in addition, is also looking for defence technology and military capability enhancement. A converging end state, therefore, is mandatory for a successful security relationship, so that both nations work towards achieving it and in the process strengthening the security cooperation. Eighty per cent of the respondents agreed that there is a degree of convergence in the objectives of security relationship of India and Japan.

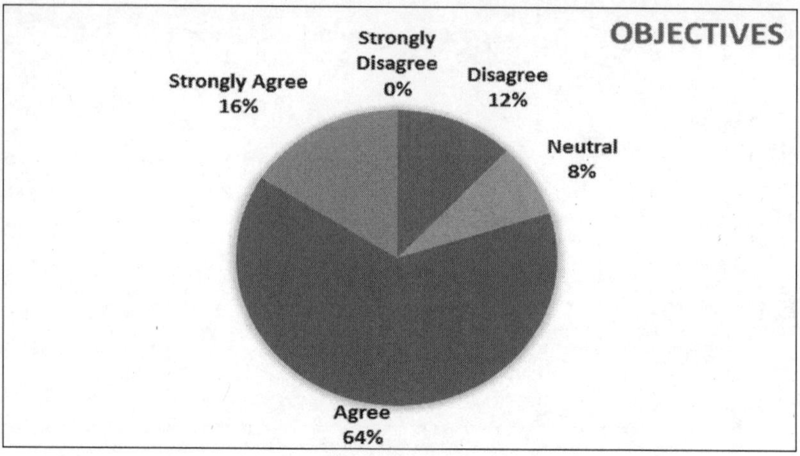

Source: Prepared by the author based on response to Questionnaire.

Economy: When security cooperation between nations contributes towards economic growth, the drive to facilitate the cooperation, increases. Defence equipment and technological cooperation resulting from security cooperation has the potential to boost economic prospects. Recent efforts by the US to ask its allies to spend more on arms procurement is an example of the effort to enhance economy through defence sales. Japan made a radical change to its defence equipment policy with the formulation of the "Three Principles on Transfer of Defense Equipment and Technology" in April 2014 and lifted the self-imposed ban on arms exports that was in place since 1976.[4] This change has opened up opportunities for the Japanese government and industries to sell Japanese military hardware to other countries and join the international arms market that previously was off-limits.[5] India, on the other hand, is on the lookout for technology and has a fledgling defence manufacturing industry. According to SIPRI data, India has been the largest importer of major arms between 2012 and 2016, accounting for 13 per cent of the global total sales. Additionally, the "Make in India" clause will boost domestic defence manufacturing and providing employment, by attracting technology to indigenous defence manufacturers. Japan, therefore, can present itself as another source of defence technology for India. Based on the question whether the security cooperation will be beneficial to the economies of both India and Japan, 100 per cent respondents agreed that it will be a win-win situation for both.

Trust: Trust is a very important criterion for any successful security cooperation. It is proportional to the level of cooperation between the countries. In the case of India-Japan security cooperation, a high degree of trust and solidarity is displayed during annual meetings and in joint statements by leaders of both countries. However, in India, deeper engagement with the US and its allies always comes with a perceived fear of loss of 'strategic autonomy'. Domestic political opposition to deeper engagement with the West has traditionally been very strong in India, though this has shown signs of ebbing during the tenure of the present Modi government. The unpredictability of the Trump regime has prompted a restraint to the Indian outreach to the West. The informal meetings with President Xi at Hunan, and with President Putin at Sochi were held to mitigate this fear of hedging. This foreign policy direction, however, contrasts with the overt dependence of Japan on the US for security and precludes generation of a high degree of trust in the India-Japan security relationship. For this trust and confidence to be enhanced, it is necessary that Japan projects itself as a far more self-asserting country that can take responsibility of its own security, when required. This trust can also be enhanced if Japan is seen committing major resources into a joint project (similar to the BrahMos missile co-development programme with Russia) or conducting joint exercises for the three Services—army, navy and air force for building up regional capability with pooled resources, say, developing a strategic lift capability for humanitarian and disaster assistance. Considering India's position on strategic autonomy, Japan needs to display a more independent approach to global events. Trust can grow over time and needs constant contribution from both sides. Otherwise this cooperation may be in danger of mere symbolism serving only the political cause of hedging against China in the Indo-Pacific. Successful cooperation requires both partners to invest when required. Implementation of planned actions should be taken with due diligence. Statements in the Questionnaire implying that adequate trust exists between the two countries was disagreed upon by 76 per cent respondents.

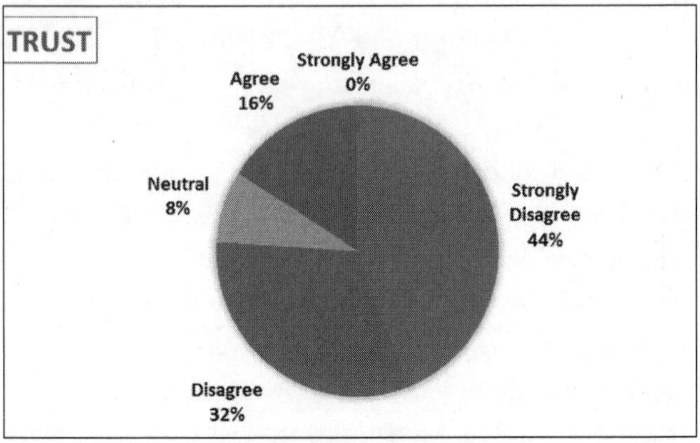

Source: Prepared by the author based on response to Questionnaire.

Partner Willingness: Willingness to share technology and intelligence inputs is an imperative for successful security relations. State of the art technology provides distinct military capability enhancement. For India, access to high end technology has been one of the drivers of this partnership. Similarly, sharing of intelligence inputs will facilitate establishment of a seamless grid across both the oceans. Willingness to share critical inputs is related to the degree of trust and the objectives of the security relationship between India and Japan. The Shinmaya US-2 offer by Japan to India, including ToT, is an example of growing trust between the two countries. This now needs to be translated to an environment where inputs pertaining to technology and intelligence can be shared seamlessly. High end technologies especially defence related or dual use technologies available with Japan require US clearance before sharing. Critical intelligence inputs are also a result of joint surveillance mechanisms in place along with the US and other allies of the US. These inputs are, therefore, unlikely to be made available to India easily. Seventy-two per cent respondents agree that partner willingness to share technology and intelligence inputs will not come easily to Japan.

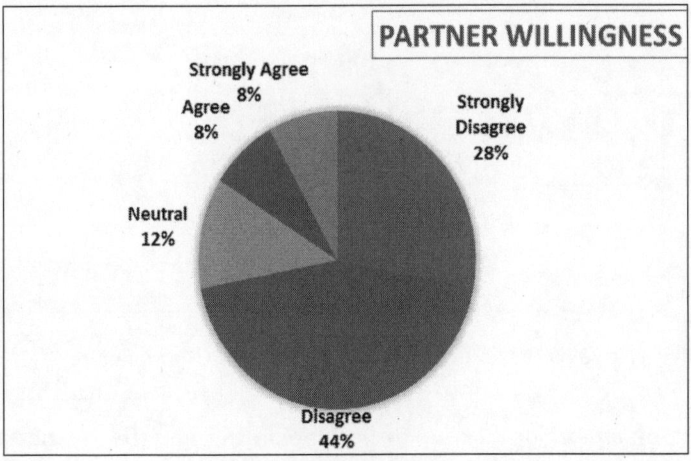

Source: Prepared by the author based on response to Questionnaire.

Military Engagements: A strong leadership at the top political as well as military level is essential for any security cooperation to succeed.[6] Simultaneously, there is also a need for dedicated engagement of military experts. India Japan security cooperation has stood the test of time from 2008 and subsequent changes in the government of both countries have not affected this relationship in any manner. Presently, the two heads of state, ministers, chiefs of the three services of armed forces, and the coast guards enjoy a very good chemistry with regular meetings being held between them. However, operational level integration of experts will ensure that the partnership continues on its own potential despite any change in political or military dispensation at higher levels. The current levels of navy to navy engagements are strong and need to be pursued by the air force and army too. Given the restrictions on the use of force by the SDF in Japan, meaningful engagements are, therefore, greater in the realms of HADR and non-traditional security. Based on the question of the levels of military to military engagements between the Indian armed forces and the SDF, 60 per cent respondents perceive that current levels of engagement are not optimal.

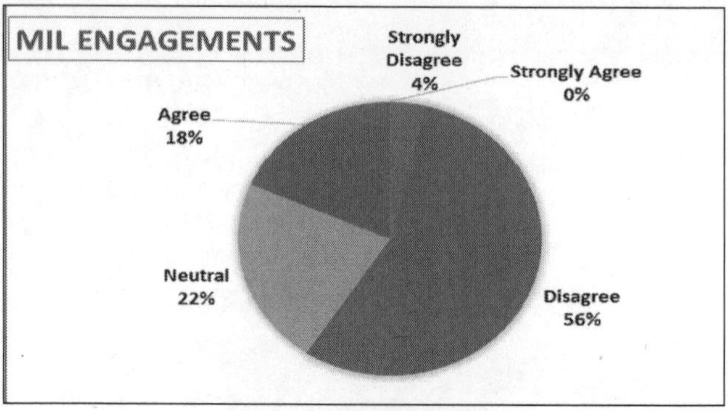

Source: Prepared by the author based on response to Questionnaire.

Involvement of Parliaments: Depending equally on national constitutions and traditions, parliaments play an essential role in decisions both on deployment of military forces as well as on defence planning and procurement.[7] Therefore, when enhancing security cooperation with each other, it is axiomatic to ensure that the law making members are involved and interact with each other. This is not only a matter of awareness and information-sharing, but can have consequences for parliamentary decision-making procedures as well.[8] In this matter, parliamentary groups of Japan and India have been visiting each other and interacting with stake holders. As both are thriving democracies, it is mandatory that there is political and public consensus with regards to a security relationship with each other. Forty-three per cent respondents agreed to the statement in the Questionnaire implying that India-Japan security cooperation has always been a priority aspect in India's foreign policy irrespective of the political leader/political party in power.

Interoperability: Interoperability between forces is directly proportional to the level at which the concepts, doctrine and equipment between them, are standardised. In particular, operating similar equipment that facilitates linkages between them allows for integration not only in the areas of training and education, but also with regard to logistics, maintenance, and the acquisition of spare parts (through-life cycle management).[9]

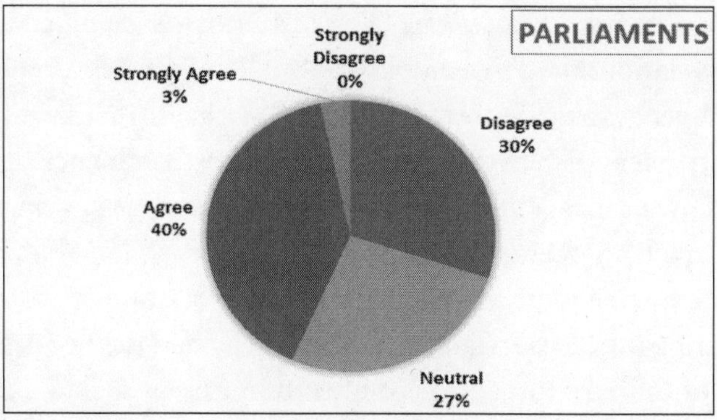

Source: Prepared by the author based on response to Questionnaire.

Recommendations for procurement of Soryu submarines by India should be seen in this context. Interoperability between the navies is being enhanced through regular exercises conducted. Such deep engagement is also desired between the armies and the air forces of India and Japan. In the logistics sphere, interoperability can be enhanced through the signing of the Acquisition and Cross Servicing Agreement (ACSA), or a similar agreement between the two countries. ACSA will facilitate easy berthing of military assets in each other's bases, maintenance and repairs, supplies and transfers of logistic material. Eighty-seven per cent respondents perceive that there is a lack of interoperability between the forces of both countries.

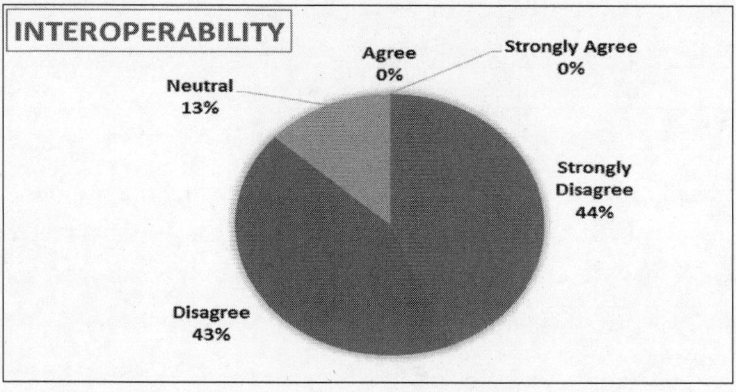

Source: Prepared by the author based on response to Questionnaire.

Expeditionary Capability: This criterion is significant for a security relationship between two 'normal' nations, especially when they are geographically separated from each other. Expeditionary capability refers both to the physical capability to influence situations far from own shores in terms of assets available as well as the 'will' to perform such an operation. In case of Japan, it is the public opinion and the enshrined pacifist Constitution that restrains such actions. Considering the heavy reliance on US security and the restrictions on the use of military force (except in certain cases), such a capability is non-existent in the case of Japan. In the case of India, there is no such legal restraint. The physical capability for expeditionary activities also exists. However, the will to go in for expeditionary support to a strategic partner depends on a case to case basis. For the purpose of quantitative assessment, this criteria has been taken as non-existent in both countries and hence, no questions in the questionnaire, have been based on this. However, the criterion has been taken into consideration while arriving at the overall levels of security cooperation between India and Japan.

Details of respondents who have populated the sample size are as under:

Researchers on Aspects Related to Japan (Civil)	03
Military Service Personnel with Experience in Dealing with East Asian aspects	09
Military Personnel dealing with Strategic Affairs in AHQ	03
Researchers on Defence Procurements and Defence Technology	01
Military Personnel with knowledge of East Asian Affairs	11
Total	27

Each of the criterion was asked to be ranked by the respondents on a scale of 10. After statistical calculations of the response received, the rank of each criterion as per weighted mean is as shown.

Rank as per Weighted Mean	Weighted Mean
Economy	729.31
Geo-Strategic Significance	695.36
Alignment of Objectives	642.05

Japan-US Alliance	556.03
Involvement of Parliaments	533.54
Historical Linkages	411.26
Restraints	405.60
Mil Engagements	393.73
Partner Willingness	361.85
Trust	331.69
Interoperability	240.72
Overall Total	5301.14
Weighted Mean = $(\sum xi^{*}wi)/\sum wi$	5301.14/84.3546
Weighted Mean	62.84
Overall Weighted Mean = (62.84 x 11)/12 (Including Factor of Expeditionary Capability)	57.6

Following deductions can be made from the statistical inference drawn.

- Economic benefits from the security cooperation are one of the primary drivers and, therefore, needs to be factored, in our interactions.
- Geo-strategic Significance of India in the IOR and of Japan in East Asia is an important consideration for closer relations between the two countries. This is a positive sign as India is likely to remain geo-strategically significant to Japan in the near future.
- Alignment of our objectives of this security relationship within the realms of realism is a must. A divergence in the desired end-states will reduce this relationship to mere rhetoric.
- The US will continue to remain a very important factor in this bilateral relationship.
- Law making bodies of both nations should ensure that adequate legal provisions (through the Parliaments) exist to build upon a strong relationship.
- Aspects of trust, interoperability, sharing and military engagements are important and take time to build up. Aspects to enhance the same must be addressed on priority.

The overall weighted mean of 57.6 (value based on a total of 100), indicates that more effort is required to focus on the important criteria (economic benefits of cooperation, alignment of objectives of cooperation and facilitating cooperation through push at the political level), to have a robust security cooperation.

A score of 57.8 out of 100 is just above the half-way mark and, thus, more needs to be done at the implementation levels for a strong India Japan security cooperation.

It also needs to be understood that golden rules and criteria do not exist. Security Cooperation is the product of many factors of influence, some of which have a more structural character—like strategic culture and historic experience, while others might be of a temporary nature such as unexpected defence budget cuts or personal relations between key political leaders.[11] The highest opportunity of success is created when the important criteria as given in the chapter above, is fulfilled and maximised by both the partner countries. This chapter, thus, provides a quantitative assessment of the levels of the security cooperation which is in congruence with the widely held opinion that though there is a huge potential, India-Japan security cooperation is, presently, still a work in progress. The chapter also provides an overview of factors where adequate focus has to be laid for keeping the trajectory of India Japan security relations, high.

Notes

1. The Clingendael Report (Netherlands Institute of International Relations) has been taken as the basis for arriving at the analyses of India-Japan security cooperation by the researcher. The report by Dick Zandee, Margriet Drent, Rob Hendriks on 'Defence cooperation models: Lessons learned and usability', October 2016 at https://www.clingendael.org/sites/default/files/pdfs/Report_Defence_cooperation_ models.pdf.
2. Christopher Paul, 'What Works Best When Conducting Security Cooperation?', RAND Office of External Affairs, October 2015, Testimony presented before the House Armed Services Committee on October 21, 2015 at https://www.rand.org/content/dam/rand/pubs/testimonies/CT400/CT441/RAND_CT441.pdf, accessed on August 13, 2018.
3. The Clingendael Report, note 1.

4. Hiroyuki Sugai, 'Japan's Future Defence Equipment Policy', Brookings Institution, October 2016 at https://www.brookings.edu/wp-content/uploads/2016/10/201610_japan_future_defense_hiroyuki_sugai.pdf, accessed on October 10, 2018.
5. Ibid.
6. The Clingendael Report, note 1.
7. Ibid.
8. Ibid.
9. Ibid.
10. Ibid.
11. Ibid.

9

Recommendations

India and Japan have grown in strength over the years since 2008, since the time the India-Japan Security Declaration was first signed between the two countries. This is reflected in the number of high-level visits exchanged and the several official dialogue mechanisms that are in place. The quality of mutual discourse is rich and there is optimism on both sides about the potential of their future ties.[1] The lack of any historical baggage and the good chemistry between the two prime ministers further facilitate this convergence.

This research has resulted in certain recommendations for enhancement of security cooperation between the two countries. The same have been covered in this chapter.

The security relationship between India and Japan needs further infusion of trust and seriousness of intentions with a realistic approach. Both nations need to build up a common end state to be achieved and spell out red lines. If India and Japan have different interpretations of the security end-state, security cooperation will remain transactional in nature. To ensure a win-win security relationship, transparent sharing of information, intelligence and technology is imperative. Also, our law-makers need to ensure that the correct environment and legal provisions exist for a robust relationship with Japan. Overall, as economic benefit from this security cooperation is one of the primary drivers of this relationship, this must be factored in the interactions.

Defence Equipment and Technology Cooperation

- Despite being expensive, the Shin Maya US-2 amphibious aircraft will be ice-breaking in terms of Japanese defence sales to India. There is an urgent need to arrive at an early decision on the Shin Maya US-2 procurement deal by resolving pending issues at the earliest. Certain *compromises on both sides* will facilitate taking the deal forward.
- Address specific Japanese concerns of sharing sensitive data with India's strategic private industry in ToT cases. Adopt *visible security measures* for protection of classified and sensitive information, reinforcing India's credibility to safeguard sensitive data and technology.
- Harness advanced Japanese technology *from Japanese manufacturers* like Mitsubishi Heavy Industries in conjunction with the DRDO or private industries for *manufacture of light tanks* under the 'Make in India' programme. This will fulfil the long standing demand of the army for a light tank that can operate with ease and flexibility in the high altitude and mountainous regions as also act as a counter to the light tank developed by China.
- Do not let procurement projects of big equipment in Defence Technology and Cooperation define India Japan relations. Smaller equipment, subsystems and components such as image sensors, Lithium-ion batteries, carbon fibre aircraft components which India needs, can be provided by Japan. *Component level procurements are simple; do not come under media glare; and the products have multiple uses.*
- *Encourage the Japanese industry* to participate in the Indian defence procurement projects. Address specific Japanese concerns in the Defence Procurement Procedures, if any. *Encourage government to government sales* with Japan where necessary. The Japanese defence attaches posted to New Delhi can play an active and important role in this regard. Ensuring active participation of Indian and Japanese defence industries in Def Expos is another constructive step in this regard. This will

provide a new source for arms and armament for the Indian armed forces and reduce dependency on certain select countries only.

Training

- *Enhance the student exchange programme* in terms of numbers of students undergoing courses in each other's military training institutions at tactical and operational levels. A deepening interaction will assist students of both countries to understand the security nuances of each other.
- *Invite Japan to utilise various institutes of expertise* for varied terrain like the High Altitude Warfare School (HAWS), the Counter Insurgency and Jungle Warfare School (CIJWS) and the Desert Battle School (DBS) for training the SDF, in India. Conduct collective training in unit and sub-unit groups, in addition to individual training. Formalise the planned ASW *training* of the Indian navy by the Japanese into an annual affair.
- *Train the SDF and the Japanese police* in countering urban insurgency and CT for the *upcoming 2020 Tokyo Olympics*. Training of *Japanese dog squads* as well as participation of Indian dog squads is an area of mutual cooperation.
- Conduct *joint amphibious training exercises* alternately in India and Japan with the newly formed Japanese Amphibious Brigade. With both the countries evolving their amphibious doctrines, joint amphibious exercises as part of the larger theatre level exercises will go a long way in enhancing interoperability, honing drills and imparting realistic training. A *trilateral format of such training exercises between the US, Japan and India* can also be thought of.

Counter Terrorism

- Formalise the planned Counter Terrorism Exercise between the GSDF and the Indian army *exercise 2018 into an annual affair*. Upgrade the exercise to include *profiling of weapons and equipment; communication systems and procedures; synergy in intelligence gathering, sharing, surveillance and optimal use of force against the identified terrorist targets.*[2] Ensuring attendance of all stakeholders dealing in counter terrorism operations including cyber experts, police and civil administration in such exercises will cater to a holistic participation with meaningful results.

- *Collaborate in technology development for anti-terrorist equipment* to facilitate rapid scanning, quick identification in a crowd, mass surveillance, close combat weapons, electronic eavesdropping on terrorist communication channels, jamming and intelligence sharing. This technology will assist in countering terrorism in India as well as assist in the smooth conduct of the planned Tokyo Olympics.
- *Establish functional counter-terror mechanisms* in order to break the nexus between terrorism, transnational organised crime, money-laundering, and illegal arms trafficking.[3]

Service to Service Engagement

- *Encourage operational and tactical level visits* to each other's military bases. Enhance visit by the aircrafts of each country to air bases of the other. Maintain and enhance visits by naval ships of both nations, including PASSEX (passing exercises).
- *Encourage regular meetings between leaders* of the countries, service to service staff talks, reciprocal visits by military leaders and operational level integration of experts.

Research and Development

- Intensify collaborative research projects and joint development between India and Japan for development of *fighter aircrafts, submarines, rocket and missile defence technology* on the lines of Japan-US, Japan-UK and Japan-Australia joint project developments.
- Incorporate civil industry in the collaboration between ATLA and DRDO for development in the field of AI and robotics for applications in the armed forces. Suggested areas of focus are

mine detection, vehicles, miniature UAVs, pilotless helicopters, swarm intelligence systems and augmented reality systems.

- The government should act as a catalyst in furthering growth by *creating an ecosystem* that is supportive of research, innovation and commercialisation of applications, revision of secondary school and university curricula to inculcate interest in AI, opening training centres focused on equipping young individuals with high-end skills in the field of analytics and Machine Learning, which in turn could be tied in with inviting data-driven global enterprises to set up their centres of excellence in India.[4] These measures will create the environment for seamless transition of AI into defence related functions.

Maritime Security

- Utilise Japanese assistance in the *development of the Andaman and Nicobar Islands into a strategic surveillance and security base* in the IOR that could allow India to create Anti-Access and Area Denial maritime exclusion zone, if required.
- Enhance *MDA through intelligence sharing.*
- Join hands with Japan in *capacity building of littoral countries in the IOR and the Western Pacific* to include training in specific aspects, sharing of resources and intelligence.
- Cooperate with Japan in the *exploration of undersea resources* in the IOR and the West Pacific.
- *Continue coordination between the navies and the coast guards of the two countries* as part of international groupings like the Regional Cooperation Agreement on Combating Piracy and Armed Robbery against Ships in Asia (ReCAAP) and Shared Awareness and Deconfliction (SHADE) on maritime threats.

UN Peace keeping Operations

- Cooperate in peace keeping operations through *composite task forces of Japanese and Indian peacekeepers,* viz. composite Japanese medical/engineer/communication units coupled with Indian infantry units.

- Offer the services of *Indian officers as liaison officers* for the SDF units in UN missions on similar lines as the Australian defence officers are presently posted.
- *Establish manufacturing hubs for UN related equipment* for Indian contingents in UN missions and integrate them with the Japanese supply chain for prompt delivery and cost effective maintenance.
- *Train larger number of Japanese peacekeepers in CUNPK.* Conduct joint training for peacekeepers in the form of joint exercises and drills in addition to class room teaching. *Conduct annual joint peacekeeping exercises* with Japan at a regional level incorporating other like-minded countries.
- Peacekeeping offers one of the finest spaces for propagating soft power. Both the countries should, therefore, *look towards propagation of soft power,* which is one of the spinoffs of peacekeeping operations and at post-conflict engagement in economic reconstruction of affected countries.
- Cooperate within the UN on peacekeeping and evolve ways to *bridge the contentious gold versus blood debate to make peacekeeping more effective.* This will also win kudos from African nations where most of the peace keeping operations occur.
- Cooperate amongst the G4 nations to *ensure that the UNSC reform process is taken up in due earnest* and is not scuttled by hardball diplomacy of the P5 countries.

HADR

- *Collaborate in HADR activities* to include Data and Statistical support and analysis, capacity development, Climate Change Mitigation and Adaptation Action, Knowledge Management, Information Sharing, sharing of best practices, sharing of earth quake resistant building technology, data and statistical analysis, early warning mechanisms, and capacity development to deal with disaster situations.

- Incorporate HADR activities including information sharing and capacity building of African nations in disaster management *as part of the activities in the AAGC.*
- Employ early warning systems of Japan and India for a *regional disaster management organisation* that can conduct annual drills, share pre-allocated resources for quick reaction to any natural disaster in the Indo-Pacific. Contribute to capacity building in the Indo-Pacific region for the use of space technology in disaster management.[5]

IT and Cyber Security

- Ease *movement of skilled IT manpower from India to Japan.* Urge Japan to overcome the restrictions of language skills, red tapism and long delays in recruitment, and enhance its immigration policies so that talent is retained. Invite Japanese students to join IITs in India and gain from the high standards of Indian engineering studies.
- *Share classified information* pertaining to cyber aspects for meaningful engagement and cyber-threat mitigation.
- Adopt an integrated and coordinated policy approach for leveraging indigenous IT talent pool.[6] Collaborate with Japan and other countries in *research and technical aspects of cyber space.*

Infrastructural Development

- Need to plan for infrastructure development through Japanese ODA loans in a manner which *aligns security benefits of enhanced connectivity and infrastructure* such as facilitating the movement of troops, side stepping in conflict, aggressive posturing, and improvement in supply chain architecture.

Space

- *Expand scope of international space cooperation for disaster management* by including a pre-disaster phase of efforts, thereby mitigating future risks of natural disasters.[7]

- Work towards establishing international policies and legal framework to regulate space, along with Japan.
- *Participate in multi-nation space missions*, wherever feasible. Invite Japan to participate in such multi-national missions too. Inviting Japan to the maritime awareness mission being planned in the IOR between India and France will speed up the project with reduced costs.
- *Explore possibilities for satellite building and launch of satellites as joint bilateral missions.* Utilise mutual capabilities for respective benefits. Cooperation between the recently established NavIC GPS system of India and the Quasi-Zenith Satellite System (QZSS) of Japan, to have an expanded coverage in the Indo-Pacific, can be explored.

Cultural Ties

- Set up *more Cultural Centres in India*. Highlight the *role of Sanskrit* in the development of the Japanese Kana script.
- Open up *Japanese language schools in India* for better people to people ties.

Demographic Profile

- Complement depleting Japanese workforce with skilled Indian workers. *Urge the Japanese government to encourage preference for Indian workers* especially in security related areas and dual use technology industry. This will be a win-win situation for both the countries.

Conclusion

Recommendations given above will go a long way in enhancing India Japan security cooperation. Some of these recommendations are already underway but there has not been much progress on ground. With bilateral visits taking place annually and political leaders of both countries looking for newer avenues to connect the scope for further cooperation increases manifold. By focusing on the positives and working around divergences, India and Japan will sustain the rising trajectory of security cooperation with each other.

Notes

1. Ministry of External Affairs, Press Remarks by External Affairs Minister at the 9th India-Japan Strategic Dialogue, March 29, 2018 at http://mea.gov.in/Speeches-Statements.htm?dtl/29735/Remarks to_the_Press_9th_IndiaJapan_Strategic_Dialogue.
2. Monika Chansoria, 'Japan-India Joint Counter-Terrorism Mechanism the Need of the Hour', Japan Forward, October 5, 2017 at https://japan-forward.com/japan-india-joint-counter-terrorism-mechanism-the-need-of-the-hour/, accessed on June 15, 2018.
3. Ibid.
4. Ibid.
5. Yuichiro Nagaia, Mukund Kadursrinivas Raob, Hideaki Shiroyamac, K.R. Sridhara Murthid, Motoko Uchitomie, Tunku Intan Mainuraf, Rogel Mari Seseg, and Tan Cheng Hai, Assessment of Space Programs and Policies for Regional Cooperation in the Asia Pacific Region, 68th International Astronautical Congress (IAC), Adelaide, Australia, September 25–29, 2017 at http://eprints.nias.res.in/1358/1/2017-MKRao-IAC-17-E3.1.8ApSpacePolicyFullPaper.pdf, accessed on September 28, 2018.
6. R. Shashank Reddy, 'Transforming Indo-Japan Relations Through Robots', *Carnegie India,* December 7, 2017 at https://carnegieindia.org/2017/12/07/transforming-indo-japan-relations-through-robots-pub-74968, accessed on September 28, 2018.
7. Monika Chansoria, note 2.

10

The Way Ahead

India and Japan have come a long way since the 6th century AD when Buddhism was introduced in Japan from India. The cultural linkages are being utilised to build people to people ties as well as security linkages. Both India and Japan are looking to triple the number of Indian and Japanese tourists in the next five years, and have been pushing bilateral travel and tourism.[1] The Japanese tourism office in Tokyo had sponsored visits of 10 Japanese tour operators, opinion leaders and even journalists to India, who had also attended the International Buddhist Conclave in 2014.[2] With the rich cultural and religious history, India is poised to draw upon the strength of this history to attract people of several faiths from countries across the globe. The Indian government has aligned itself to the Panchamrit principles to guide its foreign policy, and the fifth of these five principles is "*sanskriti evam sabhyata* (cultural and civilisational links)", which expresses the government's desire to leverage India's rich historical cultural links with other countries as part of its non-coercive soft power strategy.[3] In addition to Buddhism, yoga and Bollywood are also gradually finding place in the soft power projection of India.

The strategic relations were enhanced when realists in Japan realised the geo-strategic importance of India. In their search for "new friends" and alternative to the US security guarantee, India evolved as a suitable country with a like-minded disposition, ready for engagement. Therefore, though India did not figure in the Japanese scheme of things in the mid-20th century, the early 21st century saw an intense outreach by Japan, complemented by India to engage with each other.

Today, with the nuclear options looming in a big way, countries are averse to conflicts and wars. In an increasingly interdependent world, the role of alliances, central to strategic politics throughout history, has begun to fade.[4] Forming alliances to defeat an adversary in war or economic conflict is no longer possible since significant military or economic conflict threatens to result in a systemic collapse.[5] It, therefore, seems that alliances are a thing of the past. Currently, even the US-Japan alliance is under pressure. Japan is unsure of the extent to which US will come to its support in security aspects in case say, the Senkaku Islands are threatened by the Chinese. India-Japan relations have matured from "Global Partnership" in 2005 to a "Global and Strategic Partnership" in 2006 and thereafter to a "Special Strategic and Global Partnership". The word Strategic Partnership, therefore, holds special emphasis. They do not bind the partners to come to military assistance in case one of the partners gets committed in a conflict with its adversary. Nor is the partner nations expected to take sides in ongoing bilateral disputes of the other.

The India Japan Strategic Partnership should be seen in a similar context. India does not take sides in Japan's territorial disputes of the Senkaku Islands with China or the Northern territories with Russia. Similarly, Japan is less intrusive about Pakistan's involvement in Kashmir. In the Doklam standoff of India with China, the Ambassador of Japan to India, Mr Kenji Hiramatsu said, "What's important in disputed areas is that all parties involved do not resort to unilateral attempts to change the status quo by force, and resolve the dispute in a peaceful manner."[6] Similarly, India's statement in the South China Sea dispute was non-committal and not targeted at a particular country. To that extent, strategic partnership actually provides an opportunity to diplomatically assist in resolution of disputes, ignore certain actions based on national interests and mutual perceptions, and also present a strong front of solidarity, which can dissuade coercion by other nations. The aim of the strategic partnership should be clear and well understood by both partners.

India-Japan strategic partnership, therefore, should not be built on an anti-China plank.[7] The partnership should be based on mutual complementarities with the aim of ensuring security and stability in the region, as well as inclusive development for the people of both countries. In security terms, this translates into comprehensive capability development so that both countries are equipped to face any security challenge. A China expert in Japan observed, "India and Japan avoid direct opposition with China while having strong wariness for China and strengthen Japan and India relations for a check for China".[8]

So, where is the India Japan Security Cooperation leading to? The status today, reveals a huge but untapped potential. The qualitative and the quantitative assessments as brought out in this book indicate that the present levels of cooperation are a work in progress.

The questionnaire survey in Chapter 8 indicates that economy and geo-strategic location are two important factors for cooperation between India and Japan. The huge Indian market and the infrastructural demands in India are there to stay. Japan is gradually reaching out to areas which were earlier restricted to entry for foreign investors. The urge to maintain a perennial source of supply of raw material and energy sources will continue to dictate Japan's outreach, as deduced in Chapter 3 of this book. The geo-strategic importance is also enduring because of Japan's reliance on trade routes through the IOR. This spells a positive note for the cooperation between the two countries for some time to come.

Is the progress of this security cooperation along the correct trajectory? The answer to this lies in the understanding of the power play in Asia and the rising global significance of the Indo-Pacific region. Chapters 5 to 7 brings out the possibility of both nations deriving strength from this security cooperation through various complementarities bilaterally and regionally, and forming the foundations of a security structure in Asia that is inclusive and encompasses the vast expanse of Indo-Pacific. Infrastructural assistance and provision of latest technology from Japan to India will assist in capability building in consonance with its geo-strategic importance. India also needs the Japan and US influence in international multi-lateral organisations like the NSG to remain relevant in the global arena. This mutual dependence will ensure that the security relationship and strategic partnership stays on course in the foreseen future.

India is not ready to join any coalition against China but wants to deal on its own when bilateral issues are involved.[9] However, it is open to join a multilateral approach while dealing with regional or global issues.[10] There is widespread acceptance among the strategic community in India that its security relationship is consistent with its stand on strategic autonomy and sees no friction with Japan.[11]

Overall, both India and Japan are poised to play an important role in the security dynamics of the Indo-Pacific. Other like-minded nations like Vietnam, South Korea and Singapore are assessing this partnership for its strengths and relevance and when they realise that this partnership is aligned to their own national interests also, they will support it. The external and internal drivers of this strategic partnership as brought out in Chapter 7 will impel India and Japan to further seek complementarities to coordinate at the regional and global levels. In case the US-Japan security alliance becomes weak, or the US reduces its involvement in East Asia, India-Japan relations will need to be strengthened. Chapter 7 also brings out that both nations need to take initiatives to propel each other to enhance the levels of security cooperation and assume a major role in the Indo-Pacific. India-Japan security cooperation can form the basis of new security architecture in the Indo-Pacific. But for accomplishing the same, as brought out in Chapter 8, the factors of trust, willingness to share and interoperability will need to be enhanced. In order to leverage the combined potential of this cooperation, the relationship should be able to wield adequate influence in the region. This can be achieved by enhancing respective military capabilities and reducing dependence on other countries for security.

Any new security architecture in the Indo-Pacific would likely comprise of nations that align themselves to the rule of law, adhere to international norms in global commons and who want the Indo-Pacific to be free from the influence of any single over-arching power. The architecture will be effective only if it is able to convince the outliers to adhere to the rule of law so that they do not attempt a revision for fulfilment of individual national interests. Currently, India-Japan Security Cooperation has been progressing very well, guided by the chemistry and vision of leaders of both countries, PMs Modi and Shinzo Abe. Bilaterally, both countries need to work towards further enhancing the security cooperation. The instituted measures of multi-level engagements will ensure that the convergence of the two democracies continue irrespective of the leaders in power. What remains to be seen is with what enthusiasm, initiative and interest the engagements are carried out to achieve successful security cooperation in future.

Notes

1. Arka Roy Chowdhury, 'India is working to attract Japanese travellers, developing Buddhist circuit', *The Times of India, Times Travel,* April 1, 2018 at https://timesofindia.indiatimes.com/travel/destinations/india-is-working-to-attract-japanese-travellers-developing-buddhist-circuit/as63713037.cms, accessed on September 30, 2018.
2. Ibid.
3. Shantanu Kishwar, 'The Rising Role of Buddhism in India's Soft Power Strategy', ORF Issue Brief No. 228, February 15, 2018 at https://www.orfonline.org/wp-content/uploads/2018/02/ORF_IssueBrief_228_Buddhism.pdf, accessed on September 3, 2018.
4. R. Basrur and S.N. Kutty (eds), 'Conceptualising Strategic Partnerships', *India and Japan, Assessing the Strategic Partnership*, Palgrave Macmillan, Singapore, 2018, p. 5.
5. Ibid.
6. Statement of Kenji Hiramatsu, Japanese Ambassador to India during the Doklam standoff, *Times Now Bureau*, Japan backs India on Doklam standoff, says resolve dispute in peaceful manner, August 18, 2017 at https://www.timesnownews.com/india/article/japan-backs-india-on-

doklam-standoff-says-resolve-dispute-in-peaceful-manner-china/74406, accessed on January 23, 2019.

7. Prof K.V. Kesavan, during an interaction at the Institute for Defence Studies and Analyses, August 31, 2018.
8. Takenori Horimoto, 'Japan-India Rapprochement and Its Future Issues': Japan's Diplomacy Series, Japan Digital Library at http://www2.jiia.or.jp/en/digital_library/japan_s_diplomacy.php, accessed on September 30, 2018.
9. Rajaram Panda at http://src-h.slav.hokudai.ac.jp/rp/publications/no06/01_Panda.pdf.
10. Ibid.
11. Ibid.

Appendix A

Chinese Vessels around Senkaku Islands

(Data Taken from Ministry of Foreign Affairs, Japan Website)

Month and Year	No. of Vessels Identified within Territorial Sea of Japan	No. of Vessels Identified within Contiguous Zone of Japan
Sep 2012	13	81
Oct	19	122
Nov	15	124
Dec	21	80
Jan 2013	17	57
Feb	17	49
Mar	11	69
Apr	25	86
May	15	104
Jun	9	71
Jul	14	88
Aug	28	88
Sep	22	77
Oct	8	26
Nov	12	53
Dec	10	51
Jan 2014	6	72
Feb	9	36
Mar	6	68
Apr	8	84
May	5	49
Jun	6	42
Jul	4	59
Aug	10	89
Sep	10	110
Oct	9	48

Month and Year	No. of Vessels Identified within Territorial Sea of Japan	No. of Vessels Identified within Contiguous Zone of Japan
Nov	8	42
Dec	7	30
Jan 2015	8	32
Feb	8	68
Mar	9	57
Apr	9	66
May	9	84
Jun	8	77
Jul	7	40
Aug	6	54
Sep	9	81
Oct	7	52
Nov	8	56
Dec	7	42
Jan 2016	8	34
Feb	5	21
Mar	9	56
Apr	9	82
May	11	97
Jun	9	82
Jul	9	59
Aug	23	147
Sep	8	54
Oct	8	29
Nov	12	56
Dec	10	35
Jan 2017	10	37
Feb	7	49
Mar	10	47
Apr	12	82
May	12	94
Jun	12	60
Jul	12	98
Aug	8	58

Month and Year	No. of Vessels Identified within Territorial Sea of Japan	No. of Vessels Identified within Contiguous Zone of Japan
Sep	8	72
Oct	4	28
Nov	7	51
Dec	6	20
Jan 2018	7	25
Feb	6	30
Mar	7	52
Apr	7	78
May	8	62
Jun	8	47
Jul	7	51
Aug	8	44

Appendix B

SWOT Analysis - India Japan Security Cooperation

		Opportunities		Threats
OPPORTUNITIES (O) & THREATS (T) / STRENGTHS(S)		O1: Chemistry between leaders O2: Technology (Submarine, Aircraft Mfr, Li-Ion Batteries…) O3: Common strategic perception of security O4: Pro-active contribution to peace O5: New Security Laws O6: Professional Disaster Mitigation Org. O7: UNPKO O8:Space Tech	O9:ATLA O10:Advanced Mil Hardware O11: AI & Robotics; Strategic Electronics O12:Strong MSDF O13:Financial Power O14: SDF Capability O15: Amphibious Brigade O16: EPQI O17:Weak Littorals O18: Terrorism	T1: Aggressive Rise of China T2: Diminishing US Influence T3: N. Korean Nuclear Missiles T4: Chinese Presence in IOR T5 : Interdiction Of SLOCs T6: Terrorism T7: Need for Info/Int-SLOCs & Choke Pts. T8: Cyber Threat T9: Piracy
S1: Combat Experience. **S2:CI/CT Experience** **S3:UNPKO** **S4: Training Infrastructure** **S5: DRDO** **S6:Space Technology** **S7:HADR Activities**	**S10: Skilled and Cheap Manpower.** **S11: Robotics and Working Pot** **S12: Geo-Strat Loc in IOR.** **S13** **S14:Act East Policy** **S15:Def Policy**	**<u>SO STRATEGIES</u>** **S1O14 S4O14** - Offer available training infrastructure (ranges) and Institutions (Schools) in India to train SDF in order to utilise combat experience of Indian Armed Forces. **S3O7**-Cooperate in UN Peacekeeping activities in mission area, training of peacekeepers, logistics, soft power building. **S2,S9,O18**-Offer experience gained in Counter Terrorist operations and resources (if required) to Japanese stake holders for Olympics 2020.		**<u>ST STRATEGIES</u>** **S12T5:**Utilise Geo-strategic location to provide security to SLOCs in conjunction with other navies. Offer ACSA services to Japan **S9T4:** Assist littorals in capacity building so as not to succumb under pressure.

		Opportunities	Threats
S8: Soft Power **S9: Professional Armed Forces**	**Reforms-FDI in Defence** **S16:Make In India**	**S5O9 ;S11O11 ; S10O2** - Enhance Engagement between ATLA and DRDO in various R & D projects. Collaborate in development of mil grade robots and AI. Craft Collaborations and commence Joint Productions of defence equipment. **S6O8** - Harness complementary developments in Space Technology for regional and bilateral advantage. **S7O6**-Collaborate in mitigation of disaster risks through sharing of technology, engage in HADR activities at a regional and bilateral level. **S15,O2, O10S6** - Encourage Japan to participate in Indian Defence Procurement projects. **S8,02,013** - Utilise ODA loans for projects that have spin-off security benefits S9,O3,O14 ; S9O15; S9O12 -Conduct Joint Trg and Ex between Armed Forces; Enhanced Student exchange for Military Courses. Enhance Official Interactions and Exchanges between Armed Forces; Ex between Amphibious Brigades. **S8,O2,O13**- Exploit Indian soft power in conjunction with Japanese finance & technology to build bridges in the region. **S14O4O16**-Combine Act East with Pro-Active Contribution to Peace and EPQI in NER.	**S10T8**:Exchange Expert manpower to collaborate in IT; Deepen cyber security cooperation. **S12T9**: Collaborate with Japan other navies to mitigate non-traditional maritime threats.

	Opportunities		Threats
OPPORTUNITIES(O) & THREATS (T)	O1: Chemistry between leaders O2: Technology (Submarine, Aircraft Mfr, Li-Ion Batteries…) O3: Common strategic perception of security O4: Pro-active contribution to peace O5: New Security Laws O6: Professional Disaster Mitigation Org. O7: UNPKO O8:Space Tech	O9:ATLA O10:Advanced Mil Hardware O11: AI & Robotics; Strategic Electronics O12:Strong MSDF O13:Financial Power O14: SDF Capability O15: Amphibious Brigade O16: EPQI O17:Weak Littorals O18: Terrorism	T1: Aggressive Rise of China T2: Diminishing US Influence T3: N.Korean Nuclear Missiles T4: Chinese Presence in IOR T5 : Interdiction Of SLOCs T6: Terrorism T7: Need for Info/Int-SLOCs & Choke Pts. T8: Cyber Threat
W1: Defence Of Island Territories. **W2:** Naval Assets And Tech Of Building Naval Assets. **W3:** ASW Capability. **W4:**Infrastructure Deficit **W5:** Bureaucracy **W6:** Indigenous Defence Technology	**WO STRATEGIES** **W1O10**-Procure (with ToT) surveillance and reconnaissance equipment to assist in security of island territories. Cooperate to evolve amphibious forces into a professional element. Improve surveillance over island territories. **W2O1; W6,O2,O10**- Procure hi-tech naval assets including ToT, from Japan. Strengthen Defence Equipment and Technological Cooperation. Collaborate in ship building. **W3O12**-Collaborate in submarine training. **W4O13**-Utilise ODA loans for infrastructure development in remote areas. Collaborate in Training for ASW Capability and Def Procurements Of Submarines. The strategies arrived at through this SWOT analysis have been discussed and analysed in Chapter 4 in the context of recent incidents and the scope of cooperation that exists between the two countries.		**WT Strategy**

Appendix C

Joint Declaration on Security Cooperation between India and Japan October 22, 2008[1]

The Prime Ministers of India and Japan,

Affirming that India-Japan relations are rooted in their similar perceptions of the evolving environment in the region and the world at large;

Recognising their common commitment to democracy, open society, human rights and the rule of law;

Affirming their deep respect for each other's contribution in promoting peace, stability and development in Asia and beyond;

Recognising that India and Japan are partners with a mutual stake in each other's progress and prosperity, and that a strong and prosperous India is in the interests of Japan and that a strong and prosperous Japan is in the interests of India;

Recognising that India and Japan share common interest in the safety of sea lines of communications;

Affirming their common commitment to fight against terrorism and recognising that counter-terrorism efforts by India and Japan, including the Japan Maritime Self Defence Force's replenishment activities in the Indian Ocean, constitute an important part in the international community's effort to eradicate terrorism;

Reiterating their common commitment in pursuing disarmament and non-proliferation as partners seeking a peaceful nuclear-weapon free world and working together against proliferation;

Reaffirming their common commitment to a comprehensive reform of the United Nations, including the expansion of the United Nations Security Council in both the permanent and non-permanent categories;

Affirming the establishment of a Strategic and Global Partnership that is driven by converging long-term political, economic and strategic interests, aspirations and concerns;

Recognising the importance of the steady and qualitative upgrade of mutual cooperation; and

Committing to working together in the future by increasing practical cooperation among the foreign affairs, defence and other related agencies of the two countries;

Have decided to create a comprehensive framework for the enhancement of security cooperation between the two countries.

Elements for Cooperation

The following elements will be included in security cooperation between India and Japan;

Information exchange and policy coordination on regional affairs in the Asia Pacific region and on long-term strategic and global issues.

Bilateral cooperation within multilateral frameworks in Asia, in particular the East Asia Summit, ASEAN Regional Forum and ReCAAP processes.

Defence dialogue and cooperation within the framework of the Joint Statement signed in May 2006 between the two Defence Ministries.

Cooperation between Coast Guards
Safety of transport
Fight against terrorism and transnational crimes
Sharing of experiences in peacekeeping and peacebuilding
Disaster management
Disarmament and non-proliferation
Mechanisms of Cooperation

The following mechanisms will be included with a view to concretising the above mentioned cooperation between the two countries;

Consultations will be conducted between the two Foreign Offices by way of;

Strategic Dialogue at Foreign Minister-level,

Meeting between the Foreign Secretary of India and the Vice-Minister for Foreign Affairs of Japan,

Dialogue on Disarmament and Non-Proliferation at Director General/Joint Secretary level,

Track 1.5 Strategic Dialogue

Cooperation will be conducted between the two Defence Authorities by way of various ways such as;

Meetings between the Defence Ministers,

Meetings between the Defence Secretary of India and the Vice-Minister of Defence of Japan including Defence Policy Dialogue,

Military-to-Military Talks at Director General/Joint Secretary level,

Exchange of service chiefs,

Navy-to-Navy Staff Talks

Service-to-service exchanges including bilateral and multilateral exercises,

Exchange of students and researchers for respective defense institutions (for example, Indian National Defence College, Japanese National Institute for Defense Studies).

Consultation will be conducted between the National Security Advisor of India and the Japanese counterpart.

The two Coast Guards will continue to promote cooperation to ensure maritime safety, maritime security and to protect marine environment through joint exercise and meeting between the two Coast Guards according to the Memorandum on Cooperation between the Indian Coast Guard and the Japan Coast Guard.

In relation to the safety of transport, Shipping Policy Forum will be conducted between Maritime Authorities and private sectors, and consultation will be conducted between Railway Authorities.

Comprehensive Security Dialogue will be conducted at Director General/ Joint Secretary level.

Bilateral consultation will be conducted to promote counter-terrorism cooperation through such means as Joint Working Group on counter terrorism between the relevant government offices including the Ministries of Foreign Affairs.

Mechanism of sharing of information will be sought with regard to suspicious transaction on money laundering and terrorist financing between the two Financial Intelligence Units.

Cooperation will be conducted to develop Tsunami Disaster Map in India.

The two sides will promote capacity building in disaster prevention, preparedness, sharing knowledge and experience of both countries.

Cooperation will be conducted between the Indian Space Research Organisation (ISRO) and the Japan Aerospace Exploration Agency (JAXA) in the field of disaster management.

Implementation

India and Japan will develop an action plan with specific measures to advance security cooperation in the above areas and report to the Prime Ministers at an early date.

Tokyo,
October 22, 2008

Dr. Manmohan Singh	Mr. Taro Aso
Prime Minister	Prime Minister of Japan
of the Republic of India	

Note

1. Joint Declaration on Security Cooperation between Japan and India, available at https://www.mofa.go.jp/region/asia-paci/india/pmv0810/joint_d.html.

Appendix D

Action Plan to advance Security Cooperation based on the Joint Declaration on Security Cooperation between Japan and India December 29, 2009[1]

1. Strengthening Cooperation on Issues of Common Strategic Interest

Consolidate the Global and Strategic Partnership

Enhance information exchange and policy coordination on security issues in the Asia Pacific region and on long term strategic and global issues on the basis of the Joint Declaration on Security Cooperation

Promote open, transparent and inclusive regional cooperation in Asia, in both economic and security fields

Pursue bilateral cooperation in existing multilateral frameworks in Asia, in particular the East Asia Summit, ASEAN Regional Forum (ARF) and Regional Cooperation Agreement on combating Piracy and Armed Robbery against Ships in Asia (ReCAAP) processes

2. Strategic Cooperation Mechanisms

Annual Strategic dialogue at Foreign Minister-level

Regular Consultations between National Security Advisor of India and Japanese Counterpart

Annual Subcabinet/Senior Officials 2+2 dialogue (Ministry of Foreign Affairs and Ministry of Defence of Japan/Ministry of External Affairs and Ministry of Defence of India)

Foreign Secretary/Vice Minister level Dialogue (basically twice a year)

Foreign Office Consultations (Basically once a year)

Annual Comprehensive Security Dialogue at the level of Joint Secretary, Ministry of External Affairs (MEA) and Ministry of Defence (MOD) of India/Director General, Ministry of Foreign Affairs (MOFA) and Ministry of Defence (MOD) of Japan

Maritime Security Dialogue

Annual Track 1.5 Strategic Dialogue

Consultation on regional issues between Foreign Office and Embassy at Capital Basis

3. Defence Cooperation

Regular meetings between the Ministers of Defence

Annual Defence Policy Dialogue at the level of Defence Secretary/ Administrative Vice-Minister of Defence

Annual Military-to-Military Talks between Joint Secretary, MOD of India and Deputy Director General, MOD of Japan

Regular reciprocal visits between Service Chiefs of both sides

Regular Ground-to-Ground Staff Talks

Navy-to-Navy Staff Talks (basically once a year)

Developing of Annual Calendar of Defence Cooperation and Exchanges

1. Exercises

Annual bilateral naval exercises, alternately off India and Japan, to enhance cooperation and core capabilities for maritime operation and disaster relief

Multilateral Naval Exercises, when possible

Passing Exercise (PASSEX) during ship visits

Participation as observers in major army and air force exercises

2. Non traditional security threats

Exercise, exchanges and training on issues such as anti-piracy and transnational crimes

Cooperation in anti-piracy operations between the Indian Navy and the Japanese Self Defense Force

3. Exchanges/Seminars

Student/researchers exchange for respective defence institutions (including National Defence College, Defence Services Staff College and Institute for Defence Studies and Analysis of India, National Institute for Defense Studies, Japan Ground Self Defense Force Staff College and Japan Maritime Self Defense Force Staff College).

Participation in major defence seminars/fora/training courses/shows

Exchange of cadets/young officers through ship rider programmes and training seminars/interactions

4. Coast Guard Cooperation

The two Coast Guards will continue to promote cooperation to ensure maritime safety, maritime security and to protect marine environment through joint exercise and meeting between the two Coast Guards according to the Memorandum on Cooperation between the Japan Coast Guard and the Indian Coast Guard. The two Coast Guards will implement concrete measures based on the bilateral coordination and agreement on subjects such as the content and timing of such cooperation.

5. Safety of Transport

Shipping Policy Forum to be conducted between Ministry of Land, Infrastructure, Transport and Tourism (MLIT) of Japan and Ministry of Shipping of India, with participation from the private sector.

Consultation between Railway authorities of MLIT of Japan and Ministry of Railways of India

6. Information Exchange and cooperation in fight against terrorism and other transnational crimes

Mechanism for intelligence exchange and technical cooperation on counter terrorism such as Joint Working Group on Counter terrorism, including intelligence exchange and technical cooperation, led by MEA of India and MOFA of Japan, with participation from concerned Government Agencies.

Establishment of information exchange framework between the two Financial Intelligence Unites (FIUs) on money laundering and terrorist financing.

Workshops/training

7. Cooperation at the United Nations

Regular dialogue and cooperation on UN reform, including early realisation of permanent membership of the UN Security Council of India and Japan, at the level of Deputy Vice Minister, MOFA/Additional Secretary, MEA.

Mutual dispatch of lecturers/participants to UN peacekeeping operation related-seminars hosted by each side and exchange of experiences/information related to staff training.

Regular Dialogue and cooperation on UN peacekeeping operations, including exchanges between Japanese Central Readiness Force/International Peace Cooperation Activities Training Unit and Centre for UN Peacekeeping (CUNPK)/Units experienced in peacekeeping operations from India, training of Japanese officers at the CUNPK, and sharing experience in and information on UN Peacekeeping operations and peace building.

8. Disaster Management

Cooperation to develop Tsunami Disaster Map of India between MLIT of Japan and Ministry of Home Affairs (MHA) of India.

Cooperation to expand the capability of Asian countries to advance their ability to provide a rapid, coordinated and effective Disaster response through an active participation in the next ARF Field Exercise to be held in Indonesia in 2011.

Capacity Building through the Workshop on Water-related Disaster management conducted by the International Center for Water Hazard and Risk Management (ICHARM) of Japan.

Sharing experience in landslide disaster prevention between National Institute of Land and Infrastructure Management (NILIM), Public Works Research Institute (PWRI) of Japan and National Institute of Disaster Management (NIDM) of India.

Capacity Building for disaster management and sharing Japanese experience on disaster relief through training programmes conducted by Japan International Cooperation Agency (JICA).

Dialogue between National Disaster Management Authorities (NDMA) of India and Cabinet Office of Japan through Asian Disaster Reducing Centre (ADRC) for sharing information on disaster prevention and preparedness.

Participation as observers in Japan's nationwide disaster management drill

Sharing of disaster-related information between Japan Aerospace Exploration Agency (JAXA) and Indian Space Research Organisation (ISRO) through "Sentinel Asia" process.

9. Cooperation on disarmament and non-proliferation

Annual Dialogue on disarmament and non-proliferation at the level of Joint Secretary, MEA/Director General of MOFA

New Delhi
December 29, 2009

Note

1 Action Plan to advance Security Cooperation based on the Joint Declaration on Security Cooperation between Japan and India, available at https://mea.gov.in/bilateral-documents.htm?dtl/5089/Action+Plan+to+advance+Security+Cooperation+based+on+the+Joint+Declaration+on+Security+Cooperation+ between+Japan+and+India.

Appendix E

Identification of Drivers

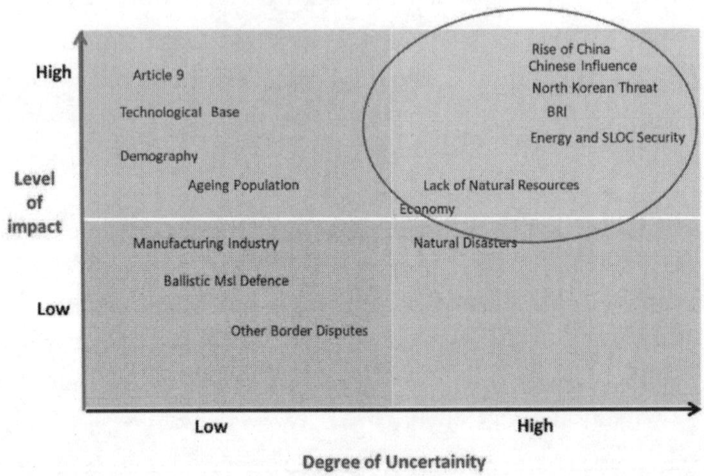

Strategic drivers can be identified by plotting the Key Decision Factors (KDF) against an Impact-Uncertainty matrix. The KDF are factors that are critical for the management of the national security of a nation. The KDFs are arrived at, after carrying out a Political, Economic, Social, Technological, Environment and Legal-Military (PESTEL-M) analysis of the country. The PESTEL-M analysis of India and Japan have been carried out during the course of research of this book (analyses has not been included) and KDFs, which affect India-Japan strategic partnership and security aspects have been identified. When KDFs are plotted as per their impact on the end-state (national security, in this case) and the degree of uncertainty of outcomes, the factors with the highest levels of impact and uncertainty become the drivers (fourth quadrant in this case).

The drivers for national security lead onto various futures. Security Cooperation between India and Japan is one such future. The drivers identified have been indicated in the graph and included in Chapter 7 of this book.

Appendix F

QUESTIONNAIRE

(The questionnaire was forwarded to respondents through Google Form. Here, the various criteria have been listed alongwith their questions (which were part of the questionnaire). The answer was sought in Likert's scale (with either the agree-disagree format or the options which were graded by the researcher during the statistical calculations, on a scale of 1 to 5. The criterion is indicated against the questions here but is not part of the questionnaire forwarded for inputs)

Q No. 1 Top of Form

Buddhism reached Japan from India through China in the 6th century AD. Influence of Sanskrit on the Japanese script is also well documented. Have the historical linkages played a role in providing a strong foundation to enhancing India-Japan security cooperation. Tick the most appropriate option. (Criterion–Historical Linkages).

(a) Historical linkages have been the most important reason for the security cooperation.

(b) Historical linkages have provided a foundation for taking this cooperation further.

(c) Cannot Say.

(d) Historical linkages are mere optics that is mentioned periodically.

(e) Historical linkages have no role to play in the security cooperation.

Q No. 2. Is the geo-strategic location of India in the Indian Ocean Region, through which Japanese maritime trade routes pass, a factor for enhanced India Japan Strategic partnership? (Criterion–Geo-strategic Location).

(a) Geo-strategic significance of India has been the most important factor bringing Japan closer to India.

(b) Geo-strategic significance is among the many but not the most important factor bringing Japan closer to India.

(c) Cannot Say.

(d) Geo-strategic significance of India is incidental. The drivers for the security cooperation are different.

(e) Geo-strategic significance has no role whatsoever to play in the India-Japan security cooperation.

Q No. 3. Does the US-Japan Security alliance have a role in enhancing the security cooperation between India and Japan? (Criterion–US-Japan Alliance)

(a) US security alliance with Japan prohibits security cooperation with India.

(b) The US Japan security alliance hinders engagement of Japan with India in security issues.

(c) Cannot say.

(d) US has encouraged Japan to cooperate with India in security aspects bilaterally and regionally.

(e) India-Japan security cooperation was initiated due to enhanced engagement of US with India in security issues.

Q No. 4. Article 9 of the Japanese Constitution prohibits threat or use of force as means of settling international disputes. This entails that Japan will not adopt an offensive deployment posture. Will this aspect be a hindrance to successful India-Japan Security Cooperation? (Criterion–Restraints (Constitutional/Political)).

(a) Restrictions of Article 9 will severely affect meaningful India-Japan Security Cooperation.

(b) Article 9 restrains the optimum exploitation of security cooperation but both countries can work through the restraints towards a meaningful security cooperation.

(c) Cannot Say.

(d) Restraints of Article 9 are not relevant to India and not a major hindrance to the Security Cooperation.

(e) Article 9 is no hindrance, whatsoever, to a successful India Japan Security Cooperation.

Q No. 5. Regional peace and security, maintaining a rules-based order, having free and open global commons could be some end-states of India-Japan strategic partnership. Is there a convergence in the desired end-state of this security cooperation for both India and Japan? (Criterion–Objectives of Cooperation).

(a) Both nations desire exactly the same end-state from mutual security cooperation.

(b) Desired end state in respect of both countries is not exactly the same. Whereas Japan desires a rules-based order and maintenance of status quo, India in addition, is also looking for defence technology and military capability enhancement.

(c) Cannot Say.

(d) Both nations have different end states as far as security environment in the Indo-Pacific region is concerned.

(e) Desired end states of India and Japan are divergent.

Q No. 6. Will the defence technology cooperation between India and Japan (as part of security cooperation) be beneficial to economies of both India and Japan? (Criterion–Economy)

(a) Technology cooperation between both countries will provide a much needed boost to the Japanese economy and enhance Indian economy immensely.

(b) Technology cooperation will benefit the economies of both Japan (through sales) and India (through ToT and employment generation).

(c) Cannot Say.

(d) Any benefit to the economy through technology cooperation is incidental.

(e) There will be no economical benefit to either country through technology cooperation.

Q No. 7. Will India stand by Japan in its territorial disputes with China? (Criterion–Trust).

(a) India will not come out openly in support of Japan in its disputes with China due to fear of getting drawn into an undesirable situation.

(b) India will issue statements that support Japan's stand in these disputes.

(c) Cannot Say.

(d) India will provide diplomatic and material support to Japan in the SCS issue.

(e) Support to Japan will be unequivocal.

Q No. 8. High end armament technology and advanced surveillance technology has been one of the strengths of Japan. As partner nation with

India in security cooperation and strategic partnership, will Japan share its high end military technology and intelligence inputs with India? (Criterion–Partner Willingness to Share).

(a) Most technologies require US permission to share being subject to IPR agreements. Critical inputs are also obtained through joint surveillance mechanisms in place. Hence, Japan is unlikely to share these.

(b) Japan may share some low end technology but not the cutting edge technology and critical inputs.

(c) Cannot Say.

(d) Limited sharing of high end military technology and critical intelligence inputs will be possible.

(e) Japan should have no issues in sharing high end technology and critical intelligence inputs.

Q No. 9. Training exchanges and exercises between armed forces enhance security cooperation. Malabar Exercise is a case in point. Are the levels of training engagement between the armed forces of India and Japan optimal? (Criterion–Military engagements).

(a) Levels of engagement for all three services are inadequate and need to be further enhanced.

(b) Presently only the MSDF and the Indian navy have adequate exercises and training exchange programmes. Training and exercises between the air force and armies are not adequate.

(c) Cannot Say.

(d) Levels of training engagement for all three services are adequate and optimal.

(e) Levels of engagement for all three services are more than adequate and can be scaled down.

Q No. 10. From the year 2008, when the Declaration of Security Cooperation was signed, India-Japan security cooperation has always been a priority aspect in India's foreign policy irrespective of the political leader / political party in power in India (Criterion–Involvement of Parliaments).

(a) Strongly Disagree.

(b) Disagree.

(c) Cannot Say.

(d) Agree.

(e) Strongly Agree.

Q No. 11. Concepts and Doctrines in the Indian armed forces and the Self Defence Forces of Japan are standardised and interoperable (Criterion–Interoperability).

(a) Strongly Disagree.

(b) Disagree.

(c) Cannot Say.

(d) Agree.

(e) Strongly Agree.

Q No. 12 Based on their importance and extent to which they influence security cooperation between India and Japan, please rank the under-mentioned factors. Same ranking can be given to more than one factor. The most important factor is to be given Rank 1.*

	1	2	3	4	5	6	7	8	9	10
Historical Linkage - Implies the influence of historical linkages (culture and religion)										
Geo-Strategic Significance (Location in the IOR)										
Japan's Alliance with USA										
Legal & Political Restrictions (Article 9-Japan and Strategic Autonomy-India)										
Objectives/End State of the Security Cooperation										
Economic Benefits from Cooperation										
Trust between India and Japan										
Sharing of Intelligence and Technology										
Training, Engagements, Exercises										
Involvement of Political Leaders (implies laws supporting the cooperation will be instituted)										
Interoperability between Armed Forces										

Overall Calculations for Weighted Mean

Step 1	**Calculation of Mean**												
	Strongly Disagree	Disagree	Neutral	Agree	Strong-ly Agree			Strongly Disagree	Disagree	Neutral	Agree	Strongly Agree	
Criteria	1	2	3	**4**	5	**SUM**	**Criteria**	1	2	3	4	5	**SUM**
Historical Linkages	1	5	**4**	14	1	25	**Partner Willingness**	**7**	**11**	3	2	2	25
	1	**5**	4	14	1	25		7	11	3	2	2	25
Average	1	5	4	14	1	25	Average	7	11	3	2	2	25
Mean	1	10	12	56	5	84	Mean	7	22	9	8	10	56
Overall Mean					3.36	3.36	Overall Mean					2.24	2.24
Criteria	1	2	3	4	5	**SUM**	**Criteria**	1	2	3	4	5	**SUM**
Geog Loc	**0**	**0**	1	17	7	25	**Involvement of Parliaments**	**0**	**9**	8	12	1	30
	0	0	1	17	7	25		1	2	4	23	0	30
Average	0	0	1	17	7	25	Average	0.5	5.5	6	17.5	0.5	30
Mean	0	0	3	68	35	106	Mean	0.5	11	18	70	2.5	102
Overall Mean					4.24	4.24	Overall Mean					3.4	3.4

Criteria	1	2	3	4	5	SUM	Criteria	1	2	3	4	5	SUM
US Alliance	1	1	6	10	7	25	Interoperability	13	13	4	0	0	30
	1	1	6	10	7	25		13	13	4	0	0	30
Average	1	1	6	10	7	25	Average	13	13	4	0	0	30
Mean	1	2	18	40	35	96	Mean	13	26	12	0	0	51
Overall Mean					3.84	3.84	Overall Mean					1.7	1.7

Criteria	1	2	3	4	5	SUM	Criteria	1	2	3	4	5	SUM
Restraints	5	8	5	14	2	34	Mil Engagements	1	15	6	5	0	27
	5	8	5	14	2	34		1	15	6	5	0	27
Average	5	8	5	14	2	34	Average	1	15	6	5	0	27
Mean	5	16	15	56	10	102	Mean	1	30	18	20	0	69
Overall Mean					3	3	Overall Mean					2.555556	2.56

Criteria	1	2	3	4	5	SUM	Criteria	1	2	3	4	5	SUM
Alignment of Objective	0	3	2	16	4	25	Trust	11	8	2	4	0	25
	0	3	2	16	4	25		11	8	2	4	0	25

Average	0	3	2	16	4	25	Average	11	8	2	4	0	25
Mean	0	6	6	64	20	96	Mean	11	16	6	16	0	49
Overall Mean					3.84	3.84	Overall Mean					1.96	1.96
Criteria	1	2	3	4	5	SUM							
Economy	0	0	0	18	7	25							
	0	0	0	18	7	25							
Average	0	0	0	18	7	25							
Mean	0	0	0	72	35	107							
Overall Mean					4.28	4.28							

Working out weightage of each criterion

FINDING OUT WEIGHTAGE OF CRITERIA

Criteria	Rank	Responders	Total	Weightage	Criteria	Rank	Responders	Total	Weightage	Criteria	Rank	Responders	Total	Weightage
Historical Linkages	10	3	30		Restraints	10	2	20		Trust	10	8	80	
	9	6	54			9	5	45			9	9	81	
	8	3	24			8	5	40			8	4	32	
	7	1	7			7	3	21			7	2	14	
	6	0	0			6	4	24			6	1	6	
	5	3	15			5	0	0			5	0	0	
	4	3	12			4	2	8			4	1	4	
	3	2	6			3	3	9			3	1	3	
	2	1	2			2	1	2			2	0	0	
	1	3	3			1	0	0			1	0	0	
	55	25	153	6.12		55	25	169	6.76		55	26	220	8.46

Geo-Strategic Significance			
	10	12	120
	9	5	45
	8	1	8

End State			
	10	7	70
	9	10	90
	8	1	8

Partner Willingness			
	10	7	70
	9	5	45
	8	6	48

	7	2	14	
	6	1	6	
	5	0	0	
	4	0	0	
	3	4	12	
	2	0	0	
	1	0	0	
	55	25	205	8.2

	7	3	21	
	6	1	6	
	5	2	10	
	4	1	4	
	3	0	0	
	2	0	0	
	1	0	0	
	55	25	209	8.36

	7	4	28	
	6	1	6	
	5	2	10	
	4	0	0	
	3	1	3	
	2	0	0	
	1	0	0	
	55	26	210	8.08

	Japan Alliance with US			
	10	2	20	
	9	7	63	
	8	7	56	
	7	3	21	
	6	2	12	
	5	0	0	
	4	0	0	
	3	1	3	
	2	3	6	
	1	0	0	
	55	25	181	7.24

	Economic Benefits			
	10	9	90	
	9	9	81	
	8	2	16	
	7	1	7	
	6	0	0	
	5	3	15	
	4	1	4	
	3	0	0	
	2	0	0	
	1	0	0	
	55	25	213	8.52

	Mil Engagements			
	10	4	40	
	9	7	63	
	8	4	32	
	7	7	49	
	6	1	6	
	5	1	5	
	4	0	0	
	3	1	3	
	2	1	2	
	1	0	0	
	55	26	200	7.69

	Involvement of Parliaments			
Criteria	Rank	Responders	Total	
	10	4	40	
	9	9	81	
	8	5	40	
	7	3	21	
	6	2	12	
	5	1	5	
	4	1	4	
	3	0	0	
	2	0	0	
	1	1	1	
	55	26	204	7.846154

Interoperability	Rank	Responders	Total	
	10	2	20	
	9	5	45	
	8	5	40	
	7	3	21	
	6	4	24	
	5	0	0	
	4	2	8	
	3	3	9	
	2	1	2	
	1	0	0	
	55	25	169	6.76

Ranking of Factors and Calculation of Overall Weighted Mean							
						RANK AS PER WEIGHTED MEAN	
CRITERIA	MEAN(FROM QUESTIONNAIRE)	MEAN (BASE 100)=xi	WEIGHTAGE (FROM QUESTIONNAIRE)=wi	WEIGHTED MEAN(xi X wi) (Base = 1000)		Economy	729.312
Historical Linkages	3.36	67.2	6.12	411.26		Geo-Strategic Significance	695.36
Geog Loc	4.24	84.8	8.2	695.36		Aln of Obj	642.048
US Alliance	3.84	76.8	7.24	556.03		Japan-US Alliance	556.032
Restraints	3	60	6.76	405.6		Involvement of Parliaments	533.5385
Aln of Obj	3.84	76.8	8.36	642.05		Historical Linkages	411.264
Economy	4.28	85.6	8.52	729.31		Restraints	405.6
Trust	1.96	39.2	8.46	331.69		Mil Engagements	393.728
Partner Willingness	2.24	44.8	8.0769	361.85		Partner Willingness	361.8462
Mil Engagements	2.56	51.2	7.69	393.73		Trust	331.6923
Involvement of Parliaments	3.4	68	7.846153846	533.54		Interoperability	240.72
Interoperability	1.7	34	7.08	240.72		OVERALL TOTAL	5301.141
		Total	84.35461538		5301.1	Weighted Mean =(∑xi*wi)/∑wi	
	Weighted Mean =(∑xi*wi)/∑wi		62.844			WEIGHTED MEAN	62.84
Expeditionary Capability					OVERALL WEIGHTED MEAN =(62.84 X 11)/12		57.6

Appendix G

Questionnaire—India-Japan Security Cooperation: Dynamics and Prospects in a Regional Context

(To be Handed over to DAs of Japan)

I am carrying out research on the subject "India-Japan Security Cooperation" at the Manohar Parrikar Institute for Defence Studies and Analysis (Manohar Parrikar-IDSA), New Delhi. This project aims to research into the dynamics of India-Japan relationship in the backdrop of the rapidly changing security environment in the Indo-Pacific region and arrive at drivers as well as a trajectory that the India-Japan security cooperation will take in the midterm (by 2035). The research will also ascertain areas that need strengthening of linkages with Japan and identify policies that the Indian establishment should adopt in order to secure its national interests.

Considering the above, a questionnaire has been prepared to have an insight into your views on the aspects as enumerated below.

1. **Joint Training and Exercises of Land Forces**—India has a number of training institutes which train for warfare in difficult and diverse terrain like the High Altitude Warfare School, Counter Insurgency and Jungle Warfare School, Desert Battle Schools and so on.
   - (a) Do you envision the Japanese Self Defence Forces (SDF) benefitting from training in these institutes in India, in section/platoon groups on a regular basis?
   - (b) Is Japan already subscribing to these courses? Which institutions/ courses are being attended by Japanese soldiers (officers and men) in India?
   - (c) Number of officers attending courses in each other's military institutions is very less. What are the measures being undertaken to increase the same?
   - (d) What other areas have been identified for joint training/exercises of the army, navy and air force?
2. **Rapid Reaction Forces**—The SDF is in the process of raising rapid reaction amphibious forces to cater to contingencies of security threat

to Japan's remote island territories.

(a) Do you feel India can contribute to the operationalisation of these forces? If yes, how?

(b) Is there a scope of joint training between the Rapid Reaction Brigades of the SDF and Indian amphibious forces? If yes, can the same be institutionalised on a periodic basis?

3. **Training Areas—**

(a) Does Japan have a shortage of real estate/ranges for manoeuvre training and firing of large calibre weapons and artillery?

(b) Is there any intent of using ranges in India in a similar manner in which the SDF uses ranges in the USA?

4. **Maritime Aspects**—It has been widely reported in the media that Japan is participating in the tender for submarines floated by the Indian navy. Currently, Li-ion batteries are being planned to be used as the power source for the Japanese Soryu submarines.

(a) Is such latest technology available for offer to India?

(b) What are the other major projects that Japan would be ready to participate in co-development with India? What niche technology does Japan have to offer to the Indian armed forces to promote capability or enhancement of the Indian army, navy and air force?

(c) Japan has been planning to develop the latest stealth fighters for the ASDF. Is co-development with India in this project, a possibility?

(d) India has a large coastline and the potential of constructing ports/ enhancing the capability of existing ports is immense. Have any ports been identified for development/capability enhancement by Japan, in India?

5. An agreement pertaining to the security of classified military information between Japan and India already exists. Is such an agreement robust enough to facilitate sharing of relevant sensitive military information? What more focussed approach is needed towards sharing of military intelligence between the two countries?

6. **India's Role in the East China Sea**—India is geographically distanced from the East China Sea. Considering this distance and the fact that Indian naval assets operating there will be stretched for support from the mainland, what role of India do you envision in the East China Sea

dispute of Senkaku Islands?

7. **Japan's Role in the West Pacific Region**—India is being projected as the net security provider in the Indian Ocean Region. Can a similar role be fulfilled by Japan in the South China Sea, irrespective of the US presence?

8. **India-Japan Security Cooperation**—It is often quoted that India-Japan security relationship is a work in progress, in which the deliverables are yet to be visible.

    (a) Which are the focus areas where India-Japan Maritime Security cooperation can be enhanced in the short term?

    (b) What additional efforts are required to build a long standing maritime cooperation?

10. What are the Japanese expectations from the defence cooperation with India? What are the means to speed up the progress so that the results are visible?

11. **North Korean Threat**—The North Korean threat is the foremost security concern for Japan in the present short term context. What role does India have in assisting Japan to mitigate/resolve the crisis?

12. **UN Peace Keeping**—Both India and Japan have been pro-actively contributing to world peace. India has been one of the major contributors to peace keeping operations of the UN and has a wealth of experience.

    (a) How can cooperation in United Nations activities between India and Japan be enhanced? Is a joint task force of India and Japan, to jointly participate in UN peace keeping operations feasible?

    (b) The SDF had two Australian officers assisting in liaison work in the peace keeping activities in South Sudan. Can a similar arrangement be worked out with India to enhance liaison and cooperation in future peace keeping activities of Japan?

13. **Cyber and Space Cooperation**—Cyber and space domains have huge potential for cooperation as both countries have their respective inherent strengths. What are the aspects of cyber and space activities where India and Japan can cooperate in the military domain?

14. **Infrastructure Development**—Japan is involved in developing roads and other infrastructure in various parts of India including North-East India. Are there any infrastructure development projects that Japan is involved in, in the Andaman and Nicobar Islands?

Index